"*The Water of Life* is an eloquent tribute to Russian folk wisdom that is destined to become a significant feature in the field of Jungian psychology. Building on the work of C.G. Jung and M.-L. von Franz, Nathalie Baratoff presents a carefully chosen collection of Russian fairytales and interprets them with a style that gifts us with a work that delights the mind and moves the heart."

    —Murray Stein, Ph.D., author of *Jung's Map of the Soul*

"Nathalie Baratoff's interpretation of the fairy tales in this volume discloses a deep understanding of Jungian psychology and a vivid interest in Russian folklore. She explores the archetypal background of her material in an enlightening and inspiring way."

    —Christa Robinson, MA, ISAPZURICH

"*The Water of Life* is written with love and sensitivity for Russian tradition and folklore. This background colors the archetypal images in the presented tales and enriches their interpretation. Schooled in the Zurich tradition of Jungian psychology, Nathalie Baratoff traces the psychic development of the characters in the tales with insight and depth."

    —Gert Oskar Alexander Sauer

www.ChironPublications.com

Interior and cover design by Nelly Murariu at PixBeeDesign.com
Printed primarily in the United States of America.

ISBN 978-1-63051-879-0 paperback
ISBN 978-1-63051-880-6 hardcover
ISBN 978-1-63051-881-3 electronic
ISBN 978-1-63051-882-0 limited edition paperback

Library of Congress Cataloging-in-Publication Data

Names: Baratoff, Nathalie, author.

Title: The water of life : Russian tales in Jungian perspective / Nathalie Baratoff.

Description: Asheville : Chiron Publications, 2021. | Includes bibliographical references and index. | Summary: "C.G. Jung's psychology provides a unique understanding of the seven tales in this volume. The archetypal images therein are many-layered. We can see them from the mythological viewpoint as dragons, demons and witches; we find them in rivers of fire, in kingdoms at the bottom of the sea, in talking animals, and in endless transformations that defy human experience. The same images mirror situations of everyday life: the joys of love, success in one's endeavors; but also, abandonment, yearning for offspring, loss of a sheltered existence, as well as the many insurmountable tasks which confront us in life. But the most significant of Jung's insights into the psyche is the realization that all such experiences rest upon an inner reality which needs to be understood symbolically. This is where the archetypal nature of fairy tales is most relevant, for it explains why people of all ages and all levels of society have been fascinated by them; people, often without much formal education, gathered around a fire at the end of a hard day and, gazing into the flames, followed the images arising from the storyteller's words. Today, many have by and large lost the capacity for such experiences. Children still do; adults are often distracted by the demands of outer life. And yet, fairy tales retell fundamental experiences of life which are timeless"~ Provided by publisher.

Identifiers: LCCN 2020051076 (print) | LCCN 2020051077 (ebook) | ISBN 9781630518790 (paperback)|ISBN9781630518806(hardcover)| ISBN 9781630518820 (limited edition paperback) | ISBN 9781630518813 (ebook)

Subjects: LCSH: Fairy tales~Russia~Psychological aspects. | Folklore~Russia~Psychological aspects. | Jung, C. G. (Carl Gustav), 1875-1961 | Fairy tales~Russia~History and criticism. | Folk literature, Russian~History and criticism.

Classification: LCC GR550 .B37 2021 (print) | LCC GR550 (ebook) | DDC 398.20947~dc23

LC record available at https://lccn.loc.gov/2020051076

LC ebook record available at https://lccn.loc.gov/2020051077

The Water of Life

Russian Tales in Jungian Perspective

Nathalie Baratoff

The author expresses her heartfelt gratitude to the Stiftung zur Förderung der Psychologie von C.G. Jung for its generous contribution towards the publication of this book.

Contents

Preface

Fairy tales provide us with images of archetypal ordering. Like dreams, they enable insights into that part of our psyche which is not readily accessible to consciousness. This is the reason why we study fairy tales in Jungian psychology, and why we include them in analytical work. In doing this, we are ever mindful of the fact that the author of fairy tales is the unconscious. Such tales were told over and over again, countless times; in the process, their archetypal core, their very essence, was distilled out of the many individual nuances which tend to find their way into the story.

The unconscious speaks to us mostly in images, rarely in words. When we *read* or, better still, when we *hear* a fairy tale we must open ourselves up to the images behind the words, for then the unconscious speaks to us directly, in its own language.

People of all ages and all levels of society have been fascinated by fairy tales; simple people, without much formal education, gathered around a fire at the end of a hard day, gazed into the flames and allowed the images to seep through the words of the storyteller. Today, many have, by and large, lost the opportunity and capacity for such an experience. In addition, children as well as adults used to enjoy hearing the same tales over and over again. Children still do; adults are often blinded by the demands of outer life: How inefficient, how redundant to repeat something two, three times when it is perfectly clear the first time?

One of the charms of such imagery in Russian fairy tales is the repetitive use of sayings or special expressions. These are experienced as ornaments, as little gems that decorate the tale and add to the atmosphere of other-worldliness.

Many such expressions appear in connection with the witch, Baba Yaga, whose proverbial hut stands on chicken legs as a sentry at the edge of the deep forest. Approaching the hut, the hero often sees no door to knock on or to enter through; he then addresses it in the familiar fashion: "Little hut, little hut, turn your back to the forest, and your front side

1

toward me" and walks in. He is greeted with "Fie, fie! Till now there's been neither whiff nor glimpse of Russians around here. Now there's one standing before me, jumping right into my mouth!" Baba Yaga's *friendly* welcome is usually followed by a question, a further attempt at undermining his courage: "Have you come of your own free will or out of need?"

Another famous figure villain of Russian folklore is Koshchey, the Deathless. In one tale, after the hero has inadvertently freed the demon from ten years captivity, Koshchey flies off to catch the hero's wife with the following words: "Never again will you see [her], as you will never see your own ears." At a later time when the hero manages to free his wife and run off with her, Koshchey learns of their flight from his horse. In answer to his question about whether they will be able to overtake them, the horse answers: "We could sow wheat, wait till it grows, reap it, thresh it, grind it into flour, bake five ovenfuls of bread, eat that bread; after that we could set out in pursuit, and even then we would overtake them."

In the tale of "Two Ivans, Soldier's Sons," as the hero rides off to seek his fortune, his mother admonishes him to offend no one without cause, or yield to evil enemies. He consoles her with the following words: "When I ride I don't whistle, when I fight, I don't yield."

The serpent is another negative character in Russian fairy tales. As the hero sets out to free the tsar's daughter from the twelve-headed monster, the serpent gives him the following words of advice: "Say farewell to the bright world and hasten into my throat of your own accord; it will be easier for you if you do!" "You lie, accursed serpent!" answers the mighty hero. "You won't swallow me, you'll choke on me!"

Very common is a tale's reference to time and place: "After they had gone a short distance or a long distance; after they had traveled a long time or a short time—for quickly is a tale told, but less quickly a deed is done..." Or again, as directions to Baba Yaga: "Beyond thrice nine lands, in the thrice tenth kingdom, beyond a river of fire, lives Baba Yaga." Typically, a tale may be introduced by the following opening sentence: "In such and such a kingdom, in such and such a land, a certain tsar...."

Should the hero be killed and dismembered, his body may be reassembled and he may be brought back to life by the sprinkling with the water of life. The hero typically responds with "How long I have slept!" and is answered with "Were it not for me, you would have slept forever!"

A lovely maiden is usually introduced with: "...such a fairy tale beauty as neither tongue can tell nor pen describe." In the tale of "The Seven Simeons" we hear of Elena the Fair, "a tsarevna (princess) of unimaginable beauty; red color spreads over her face, white down covers her breast, and one can see the marrow flowing from bone to bone."

Apart from such vivid imagery, fairy tales frequently impress us with their wealth of wisdom; revisiting a fairy tale, we are humbled by the realization of how much more lies within, still waiting to be recognized. This testifies to the symbolic nature of the fairy tale which only reveals what we are capable of seeing.

The tales appearing in the present volume stem from the collection of Alexander Afanas'yev.[1] Although a lawyer by profession, Afanas'yev (1825-71) had always been fascinated by folklore; it was his firm belief that therein laid the roots of his people's soul. In part, this can be explained historically, for until the reforms of Peter the Great in the eighteenth century, the printed word in Russia was the prerogative of the Church; as a result, the pre-Christian tradition could only have survived through oral transmission. It was this mythological and pagan backdrop that Afanas'yev was forever trying to unveil through folklore in general, and through fairy tales, in particular.

Afanas'yev was strongly influenced by the spirit of the Romanticism of his day, and greatly impressed by the work of the Grimm brothers. He was one of the foremost advocates of the Mythological School, founded by, among others, Jacob Grimm. His first collection of fairy tales was published in the years 1855-1864.[2]

Afanas'yev's interest in the historical and cultural roots of folklore resonates with the Jungian approach to fairy tales. Especially notable is the importance ascribed to a country's heritage in the interpretation

---

1 Afanas'yev, Narodnye russkiye skazki.
2 Lutz Röhrich, Nachwort zu Afanasjew Russische Volksmärchen. Munich: Winkler Verlag, 1985, 915-18.

of its folklore. Although it is possible to work almost instinctively with tales of one's own cultural background, there is a danger in projecting the same expectations onto tales of other cultures. This is supported by Jung's insistence on including ethnology and religion into his view of psychology. With this in mind, I have tried to include such background material in the interpretations of the tales presented here.

And yet, such considerations can never be at the expense of the universal human patterns underlying the *skeleton* of all tales, even though the size of the bones may be different, there may be deformations, or some parts may be missing. Carrying such a template within our psyche allows us to better recognize the differences and draw conclusions from any particular deviation. Psychologically, this inner model represents the archetypal structure which resonates with the psyche of each human being.

The front cover of this book is an adaptation of Ivan Bilibin's painting of "The Little White Duck" from 1902. Bilibin is best known for his illustrations of Russian fairy tales. Looked at from a Jungian perspective, this painting is more than an illustration of a particular tale; it is an image of a soul landscape that introduces us to the world of fairy tales.

We note, for example, that the better part of this painting is forest and water, both symbols of the unconscious. The piece of land on which the children stand is an apt image of the conscious part of the psyche. The unconscious is given more space and, thereby, greater importance. This supports the earlier statement about the unconscious origin of fairy tales. Like dreams, these provide glimpses into a part of our psyche that lies in the dark.

These two realms are clearly separated in Bilibin's painting. This is most noticeable in the way the children are placed at the very edge of the water. They neither swim or play in the water; they just stand on the shore, close to one another. Psychologically, this is significant, for the transition between consciousness and the unconscious is not without its dangers.

And yet, there is a visible connection between water and land: the little white duck is shown swimming toward the children and they turn in its direction. Furthermore, even though the children remain on land, their images are reflected in the water. Here, we can speak of the children's reflection in the water, but we can also say that the water reflects their images.

The water also reflects the duck and the large tree at the bottom left. Among its many symbols, the tree stands for life and for the mother; here it carries fruits or flowers. The duck, because it can move in all three elements—land, water and air—symbolizes the soul, or, in general, the transcendent. Thus, without having read the tale, we will know that it will include all these aspects.

Apart from describing a physical phenomenon, "reflection" refers to pondering, to allowing one's thoughts to ripen in one's mind. This is quite different from focusing on a goal, for it implies an openness towards the unexpected and unknown. Psychologically, this represents a process of thought that includes the unconscious.

Thus, independently of the narrative, Ivan Bilibin's painting unveils the underlying essence of fairy tales. It confirms their unconscious origin and emphasizes the "otherness" of this part of the psyche. At the same time, it invites the observer to shift onto another level which can bridge these different realms.

Because the Cyrillic alphabet is transcribed in different ways, I would like to call attention to the fact that all Russian transliteration in this volume follows the U.S. Board on Geographic Names. All translations are mine.

The book is divided up into seven chapters, each devoted to a single fairy tale from the Afanas'yev collection followed by an interpretation based on Jung's view of the psyche.

Because of the archetypal nature of fairy tales, some motifs inevitably appear in more than one of these chapters, and therefore require repeated amplifications. To make each chapter reasonably self-contained without excessive repetition, I have sometimes cross-referenced between chapters in such instances.

I dedicate this book to all students of Jungian Psychology, and to those with an interest in the work of C.G. Jung as well as in Russian fairy tales and folklore. The tales and interpretations included in this volume were first presented at the International School of Analytical Psychology in Zurich (ISAPZURICH), AGAP's Post-Graduate Jungian Training. May the school continue to flourish and enrich the lives of those who take part in its program. I am grateful for having had the opportunity to take part in its development and I cherish the many friendships that resulted from this endeavor.

Acknowledgements

My heartfelt gratitude goes to all who accompanied me in the writing of this book, to all who read and shared their impressions, and to all who helped with the more technical aspects of preparing the manuscript. My thanks also go to those who patiently supported me throughout the long gestation period, enabling this child to finally see the light of day.

- To my mentors and guides René Malamud and Elisabeth Rüf ... Thank you!

- To my colleagues and friends Christina Altmann, Eugenia Arensburger, Anita Chapman, Paul Brutsche, Nancy Krieger, Jody Schlatter, Christa Robinson, Murray Stein, Wendy Wilmont and Stacy Wirth ... Thank you!

- To Carol McGinty, and Anita Mihalek, librarians of ISAPZURICH and the Slavic Department of Zurich University ... Thank you!

- To Lyudmila Litvinova, and to Inna and Michael Boboshko for their invaluable assistance in providing me with Russian literature ... Thank you!

- To Andrew Fellows for his careful and knowledgeable editing ... Thank you!

- And last, but not least, to four Baratoffs: to my husband, Alexis, and to my digital natives, Cyril, Gregory, and Isabel ... Thank you!

I. The Water of Life

There once lived a tsar (king) with his tsaritsa (queen). The tsar had three sons. One day he sent his sons out to search for his youth. The tsareviches (princes) set out on their journey. Soon they came to a pillar from which ran three roads. On this pillar was written: "Go right and you will be sated, your horse hungry; go left, you will be hungry, your horse sated; go straight ahead and you will lose your life." The eldest tsarevich took the road to the right, the middle one turned left, the youngest rode straight ahead. After traveling for a long or a short time, the youngest brother came to a deep ditch. He lost no time wondering how to get over the ditch: crossing himself, he spurred his horse and jumped over to the other side. There, at the edge of a dark forest, he saw a hut, standing on chicken legs. "Little hut, little hut, turn your back to the forest, and your front side toward me." The hut turned around and the tsarevich walked in. Inside sat Baba Yaga. "Fie, fie!" said Baba Yaga. "Till now there's been neither whiff nor glimpse of Russians around here. Now there's one standing before me, jumping right into my mouth! Well, well, my good fellow, have you come fleeing duty or seeking it?" "Oh, you old hag, you, had you not spoken these words, had I not heard them! First offer me food and drink, then ask me questions." Baba Yaga gave him to eat and drink, interrogated him, and gave him her own winged steed, saying: "Be on your way, my good man, and go to my middle sister."

After a long or a short time, he came to a hut. He went in. There sat Baba Yaga. "Fie, fie!" said Baba Yaga. "Till now there's been neither whiff nor glimpse of Russians around here. Now there's one standing before me, jumping right into my mouth! Well, well, my good fellow, have you come fleeing duty or seeking it?" "Ach, woman, first offer me food and drink, then ask me questions." Baba Yaga gave him to eat and drink, then began questioning him: "What fate has brought you to this distant land?" "My father has sent me in search of his youth." "Very well then, change over to my best steed and ride to my elder sister."

The tsarevich immediately set out. After a long or a short time, he once again came to a hut on chicken legs. "Little hut, little hut, turn toward me, with your back to the forest!" The hut turned around and the tsarevich walked in. There sat Baba Yaga. "Fie, fie!" said Baba Yaga. "Till now there's been neither whiff nor glimpse of Russians around here. Now there's one standing before me, jumping right into my mouth! Well, well, my good fellow, have you come fleeing duty or seeking it?" "Oh, you old hag, you, you've neither fed me nor given me to drink, but are already questioning me." Baba Yaga gave him to eat and drink, asked him for news, then gave him a steed better than the first two. "God be with you," she said, "not far from here is a kingdom; when you get to it, don't go through the gates, for they are guarded by lions; give your horse the whip and jump over the stockade, but be careful not to catch any of the strings as you go over. If you do, the whole kingdom will be in an uproar and you'll never make it out alive. After jumping over the stockade, go immediately to the castle, into the furthermost room. Open the door ever so quietly and there you'll see the sleeping tsar maiden. A phial with the water of life lies hidden under her pillow. Take this phial and go back quickly; beware of being tempted by her beauty."

The tsarevich did everything Baba Yaga said. There was only one thing he could not resist doing; he was tempted by the maiden's beauty... As he mounted his steed, the steed staggered; as he swung over the stockade, he caught one of the strings. Instantly the whole kingdom awoke. The tsar maiden also awoke and ordered her steed saddled. By this time Baba Yaga already knew what had happened to the valiant youth, and prepared herself for what was to come. No sooner had she sent the tsarevich on his way than the tsar maiden stormed in. She found Baba Yaga all disheveled and in disarray. "How dare you allow such a scoundrel into my kingdom," said the tsar maiden.

"He entered my quarters, drank kvas (beer) and left without covering it up again!" "Oh, my dear mistress, can't you see how disheveled my hair is? I fought him for a long time but could not subdue him." The other two Baba Yagas both said the same thing. The tsar maiden now sped on in pursuit of the tsarevich. She was just about to seize him when he jumped over to the other side of the ditch. "Expect me in three years," she called out after him, "I will be coming by sea."

From sheer joy, the tsarevich didn't realize that he had arrived at the pillar and turned left. Soon he came to a silver hill. On the hill he saw a tent; by the tent stood a steed eating summer wheat and drinking honey water. In the tent he found a valiant youth, his own brother. "Let us go look for our elder brother," said the youngest tsarevich. They saddled their horses and took the road to the right. Soon they came to a golden hill. On the hill they found a tent; by the tent, a steed eating summer wheat and drinking honey water. Inside they discovered a valiant youth, their elder brother. They roused him and rode together to the pillar where the three roads came together. Here they stopped to rest. The two elder brothers started questioning the youngest. "Did you find our father's youth?" "Yes, I did." "How and where?" He told them everything that had happened, lay down in the grass and fell asleep. The brothers cut him up into small pieces and strew the pieces in an open field. They took the phial with the water of life and made their way to their father.

Suddenly the firebird came a-flying. She gathered the pieces and laid them properly one to another. Next she brought some water of death in her mouth, sprinkled the pieces, and they grew back together. She now fetched some water of life, sprinkled it on the body and the tsarevich came to life. Getting up he said: "How long I have been sleeping!" "Were it not for me, you would have slept forever!" said the firebird. The tsarevich thanked her and made his way home. His father scorned him and banished him from his house, and so he strayed, homeless, for three years.

As the three years drew to a close, the tsar maiden arrived, sailing on a ship. She sent the tsar a letter, demanding that the guilty one be delivered to her and threatened to burn down and destroy the whole kingdom if he didn't comply with her wishes. The tsar sent his eldest son. Two boys, sons of the tsar maiden, saw him coming and asked their mother whether this was their father. "No, this is your uncle." "How shall we greet him?" "Take a whip, each of you, and send him back to where he came from." Inglorious was the eldest tsarevich's return! Repeating her threats, the tsar maiden once again demanded the surrender of the guilty one. The tsar sent his second son. The same happened to him.

The tsar now ordered a search for the youngest tsarevich. As soon as he was found, the tsar bid him go to the ship of the tsar maiden. The tsarevich replied: "I will not go until a crystal bridge is built all the way up to the ship. This bridge must be laden with an abundance of food and wine." The tsar had no choice but to have the bridge built and to provide the food, wine and mead. The tsarevich gathered his comrades and said to them: "Be my escorts, eat and drink to your hearts' delight!" As he walked up the bridge, the boys cried: "Mother dear, who is that coming?" "That is your father." "How shall we greet him?" "Take him by the hand and lead him to me." They embraced, they kissed, they caressed each other. Then they went to the tsar and told him everything as it had happened. The tsar banished his elder sons and lived on with his youngest in joy and plenitude.

Alexander Afanas'yev, Russian Folk Tales, #172, trans. NB.

INTERPRETATION

This tale is one of eight variants given by Afanas'yev under the title of "The Tale of the Valiant Youth, of the Rejuvenating Apples and the Water of Life." The present version below is § 172 and will be referred to as "The Water of Life."

A father, a mother and three sons: How nice that this tale starts out with a family that is whole, intact. The foundations of life have been honored. The future has been provided for. The number five stands for the natural man, for a development which is in harmony with nature.[3] The five fingers on each of our hands and five toes on each of our feet make it possible for us to move from one place to another, to provide for our needs, and to interact with the world. It is likewise the basis for the decimal system. We have, moreover, five senses with which we perceive the concrete world. All this helps us to establish ourselves in life, which Jung saw as satisfying the demands of the first half of life.[4]

But then we learn that the tsar (king) sends his sons to "search for his youth." He is looking back on his life and missing something he once had. This is a typical scenario for the transition into the second half of life. One realizes that something is not the way it was before and one tries to recapture what has been lost. This is an understandable wish because youth, with its abundance of physical energy and its seemingly unlimited potential, is the summit of man's biological development. After this summit has been reached, the biological development begins to slacken. As Jung shows in "The Stages of Life," a shift occurs in the human psyche and the psychic energy now begins to flow in a different direction. Man finds himself standing before a new challenge for which the criteria of the first half of life are no longer sufficient. All too often, he tries to recapture his youth too concretely, without

---

3   Jung, *Archetypes*, CW 9i, § 680.
4   Jung, *Structure and Dynamics*, CW 8.

realizing that, in the overall plan of the psyche, the focus should now be on the inner world and on cultural values.[5]

Let us for a moment consider the symbolism of the number three, for it is the *three* sons who are charged with the task of searching of the tsar's youth. In number symbolism all odd numbers are considered masculine and dynamic, in contrast to even numbers which are feminine and passive. The number three is also connected with our notion of time: the past, present and future, and can therefore represent developmental or historical movement. In many cultures, this is mirrored in the goddesses of fate, for example, the three Greek *Moirai* who spin the thread of life, measure it and cut it, thereby bringing a life to its end. The Moirai stood for a natural measure of time, over and beyond the collectively determined one, so that even Zeus could not overrule their verdict. This number also reflects our perception of space, measured in length, height, and depth.

We can, therefore, say that the appearance of the number three in any symbolic material always heralds a fateful, dynamic development in time and space. It is a signal that some new process has been constellated which will bring about change. This is very much in keeping with the impending transition into another phase of life.

The three sons are the product of the first part of the tsar's life, both in a concrete as well as symbolic sense. It is, therefore, meaningful that the tsar relies on them at such an important moment in his life. But they also represent his future: Concretely, they are his heirs and will rule the kingdom upon his death; symbolically, they represent the energy and potential he now finds lacking, experienced as his youth.

But energy and potential alone do not necessarily bring success. Soon after starting their journey, the three brothers arrive at a pillar, a signpost, indicating the direction of the three roads that lie before them. Signposts usually give directions to specific destinations. The traveler only needs to decide where he wants to go. There is no such information on the signpost in the present tale. Instead of a final destination they are informed about what awaits them along the way: "Go right and you will be sated, your horse hungry; go left, you will be hungry,

---

5 Jung, *Structure and Dynamics*, CW 8, § 772 ff.

your horse sated; go straight ahead and you will lose your life." This is less concrete but more existential. In a way, it is closer to the orientation given by a compass which is based upon the North Pole and hence always relevant and universally applicable.

The choices made by the three brothers provide information about each of them. The first brother takes the road to the right. This may refer to the *right* road, the road which would be in conformity with collective principles. As heir to the throne, this brother is usually concerned about upholding existing principles.

There are at least two possible reasons why the middle brother now chooses the road to the left: Firstly, if the eldest goes to the right, the left is the only direction this brother can take if he doesn't want to "lose his life," as the sign indicates. A symbolic view would be to see the left as the way to the unconscious, to a deeper experience; it can, however, also refer to remaining unconscious.

Without hesitation, the third brother rides straight ahead, following the road which leads to death. It is typical for the hero to make decisions which are difficult to understand rationally. The fact that the hero is usually victorious suggests that he is guided mostly by irrational impulses. It is for this reason that Marie-Louise von Franz defines the hero as the model ego for he/she shows the way out of a dilemma which is in accordance with the Self.[6]

In choosing the way to the right, where he will be sated, his horse hungry, the first brother shows little concern for the animal carrying him. He thinks only of his own well-being and is ready to sacrifice an instinct that could be a valuable support and friend in the task ahead. The second brother goes to the opposite extreme; he puts all his trust in his instinct and neglects himself. But a horse symbolizes a powerful instinct and can easily panic and get out of hand if not guided by the rider. This would amount to giving up ego control and living according to one's instincts. And lastly, in choosing to go straight ahead, the third brother entrusts himself to fate.

This imagery is easily translatable into concrete life experience: In a difficult situation when one must orient oneself and make a decision,

---

6   von Franz, *Interpretation of Fairy Tales*, 45.

going the way of the collective or shutting one's eyes to the difficulties, that is, choosing to remain unconscious, is often the way chosen because it carries the least personal responsibility and requires a minimum of effort. If we now skip ahead to the scene where the hero returns from his encounter with the tsar maiden, we can see that this is indeed a very fitting interpretation for the choice taken by his two elder brothers; the hero finds them resting in their tents with their steeds "eating summer wheat and drinking honey water." They have accomplished nothing since they parted at the crossing; they did not even venture far from that place. The only thing they did was make themselves and their horses comfortable. It is, moreover, by their hand that the hero loses his life, as predicted on the signpost.

The information given in the first few sentences suggests interpreting this tale from a masculine perspective: "Once upon a time there lived a tsar with his tsaritsa (queen). The tsar had three sons..." We are not introduced to a tsar and tsaritsa with their family but with a tsar who had a wife and three sons. Needless to say, such a description discloses a definite patriarchal bias.

Psychologically, the sons would be seen as the tsar's youthful shadows. At the end of the tale we can see that the two elder ones are not only incapable of finding the tsar's youth, but that they endanger the life of the third brother, who can. This reveals vital information about the tsar: It shows that the impulse to recover his youth is in large part colored by very dubious aspects of his personality. The two elder brothers are shown to be lazy, opportunistic, unfaithful, murderous, and deceitful.

It is somewhat surprising that the tsaritsa is mentioned at the beginning but plays no further role in the tale. She could have seen her sons off on their quest, opposed the eviction of the third son at the end of the tale, or joined the tsar in welcoming the hero and his family at the end. None of this takes place, nor is the reader given any explanation for her absence.

There are many tales where the queen is never mentioned at all. One doesn't even know if she is dead or alive. She is simply not there. In interpreting such a tale symbolically, one would have to assume that the ruling Eros, represented by the queen, is non-existent. This is, most often, the case in patriarchal societies where Eros is repressed by the Logos principal, and, consequently, unable to survive.

Our tale presents this situation in a more differentiated form. The tsaritsa appears to be there as long as her activities are limited to the concrete aspects of life, for example, her role in court and her responsibility in providing heirs to the throne. This is all part of the first half of life. As soon as the tsar is confronted with the psychic need for wholeness, which is a demand of the second half of life, the tsaritsa vanishes: she becomes a nonentity, she is not acknowledged; she is not allowed to live.

Seen symbolically, the tsaritsa represents the tsar's anima and, as such, would rightly be the one to bridge the gap to the inner world and to connect him with the flow of energy from within. Why does she disappear when she is most needed to make the transition into this second half of life? Might this explain why the tsar is stuck in the first half of life and unable to see beyond its concrete, biological needs? The absence of the tsaritsa-anima would suggest that this is so.

Such a state of affairs may be interpreted as the ego's fear of succumbing to the unconscious; after all, the task of the first half of life is strengthening the ego and freeing it from its initial contamination with the collective unconscious. All too often this results in a one-sided rational attitude, a swing to the other extreme which leads to a denial of the irrational and symbolic. In the second half of life, where wholeness is a priority, excluding the inner experience narrows a person's psychic horizon and often leads to neurosis.

Accepting the reality of both aspects of the psyche broadens one's understanding of life; in the case at hand, it allows one to see that if the tsaritsa can conceive concretely and bear a child, there is no reason why she cannot bear an inner child. This symbolic interpretation implies that through Eros something new could enter the tsar's life, enriching him and making him more creative.

Common to both realities is a simple but very important fact that no child can be conceived without a man *and* a woman. This holds true in the inner world as well as in the outer. However, whereas in the outer world, the patriarchal man may be able to determine the rules of the game, he cannot expect to do so in the world of the anima. The reason for this is that here he is dealing with an archetype, and that whatever he does affects his own psyche. This combination has serious consequences for his well-being. The anima is the principle of life and of relatedness. If a man suppresses this part of himself, he will become rigid and inhuman; moreover, he will thereby be standing in the way of his own individuation.

From all the above we can conclude that all is not well in this masculine psyche: two of the tsar's sons are shadowy figures and the tsaritsa is unable to fulfill her proper role as anima. Fortunately, the tsar has a third son and it is he who provides the ray of hope in the story ahead: After the three brothers arrive at the fork and read the signs on the posts, this brother loses no time in pondering the possible dangers before him but rides straight ahead, taking the road which forebodes death.

"After traveling a long or a short time" is a frequent fairy tale phrase which alerts the reader to the closeness of the unconscious, for in this realm the human concepts of time and space do not exist; this is something we often experience in dreams. And indeed soon afterward we learn that he comes to a deep ditch. This is definitely a euphemism, for if it really was a ditch, even a deep one; he would not need to spur his horse to jump over it. His crossing himself beforehand also points to the precariousness of this obstacle. As it soon becomes clear, this ditch marks the boundary with the unknown to which the hero's search for the tsar's youth now leads him.

There is something very heroic about this third brother; he shows a boldness and courage reminiscent of the Russian epic heroes. His jumping over the ditch is just the first of many examples. As we follow him on his journey we will witness more. It is possible that some motifs from the epic tales infiltrated this fairy tale. It is also possible that the task ahead could only have been performed by a hero of such caliber.

No sooner has our hero jumped over to the other side then he finds himself at the edge of a dark forest. Before him stands the proverbial hut of Baba Yaga. This hut on chicken legs, spinning round and round is a familiar motif in Russian tales. Psychologically, it may refer to an automatic, never ending churning in the unconscious which can only be stopped if recognized by consciousness.[7] Baba Yaga seldom welcomes her human guests, except if she intends to eat them. Neither is she willing to surrender

---

7   Jung, *Nietzsche's Zarathustra 2*, 956.

her power or her secrets, some of which turn out to be rather shadowy as we can see from a tale like "The Beautiful Vasilisa."

In many tales Baba Yaga has the important function of screening those who venture into her realm. This now explains why she appears immediately after the hero has jumped over the ditch. It is not every one who can get past her. So, also, in the tale at hand, where she first tries to intimidate her guest: "Till now there's been neither whiff nor glimpse of Russians around here. Now there's one standing before me, jumping right into my mouth!" Incidentally, *Russians* doesn't indicate nationality; it simply refers to those who come from another world.

Her asking the hero if he comes "fleeing duty or seeking it" is another frequent motif. By this she means to test his resolve and seriousness of purpose. But even though the hero has a very legitimate reason for being there, he shows no intention of answering her question and pro-viding her, thereby, with a hook for further interrogation. He curses her and puts her in her place for not extending him, a guest, a proper welcome. "Oh, you old hag, you! Had you not spoken these words, had I not heard them! First offer me food and drink, then ask me questions." His assertive manner makes her change her tone. She provides him with food and drink, interrogates him; then gives him her winged steed and sends him off to her sister.

Jung warned of the danger of panicking in the face of the unconscious, for to panic is to lose ego control, thereby, giving the unconscious added power.[8] Here the hero responds instinctively by using Baba Yaga's own provocative language. His response is not rational, nor does he appeal to her compassion, for this would be taken for weakness, and he would surely have landed on her plate.

Like every archetypal figure, Baba Yaga is ambivalent, and it is the hero's task to induce her to turn her more positive or related side toward him. In a way, he has already done this by commanding the hut on chicken legs to turn its back to the forest, its front side toward him.

Arriving at the hut of the second Baba Yaga, the hero is met with the same stereotypic greeting, but he no longer curses her, he just asks that she first feed him and give him drink. Here, her questioning is

---

8   Jung, *Dream Analysis*, 205.

friendlier. "What fate has brought you to this distant land?" she asks, and he now tells her that his father has sent him out in search of his youth. In parting, this Baba Yaga gives him her best steed and directs him to her elder sister.

Despite the fact that the hostility of the hero's encounter with the first Baba Yaga is repeated with the third, the results of their meeting testify to a gradual rapprochement with the three sisters. The last Baba Yaga gives him a steed better than the first two, provides him with information on how to secure the water of life and cautions him of the dangers involved. Most importantly, she divulges the connection between the water of life and the tsar maiden. Finally she sends him off with "God be with you," a rather unusual farewell for a witch!

It should not surprise us that the water of life is in the possession of the tsar maiden. This equates the anima with life. As we shall see in what follows, however, this new life is very different from the one represented by the tsaritsa-anima. The tsar's youth which the three brothers were sent out to find comes from another world, from the world beyond the deep ditch.

Let us for a moment consider the three Baba Yagas. Parallel to the three brothers, they are three sisters but, in contrast to the tsareviches (princes), they are in the service of a feminine ruler. Psychologically this makes perfect sense, for the masculine order of the outer world is compensated by the feminine in the inner world. The number three appears again, heralding a new phase of a dynamic, fateful development in the psyche.

The Baba Yagas are initially hostile to the hero's intrusion into their realm. They seem to see this as meddling in their affairs. On the other hand, they are also interested in the hero and ask him questions. The motif of Baba Yagas eating their guests is really quite similar, for eating something or someone symbolizes integrating this content. Furthermore, as this fairy tale discloses, if the hero meets with their expectations, they change their attitude toward him and even help him in delving deeper into their world.

Such a cautious attitude toward a stranger is good advice for any analyst for if a person comes into analysis for the wrong reasons or is unwilling to acknowledge another reality because it does not correspond to that of consciousness, then the work will either be superficial and fruitless or, possibly, even dangerous.

We return for a moment to Baba Yaga's interrogation of the hero, something we note with all three sisters. This suggests that they are not aware of what goes on in this part of the psyche. Interestingly enough, the opposite appears to be true where their world is concerned. For example, they are prepared for the arrival of the tsar maiden who storms into their huts after the hero's visit. Here they seem to know the reason for her fury; they realize, without being informed, what took place in her chamber.

This is supported by the experience of active imagination. In speaking of this technique, Barbara Hannah emphasizes the need to acquaint the figures of the unconscious with the concrete situation.[9] It is indeed a major requirement of active imagination that the two parts of the psyche interact with one another, for the goal is to heal the split between the ego and the unconscious and to establish the right relationship between the two.

We can see the implications of this for the analytical situation, for important as it is to be open to the reality of the inner world, this should never be at the expense of the conscious situation. Therefore, when working with dreams we want to know about the context in which the dream appears, we ask for personal associations to the different symbols and for feeling reactions to different aspects of the dream. Dream interpretation is concerned with wholeness, with understanding the message of the unconscious and finding a place for it in consciousness.

The motif of eating and drinking in the other world is a familiar one in fairy tales. Concretely, eating or drinking can strengthen and energize body and mind. There is also a strong social component to eating and drinking for it furthers communion with others; baptisms, weddings, funerals are examples of archetypal situations affecting the lives of all human beings and extending beyond the purely personal. In such situations, the collective lends its support to the individual and thereby fixes it in outer reality.

The transition from the first to the second half of life is another such archetypal experience. Because it is a process rather than a relatively

---

9   Hannah, *Encounters with the Soul*, 101 f.

sudden event, it lacks the same social recognition as other transitions. This deprives the ego of the support of the collective and leaves it to adjust to this archetypal demand on its own. In our day we have mostly lost awareness of the initiatory significance of this transition. An initiation is always connected with passage from one state to another, the exchange of the old way of life for a new one. It is a process of development, not only in a physical but also in a spiritual sense, and, hence, a broadening of consciousness.

However, as everything archetypal, initiation has negative as well as positive aspects. Through eating and drinking, one will not necessarily be nourished and strengthened, but can also be drugged or poisoned. A famous example of this danger can be found in the *Odyssey* where some of Odysseus's men are offered the lotus fruit to eat. This causes them to forget their intention of returning home; they can only be saved by being tied and dragged onto the ship by their comrades. Psychologically this would describe a state of addiction or a situation where the ego is overwhelmed and dissolved by the unconscious.

We find a similar example in the story of Persephone. Kerényi tells how Pluto forces Persephone to eat a pomegranate seed before releasing her from the Underworld. Interestingly enough, Demeter's very first words to her daughter are to ask if she had eaten anything in the world of the dead. This is presented as the reason for Persephone's having to return to the Underworld for one-third of every year.[10]

Such examples show that to incorporate unconscious contents, that is, to eat and drink in the other world, is potentially dangerous for the ego. It takes a hero with enough ego strength to enter this world, to conduct himself properly toward its inhabitants and to be able to return unharmed with the gifts he gleaned from his journey.

As Jung pointed out, although the unconscious is the source of all new development in consciousness, it also has a destructive side which all too often tries to take back its own creation. We find this exemplified in the myth of the Greek Titan, Cronos, who swallowed all the children born to him by Rhea until he was subdued by his son,

---

10   Kerényi, *Gods of the Greeks*, 240.

Zeus. This was a deed of such great importance that it heralded a new collective order of the Olympic gods.

Psychologically, this testifies to the ambivalent nature of all unconscious contents. Jung described this as a *horror vacui*, a fear of the void, experienced by the unconscious upon release of its contents to consciousness.[11] Giving such contents concrete substance is hence the last and most important challenge in integrating them into consciousness. It is also the *sine qua non* of working with dreams. It is not enough to appreciate their insight and wisdom; we must incorporate their contents into our lives lest they slip away from us and be swallowed up again by the unconscious.

The hero's repeated demands for food and drink in Baba Yaga's world may hence be seen as proof of his serious intentions for the journey ahead. They also provide an indirect answer to the first Baba Yaga's question of whether he has come fleeing duty or seeking it. As we can see, all the Baba Yagas' responses indicate that they find the hero worthy of their trust. They change their attitude toward him and start to treat him in a more benevolent way.

Each of the three sisters gives him a horse for his further journey through the forest. A horse stands for tremendous instinctual carrying energy. Horses are also very sensitive and intuitive creatures and can find their way in difficult and dangerous situations. They cannot be looked upon merely as mechanical horsepower. A horse can become a true partner, and a relationship can develop between it and the rider. Folklore has attributed mantic powers to this animal. They are believed to see ghosts and intuit their master's wishes and intentions. Such beliefs bespeak the ability to know or sense things which are normally not accessible to consciousness and which would hence be invaluable in situations outside the ego's sphere of influence.

All three brothers start their journey on horses from their father's kingdom. The powerful instinct these horses symbolize is hence connected to this collective. It is, therefore, very meaningful that the hero receives a new horse from each of the three Baba Yagas. The first sister gives him a winged steed, a horse that can fly like the Greek Pegasus. The

---

11   Jung, *Archetypes*, CW 9i, § 426.

instinctive force symbolized by this animal now receives a spiritual dimension.[12] The second Baba Yaga replaces this steed with her best one, and
the third, with a steed better that the first two. This intensification of
the motif confirms that, despite their original hostility, the Baba Yagas
have come to respect and trust the hero. He has been tested and found
worthy.

The third Baba Yaga not only provides him with a steed better than
the first two, she also directs him to the goal of his quest. The hero now
learns that the tsar maiden, the virgin queen of this kingdom, lives in a
well-guarded castle, and that a phial with the water of life lies hidden
under her pillow. No one can get past the lions at the castle gates, and a
high stockade is wired with strings which are meant to rouse the whole
kingdom if struck. The hero is instructed to whip his horse over this
stockade and to proceed to the furthermost room of this castle where
he will find the sleeping tsar maiden.

A fateful meeting with the anima is drawing close. The mother is a
man's first experience of the anima. In our tale, she is mentioned up to
the time when the three brothers set out on their quest, but not afterward.
This shows that the three brothers did have a mother to mirror this
aspect of the archetype. As we have previously seen, the constellation
in this tale is the transition from the first to the second half of life. At this
time the mother aspect of the anima is superseded by that of a partner;
the role of the feminine now shifts from giving birth to a man, to giving
birth *together* with a man. The first, biological function is clear; the second
can only be understood symbolically. Psychologically, this implies that
a man in the second half of life can only be creative through union
with the anima.

This is the threshold at which the hero now stands. The challenges
posed by the three Baba Yagas tested his resolve, his courage, and his
ability to stand his own against the feminine in its negative manifestation; these are all trials belonging to the first half of life. For this
reason, the confrontations with the Baba Yagas could not bring the tale
to its desired end, for the mystery of youth which the hero is seeking

---

12   Jung, *Archetypes*, CW 9i, especially §§ 419-434.

is a mystery of rebirth, and this cannot be attained concretely but only in a symbolic sense.

It is clear now that the way to the water of life, the renewal which the tsar sends his sons out to find, turns out to be the way to the anima. From what the third Baba Yaga tells the hero, this will be no easy task. He cannot expect to succeed just because he has shown himself to be such a valiant hero; this would amount to naiveté and inflation. His ability to cope with the Baba Yagas, however, will pay dividends, for he succeeded in turning their initial malevolence to his favor. Without their help and advice he would never have gotten this far.

Psychologically, this shows that learning to cope with the negative aspect of the archetypal feminine integrates it into one's psyche. A man's experience of the feminine becomes more holistic and closer to the instinctual nature of this archetype; indirectly, this also strengthens his own instinctual masculinity.

Let us return to the advice the hero receives from the third Baba Yaga. Firstly, he is warned against going through the gates guarded by lions. This is another familiar motif in fairy tales. The lions symbolize passionate power and lust which are capable of tearing a person apart. In *Individuation in Fairy Tales,* von Franz writes that this state can actually lead to suicide.[13] In most tales, the hero is advised to bring some meat to distract the lions while he slips by. Here the solution lies in substituting meat for the human being. Psychologically, this amounts to differentiating between what can be integrated and lived in a human way, and what must be rejected. This bears similarity to the foregoing commentary about the Baba Yagas. In each separate case, the hero must be able to choose the right way of confronting the negative archetypal forces; in this latter case, he does so by standing up for himself.

We can well imagine that the prospect of obtaining access to the tsar maiden and to the water of life may have triggered such shadow aspects in our hero. The solution given in the tale, however, is not to distract the lions by throwing them pieces of meat, but to bypass all confrontation with them. In this case, the emphasis appears to be on not awakening the tsar maiden, for this is presented as a far greater

---

13   von Franz, *Individuation in Fairy Tales,* 38 ff.

danger than the one posed by the lions. The hero is called upon to focus all his attention on getting to the tsar maiden's chamber and stealing the phial of the water of life from under her head. To accomplish this he is dependent upon the third Baba Yaga's assistance and explicit directions. She provides a horse which is capable of jumping over the stockade and tells him where to find the tsar maiden in the castle. It is highly significant that in doing so she takes the hero's side against that of the tsar maiden; psychologically, we can say that she is supporting consciousness.

Arriving at the tsar maiden's castle, the hero gives his horse the whip and manages to get over the stockade without touching any of the strings. Going quickly to the tsar maiden's chamber, he opens the door quietly so as not to awaken her and steals the phial with the water of life from under her pillow.

But then something happens that affects the whole outcome of the tale: the hero is so impressed by her beauty that, contrary to Baba Yaga's admonition not to be tempted by the tsar maiden, he succumbs. And still the tsar maiden sleeps. Fairy tales are very economical in their description of feelings. We are told nothing about the hero's experience of this moment; it is only from the reaction of his steed that we can sense the intense, even numinous nature of what has taken place: The animal staggers as the hero mounts and catches one of the strings as they jump over the stockade.

As previously mentioned, a horse is a highly intuitive animal. This one originally belonged to the third Baba Yaga, and witches themselves are extremely intuitive. Horses compensate for their poor vision with strong sense of smell; they have a nose for things. The tale of "Vasilisa the Beautiful" provides one such example: as Baba Yaga returns home, she stops at the gate, sniffs the air and says "Fie, fie! I smell a Russian smell! Who is here?" As mentioned earlier, here too *Russians* refers to strangers (p. 19). Baba Yaga doesn't see Vasilisa who is standing right in front of her but she senses her presence. Here the English verb to *sense* is really to *intuit*.

The horse that the hero is riding was given to him by the Baba Yaga; she gave it to him as a gift. We may say that he inherited this horse from her or, psychologically, that this is something he integrated from the Baba Yaga.

If we now take this horse for the hero's intuition, we can say that in some deeply unconscious, or only partly conscious part of his psyche, he realizes that something powerful and highly significant has taken place at the moment of his union with the tsar maiden, something that goes far beyond a man who could not resist a beautiful girl.

But what could it mean that he finds the tsar maiden sleeping? We find the motif in the Grimm fairy tale of "The Sleeping Beauty." There we learn that this was the result of the heroine pricking her finger on a spinning wheel, and that this was arranged by the angry fairy god-mother, another negative feminine figure. In the present tale, we are given no such explanation, for the Baba Yagas were only initially hostile toward the hero. Was she asleep because it was night time? If that were so, wouldn't the Baba Yaga have warned him to leave before dawn?

None of the above examples help us understand why the tsar maiden lies sleeping in the furthermost room of the castle. If, however, we see sleep as a state of unconsciousness, we might say that this anima figure, with the water of life under her pillow, cannot or will not enter consciousness. And here we must ask *why*? What is the psychic constellation mirrored in this tale that would explain this state of affairs?

The initial situation of this tale presents us with an image of a patriar-chal society where the feminine has a place in the first half of life but disappears on the threshold to the second. As mentioned earlier, the goal shifts from a need to strengthen the ego and establish oneself in the outer world to one of wholeness. This is a cultural development, open only to the human being. It requires a return to proximity with the unconscious from which all life began. No animal is included in this development because no animal ever leaves it; for man it is a return with consciousness, whereas the animal retains its instinctual nature throughout.

The movement toward wholeness is initiated by the unconscious psyche but it is only the one who is receptive to this reality that will hear its call and follow its lead. This is the essence of the hero in fairy tales, a model for the ego who, consciously or unconsciously, reestab-lishes the connection with the Self and accepts Its guidance.

In our tale, the tsar experiences this call but understands it literally; he misinterprets it as a longing to retrieve the concrete energy of his youth. The tsar's energy is slackening because it is being forced into the old direction, while his unconscious has already changed its course toward the inner world. When this condition becomes extreme or lasts too long, the psyche loses its equilibrium and the unconscious begins to send out warning signals. As we know from dreams, these signals are the response of the unconscious to what is happening in the outer world. We often speak of compensation in dream interpretation and we know that if these messages are not heeded, more serious problems may follow; the unconscious may then turn to obstruction and sabotage. Most often this leads to neurosis, where a split takes place within the psyche.

Summarizing, we can say that if a person standing on the threshold to the second half of life does not heed the call for turning inwards, unconscious forces, infinitely more powerful than their ego, may be triggered. The consequences of such an attitude are considerably greater if this person is a tsar, for then it affects the whole collective.

Returning to the sleeping tsar maiden, we may deduce that it is the inability of consciousness to accept the challenge of the second half of life that forces the anima to regress into the deeper levels of the unconscious, and that this deprives a man of the renewal she is capable of bestowing.

In our tale, it is only the hero who has made it thus far; furthermore, because he acts in harmony with the Self, he now dares to disobey the advice of the third Baba Yaga. The coniunctio with the anima goes beyond his fascination for the beautiful woman he sees before him; it takes priority over Baba Yaga's admonition not to be tempted by her beauty. The impact of this transgression makes the mighty steed stagger as the hero mounts, and results in its catching one of the strings as the hero jumps over the stockade. We can imagine the power emanating from this contact if it awakened the whole kingdom.

Earlier we compared the motif of the sleeping maiden in "The Sleeping Beauty" with our tale. After the princess in the Grimm tale pricks her finger on the spinning wheel and falls asleep, all life comes to a halt. And at the end, it is the prince's kiss that reawakens the whole castle. These examples, as well as the one in our tale, show that information travels differently in this world than in the world of consciousness.

This is further confirmed by the observation that all three Baba Yagas appear to know what took place in the tsar maiden's chamber even before she arrives at their door. We can see this as a characteristic of the unconscious psyche where all things are contaminated with one another and where a-causal connections predominate.

A variant of this tale, (Afanas'yev, § 174) suggests a slightly different explanation for the Baba Yagas' knowledge of the hero's transgression. Here we learn that, when fleeing the tsar maiden, the hero revisits all three Baba Yagas with the purpose of switching horses. Such changing of horses is normally undertaken when the journey is long and arduous. The tsar maiden notices the sweating horse and asks Baba Yaga for an explanation. Covering up for the hero, Baba Yaga answers that she, herself, was out riding.

In that variant, the sweating horses make the tsar maiden suspect a connection between the hero and the Baba Yagas. Indeed, we know from the tsar maiden's own words that the three Baba Yagas are responsible for guarding her kingdom from intruders. This knowledge was attributed to the intuitive nature of the unconscious where everything is contaminated with everything else. Considered from the point of view of consciousness, we could say that the variant with the sweating horses is indicative of the sensation function, whereas the present version implies intuition. In consciousness these functions are opposites; by the very nature of the unconscious, however, they are united in their polarity. And since this scene clearly takes place in the unconscious, we can see that the two versions offer complementary descriptions of the same phenomenon. The symbol of the horse unites these two scenarios for, like the unconscious, it, too, possesses a strong intuition.

This incident provides additional psychological insight. It may well be that the hero needs a fresh horse to continue his journey home, but this is not necessarily the only explanation. Another possibility is that he must gradually down-scale the tremendous libido generated by the meeting with the tsar maiden and the Baba Yagas; it could even be dangerous for him to return to the conscious world with such (horse) power at his disposal.

We see a parallel in the tale of "Vasilisa the Beautiful": upon receiving the burning skull from Baba Yaga, she uses it to illuminate her way home and to relight the fire in her step-mother's house, but buries it when she witnesses its destructive potential.

Jung speaks of the tradition in certain African tribes never to permit a victorious warrior to enter his village immediately upon returning from battle; he was obliged to stay in a little hut where he was kept on a vegetarian diet for several months before reentering his village. This was due to the danger he posed to his own people while in the frenzy of war.[14]

After this short digression, let us return to the scene where the hero's horse catches one of the strings while jumping over the stockade. Considering the response of the tsar maiden upon awakening, we can hardly imagine that she would have welcomed the hero into her bed. From this we can deduce that this was the only way of achieving union with the anima at this particular moment. Had he asked, the answer would probably have been "no," in fact, it would probably have cost him his life. This episode reminds us of the virgin goddess Artemis, caught bathing in her secret cave by Actaeon. Furious over the invasion of her privacy, she turns Actaeon into a stag and allows him to be torn limb from limb by his own hounds.[15]

In our tale, it is the Baba Yagas who suffer the brunt of the tsar maiden's anger, but they appear to know how to cope with their mistress, and, after all, they are women. This episode discloses the Amazon in the tsar maiden, a proud and independent woman, who is focused and goal oriented; who unites with men when she decides to do so; a partner rather than a subservient wife.

It is not difficult to see how such an image of the belligerent and vengeful woman appears in compensation to the patriarchal view of the feminine. It becomes constellated when the woman, and the Eros principle she embodies, is not given its due. This is the reason why the missing queen is such a widespread motif in the tales of our Western culture and why the tsaritsa in our tale fades out of sight on the threshold to the second half of life. To be sure, vanishing is not the same as fighting, but it may be symbolized by sleeping; both images witness to the difficulty for this part of the feminine to survive in a patriarchal society.

---

14   Jung, C.G. *Jung Speaking*, 33.
15   *Bulfinch's Mythology*, 34 f.

Vanishing can also be seen as vengeance; not as much as passive aggression, but as the loss of relatedness. The motif of the Amazon in Russian culture will be discussed at greater length in connection with the tale of "Mar'ya Morevna."

We now return to our raging tsar maiden where we find her questioning and rebuking the Baba Yagas in no uncertain words: "How dare you allow such a scoundrel into my kingdom?" The Baba Yagas escape her wrath by feigning innocence; they appear before their mistress "disheveled and in disarray" and claim that they had been unable to subdue the "scoundrel."

The tsar maiden now races after the hero, but he manages to jump over the *ditch* just before she catches up with him. It will be remembered that this was the ditch he had come upon shortly after parting from his brothers at the crossing. We had seen this crossing as a border between the conscious world and that of the unconscious. This explains why the tsar maiden is unable to jump over this ditch, for she is still very much a part of that other world; psychologically, she represents an unintegrated part of the hero's anima. As she speaks to the hero, however, we note that her fury gradually subsides. Instead of threatening or cursing him, she tells him to expect her in three years, adding that she will be coming by sea. We may ask whether, standing on this border, she is becoming conscious of what has taken place; perhaps she is even beginning to reconcile herself with this world.

The very next sentence in our tale speaks of our hero experiencing "sheer joy"! He is in his own world, on familiar ground, so to speak; he has managed to procure the water of life for his father and, most importantly, he has had an indescribable experience. It should be noted that this is the first sign of any kind of emotion from our hero.

As already mentioned, fairy tale heroes are very economical in their expression of feelings; in our tale, the hero shows no fear in following the road which leads to his death; he does not hesitate in jumping over the ditch, nor is he cowed by the menacing words of the Baba Yagas. The same holds true for his experience with the tsar maiden.

Not only is there little expression of feelings, but also a lack of rational deliberation. In fact, the hero responds to whatever confronts him by following his instinct. He reacts instinctively in standing up to the Baba Yagas; he follows his instincts upon entering the tsar maiden's chamber; he is led by the instinct of self-preservation in fleeing the tsar maiden's wrath. Psychologically, this last would amount to safeguarding the ego from extinction. Had he not succeeded in escaping the tsar maiden, all the long and arduous journey into the world on the other side of the ditch would have been in vain.

Many a hero has failed to retrace his steps into the world from which he came. He either perishes in that other world, which would be equivalent to a psychosis; or he returns to outer reality but cannot free himself from the images of the inner world, and lives a life of fantasy. In both cases he is unable to bring back his experiences and integrate them in the conscious world.

This emphasis on instinct explains why the animal so often appears after the hero has done everything possible to solve the problem confronting him. Marie-Louise von Franz holds that in fairy tale interpretation there is but one rule without an exception, and this says that one must never hurt a helpful animal, or ignore its advice.[16] By turning to our instincts we connect up with our psychic roots and this anchors us in life-threatening situations when the ego is powerless.

The "sheer joy" experienced by the hero upon hearing the tsar maiden's promise to visit him in three years' time is apparently so strong that it hinders his orientation in the conscious world. He makes his way as if in a trance, past the pillar where he parted from his brothers, turning left to the silver hill where the middle brother had pitched his tent. Here he sees his brother's horse "eating summer wheat and drinking honey water" and finds his brother resting inside his tent. Together with this brother he goes to look for the elder one. Once again, the reader receives very scanty information on his state of mind and his feelings. As all three brothers ride to the pillar and stop to rest, he senses nothing of the danger ahead; he willingly recounts the experiences of his journey and, most importantly, of having procured the water of life. Then, exhausted from his experiences, our valiant hero drops off to sleep. This sleep is an appropriate image for the state of unconsciousness which now envelops him.

Gold and silver are royal metals symbolizing the highest masculine

16   von Franz, *Shadow and Evil in Fairy Tales*, 119 f.

and feminine values respectively. The two elder brothers have done nothing to be worthy of such attributes. At best, we can see these symbols as their unrealized potential, or as their royal persona. The latter would suggest that the brothers only understand gold and silver in their concrete, outer manifestation. This is in contrast to the hero's experience of the *coniunctio*, his bringing about a union of the masculine and feminine in the world beyond the ditch. We may, therefore, assume that the gold and silver hills reintroduce the hero into a kingdom where there is no understanding of such inner values.

Evil often succeeds because it has no scruples about misusing power. The evil brothers do not shy away from killing the hero and cutting him into pieces. Returning to their father, they take credit for finding his youth and, in so doing, win the tsar's favor and secure their position as heirs to the throne. The water of life, which belongs to the anima and which, at this point in life, should rightly be turned toward inner development, is rerouted to serve their shadowy outer purposes.

The tsar has more power than any other person in the kingdom. He is given this power because he has a responsibility for the well-being of his people. What is often forgotten, however, is that, as the anointed, the tsar is responsible to God for the way he uses this power. In our tale, his two elder sons prove themselves unworthy of such power. It is only the third son who is capable of fulfilling this condition of kingship.

It is crucial to the interpretation of this tale that all three brothers are seen as shadows of the tsar. They are not individual egos but are all parts of the tsar's psyche. The tsar is the current dominant of collective consciousness; this means that it is his view of the world that determines the *Zeitgeist*. As we have seen, two of his three shadow sons are negative and only capable of perceiving reality in a concrete way.

As all three sons make their way out into the world in search for the tsar's youth, the hero, the tsar's positive shadow, chooses the road that foretells his death. Crossing the threshold from his father's world into that of the tsar maiden, he becomes exposed to another *Weltanschauung* and has to adapt himself accordingly. Returning to his father's world, he needs to do the same. We saw how dazed he was at the beginning as he retraced his steps to the pillar. The experiences of the other world were still very present in his mind and in his heart. When he met up with his brothers, he had not quite made the transition back to his father's world. As the story now shows, this is of such vital importance that the hero's inability to do so results in his death and dismemberment.

Dismemberment is a central motif in the shamanic initiation rites of many cultures, as well as in alchemy. It symbolizes a fundamental disruption in the prevailing conscious attitude, marking a point in the individuation process where nothing but a completely new orientation can enable the hero to find his way out of the dilemma he finds himself in. It is an intervention by the Self with radical consequences for the personality, and experienced as total destruction (of the former conscious attitude).

What we see here is the extraordinary importance ascribed to consciousness, and to the danger of not taking responsibility for anything one has experienced from the unconscious part of the psyche. In *Methods of Treatment in Analytical Psychology*, von Franz compares the drug fantasies of two brothers with the dream of a student on a similar theme.[17] Both scenarios are apocalyptic but the dreamer appears to have a goal, a task to perform, whereas the drug fantasy presents an image of sheer annihilation with no hope for the individual. "A more constructive aspect of the unconscious," writes von Franz, "is probably only constellated when it has a conscious ego as vis-à-vis."[18]

We have seen the hero prove himself many times in the other world. He is not afraid of jumping over the ditch which, psychologically, separates the two parts of the psyche; he shows himself capable of standing up to three Baba Yagas; he unites with the tsar maiden, even when the third Baba Yaga explicitly warns him against doing so; and he flees from this same furious being when she threatens to destroy him. In all these cases he follows his instinctive reaction and is successful. And then, arriving in familiar surroundings and being reunited with his brothers, his instinct appears to have abandoned him; he doesn't realize the danger posed by his brothers, and he must pay for this with his life.

And yet, seen from what follows, this is more chastisement than destruction for, no sooner have the brothers made off with the water of life, than a firebird flies in to save him. The firebird is a well-known

---

17   von Franz, *On Active Imagination*, 92-94.
18   von Franz, *On Active Imagination*, 95.

image in Slavic tales; because of the bird's beauty and its bright, burning colors, it is the goal of many a heroic quest. One of its feathers is capable of lighting up a whole room at night; it feeds on golden apples which restore youth; and, as in the present tale, it has access to the water of life. Symbolically, the firebird can be seen as a spiritual image of the anima or of the Self.

In our tale, the firebird first reassembles the dismembered hero; it then sprinkles the body with the water of death, whereupon the pieces grow together; lastly, it brings the hero back to life by sprinkling it with the water of life. Often this procedure is restricted to the water of life, but in this tale we find a nuance which provides a more differentiated psychological interpretation. First the different parts must be pieced together in the proper order, a restoration of the original body with no parts missing. Very concretely, it would make no sense to revive a foot here, the head there, an arm behind the tree, or to leave out some important organ or body part. Sprinkling the reconnected body parts with the water of death would then mean that this body, in its entirety, must die, that is, that the transformation into another attitude cannot take place in a partial or one-sided way. Only after this has been guaranteed can the body be revived.

The hero then thanks the firebird and makes his way home. Deceived by the reports of the two elder sons, his father banishes him from the kingdom. It is worthy of note that the hero does not attempt to justify himself or to share any of his experiences. In fact, he appears to realize that there is no understanding for what he had experienced on the other side of the ditch. No one apparently wants to know; no one is ready to listen.

This is a very real situation for anyone who gets insight into the unconscious. When we begin to work on our dreams and experience their influence in our life, when we learn to recognize the appearance of synchronistic phenomena or catch some indication of a complex reaction, or when something is revealed in active imagination which we cannot attribute to the ego; when such things happen to us, it is often difficult to convey them to someone who has not experienced this side of the psyche. This leads to isolation and estrangement from those to whom one had formerly been close. On a collective level, creative people, for example, writers, musicians, painters, often produce material which is not understood in their time. They are heroes because they have been able to access the source of life and manage to give it a form in the outer world. They, too, are often misunderstood and undervalued, but mostly they are not swayed by collective opinion, because of the inner experience they have been through. Such is the case with our hero: "...and so he strayed, homeless, for three years."

As mentioned earlier, the appearance of the number three in any symbolic material always suggests a fateful, dynamic development in time and space. It is a signal that some new process has been constellated in the unconscious. And so now, after three years have gone by, we learn of the arrival of the tsar maiden at the shores of this kingdom. It will be remembered that, standing on the other side of the ditch, she herself told the hero of this.

That the anima should move about on water is not difficult to understand for she is the archetype of life and all life originates in water. This would also explain why the phial with the water of life is in her possession. That she comes by sea shows that she is still in the unconscious part of the psyche. Her entering the conscious world will depend upon how she will be received in this kingdom, that is, whether collective consciousness, represented by the tsar, will appreciate her and give her the respect she deserves and, in a more general way, whether the tsar will be open to a psychic reality beyond the outer world.

The tsar maiden's asking for "the guilty one" leaves no doubt that it is the hero she has come for and no one else. He is the one who dared to enter her kingdom and her chamber at great peril to his life, awakening her from sleep and affecting a bond between them that materialized in the sons she bore. She is now bringing the product of their union into the outer world, but we would do well to remember that she is an Amazon and, as such, will insist on her conditions.

This becomes clear in her very first contact with the tsar. She stipulates in no uncertain terms that if "the guilty one" is not sent to her, she will "burn down and destroy the whole kingdom." At this point of the story, the tsar knows nothing of his elder sons' shadowy dealings. Psychologically, it shows how ignorant he is of this part of himself, for such an attitude is only possible when one's shadow is either completely repressed or split off. Moreover, if we see the tsar as representing collective consciousness, then we cannot but realize that this attitude is the prevailing one in the society over which he rules.

In the case at hand this blindness or misconstrued reality is directed toward the tsar maiden, a divine feminine being, psychologically the anima, who stands for the Eros principle. The anima is the inner woman for the man, the one who acts as a bridge to the unconscious part of the psyche.

Let us return for a moment to the beginning of our tale and review what had been said about the transition from the first to the second half of life. We saw this as an important threshold where psychic development shifts from the outer to the inner world. Here one must clean up one's household and, in the interest of wholeness, face whatever was ignored or rejected in the first half of life. The shadow must be dealt with if it hasn't been dealt with before and, for a man, the relationship with the inner feminine must be sought.

We see no signs of this happening in the present situation: upon receiving the water of life from his elder sons, the tsar had not questioned their account, but he banished the only one who could have challenged them. Now, threatened by total destruction, he behaves pragmatically by sending the elder son to the tsar maiden. In all these actions, he avoids confronting his shadow.

This is a common reaction to the shadow; we experience it as a disturbing uneasiness, and respond by repression or projection. It is an awkward feeling with negative energy that doesn't fit into our view of ourselves. We therefore assume that even if it does exist, then it must be outside of us. This diverts the irritation and we can get on with life. Such a reaction is most often triggered by impending danger where the ego is thrown back upon itself to provide a solution which goes beyond the concrete experience of reality.

In our tale, the tsar is faced with the destruction of the whole kingdom—psychologically, his worldview and his power—if he does not comply with the tsar maiden's wishes. He tries to solve the dilemma by sending his eldest son, his immediate heir. In a way, both the eldest and the middle son fulfill the tsar maiden's requirements: They *did* deliver the water of life and, since this was stolen from her, they would both

THE WATER OF LIFE

qualify as "the guilty ones." This is, of course, only part of the truth, the part provided by the tsar's eldest sons. From the point of view of the whole psyche, however, this is a one-sided explanation, favoring the shadow. The eldest son is understandably pleased with the prospect of acquiring such a beautiful and prestigious wife with whom he would reign upon his father's passing.

Unfortunately for both father and eldest son, this outcome is not acceptable to the tsar maiden. As the elder brother approaches, she instructs her twin sons to take whips and send their uncle "back to where he came from."

As noted earlier, the tsaritsa is no longer present in this latter part of the tale. We saw her as an aspect of the tsar's anima which disappeared on the threshold to the second half of life (p. 17). As we have seen, the tsar is not capable of making this transition. In patriarchal society, a woman's role is restricted to her biological and social function. She is subordinate to man and never acknowledged as an equal partner. Because her function is restricted by the collective to concrete reality, she can never fulfill her role as the anima that connects a man to the other, unknown part of his psyche. Her disappearance would, therefore, be supported by the hero's finding the tsar maiden asleep with the phial containing the water of life under her pillow (p. 28).

After the second attempt to appease the tsar maiden proves unsuccessful, the tsar is forced to consider other possibilities to save his kingdom. Only now does he order a search for the banished son; when the hero is found, the tsar bids him go to the tsar maiden. But here he is met with unexpected resistance. The hero does not fly into the arms of the tsar maiden as might have been expected. He sets conditions which show that the transformation he had undergone upon his dismemberment had far-reaching consequences.

His first demand is for a crystal bridge to be built connecting the tsar's kingdom with the tsar maiden's ship. Crystal is transparent and extremely strong. These qualities attest to the spiritual eminence of the anima. No one else thought of welcoming her in such a worthy fashion; no one seems to have realized who it was that had approached their shores.

As escorts on his way to the tsar maiden, the hero does not take his brothers or court officials but those simple men who had become his comrades in his three years of exile. They are to eat and drink and rejoice together with him. In so doing, he is bringing together the highest and the lowest of the collective, thereby implying that, when he ascends to the throne, the development which he had undergone will not be restricted to the nobility. This is an example of the Eros so badly missing in this kingdom.

Likewise interesting is the way the tsar maiden welcomes the hero: "They embraced, they kissed, they caressed one another." This is certainly a changed woman who greets him. Psychologically, it demonstrates the reciprocal transformation of the masculine ego and the anima which has now taken place.

The tsar maiden and the hero, together with their children, return over the crystal bridge to the tsar and tell him "everything as it had happened." Then justice is done and the evil brothers are banished. The final sentence of the tale now recounts how the tsar lives on "with his youngest in joy and plenitude." This is an unusually brief account which focuses on the tsar, even to the point of not mentioning a royal wedding.

It is a bit surprising that the hero doesn't succeed his father on the throne. It is likewise difficult to understand why the tsar maiden somehow fades into the background and is not even mentioned in the final sentence along with the hero or, indeed, that the hero is only referred to as the tsar's "youngest." After all that had taken place, after the way the hero had honored the tsar maiden in front of the whole kingdom, one might have expected that the couple would be given the final bow in this performance. From outer appearances, it now looks as if the tsar maiden has taken her place in this patriarchal society and stands quietly behind her man. Viewed psychologically, this is a very realistic scenario. It mirrors a situation where one has had the most amazing inner experiences but is unable to incorporate them into one's life. It all remains a fantasy and one goes over to the business of the day.

From the inner perspective, we see the ego of the tsar surviving a life-threatening assault from out of nowhere (the tsar maiden arrives by ship, asks for the guilty one and threatens to destroy the kingdom if her demands are not met). This forces him to realize that he has been putting his trust in dubious assumptions (his two elder sons) and underestimating those he had earlier scorned and abandoned (his youngest son). He distances himself from his former beliefs, that is, he represses them (he banishes his two elder sons). Finally, with the help his youngest son, he is able to reestablish his authority and capitalize on the new potential at his disposal (new energy provided by the water of life).

Both the outer as well as inner description indicates that no transformation has taken place within the tsar's psyche; it was only the hero who became transformed through his experiences in both worlds. The tsar who still sits on the throne and determines what goes on in his kingdom has not understood the implications of the water of life which his youngest son was able to procure for him. He has only seen that his elder sons were dishonest in stealing the phial, and for this he banished them from his kingdom. Most importantly, he has not given the tsar maiden the recognition she deserves; his response to her shows that even such existential danger did not open his heart to the inner reality of the psyche.

Viewed from an inner perspective, all this takes place within the tsar's psyche: the hero is but a part of this psyche; he is the positive shadow who has fathomed the depths and brought up the treasure. However, as long as the tsar maiden is not acknowledged and the hero is referred to only as the tsar's "youngest," this episode will remain a split-off part of the tsar's personality. In analysis, this would be comparable to having an archetypal dream of great significance and not being able to integrate it into one's life. This does not preclude the possibility of something changing in the tsar's psyche at a later time, but the present lysis shows that the essence of this experience has not been grasped.

There are other tales with a similar scenario where the couple does not even remain in the hero's kingdom but returns to that of the anima. One such example is the Russian tale "The Maiden Tsar." In this fairy tale, the hero presents the tsar with the water of life and death, and the rejuvenating apples; he wishes the tsar a long life and asks his blessings to marry the tsar maiden, with whom he then returns to her kingdom. Here the split becomes even more obvious and the lysis shows this hard-won treasure receding into the unconscious.

Von Beit attributes such a regression to the ego's difficulty in accepting the reality of the psyche, that is, of its unconscious as well as its conscious aspect. It is unable to integrate unconscious contents because it cannot find a place for them in its understanding of life.[19] In his *Zarathustra Seminars*, Jung quoted a sixteenth century Latin text of one of the Hermetic philosophers: "*In habentibus symbolum facilior est transitus...* For those who have a symbol," meaning, for those who are capable of thinking symbolically, "...the passing from one side to the other, the transmutation, is easier."[20] It is worthy of note that Jung translated "*transitus*" not as transition but as transmutation, for this latter, according to Webster, indicates a change into another nature, substance, form or condition," hence into another part of the psyche. This explains why Jung placed such importance on the ability to work with symbols for, being of both worlds, they provide a bridge allowing us to experience the psyche in its wholeness.

In the present tale, this is expressed by the twin motif. For the purposes of the tale, it would have been sufficient for the tsar maiden to have borne one child. This would have confirmed the union between the tsar maiden and the hero or, psychologically, between the two parts of the psyche. The fact that she bears twins suggests some additional meaning that is less readily discernable, that is, which must be considered symbolically.

The twin phenomenon will be discussed in more detail in connection with the tale "Two Ivans, Soldier's Sons." For now, suffice it to say that this motif signals the surfacing of some unconscious content. We know that the opposites are united in the unconscious, something that is impossible in consciousness. When such contents reach the threshold of consciousness, they break up into two, identical images, for this is the initial phase of their manifesting as opposites. This is the case in the tale at hand: The tsar maiden has born two identical sons. There is no difference between them either in their physical appearance or in their behavior.

Thus, we can say that this stage represents only a potential development because, being on the threshold, they can just as easily slip back

---

19   von Beit, *Symbolik des Märchens*, 444.
20   Jung, *Nietzsche's Zarathustra 2*, 1248.

into the unconscious as pass over into consciousness. An example for this is the way we experience dreams. We wake up in the morning and may have a clear image before us but, if we do not write it down or otherwise fixate it in our memory, it may soon disappear. This implies that, if we don't want to lose such new contents, we need to give them sufficient attention so that they can become established in consciousness.

The birth of twins therefore witnesses to the tentative nature of this new undertaking; more precisely, it shows that the tremendous psychic development which resulted from the union of the hero with the anima is still in danger of being swallowed up by the unconscious. The arrival of the tsar maiden and her loving response to the hero suggests that the unconscious is supporting this development; the crystal bridge, the costly preparations for welcoming the tsar maiden into this kingdom are evidence of the hero's commitment. However, as we see from the lysis of this tale, the tsar—the one who has the most to benefit from this transformation and who can best pass it on to his people—doesn't really understand the implications of what has taken place.

Psychologically, banishing his elder sons is equivalent to repressing the shadow, and living on with his youngest in joy and plenitude without mentioning the tsar maiden, completely ignores the role of the anima. The fact that there is no mention of a marriage, which might have anchored the couple in this kingdom, suggests that the birth of the twins remained a potential development to which the tsar, as collective dominant, was not receptive.

One small detail places the experiences mirrored in this tale into a broader context. We note that none of the characters have personal names. This is not the case in either of the other tales mentioned here, nor in any of the Afanas'yev variants. In the present tale we have a tsar, a tsaritsa, a tsar maiden, the eldest, the middle and the youngest tsarevich. This lack of personal names makes the characters more general and hence more archetypal. The only information we can glean from these titles points to their royal status; they are the elite, the best educated, cultured, most differentiated members of society. From this we can deduce that the problem constellated in this tale, that is, that of the transition from the first half of life to the second half of life, sets higher demands upon the individual. This corresponds to what Jung wrote in "The Stages of

Life," namely, that the first half of life is concerned with the biological and social demands of life, anchoring the individual in outer life, whereas the second half of life is a process of inner development, reconnecting man with his psychic roots in the unconscious.

II. The Speedy Messenger

In a certain kingdom, in a certain land, there were many impassable swamps. A road surrounded these swamps; riding fast, one needed three years to get around them; riding slowly, even five were not enough! A poor old man lived at the very edge of this road with his three sons. The first son was called Ivan, the second Vasiliy, and the third, Semën, the young lad. One day the poor old man decided to clear the swamps, lay a road for travelers on foot and on horseback, and build wooden bridges out of snowball bushes (*L. viburnum*); in this way, the journey would take three weeks on foot and three days and nights on horseback. He set to work with his children, and after a short time the wooden bridges were paved and the roads cleared.

The old man returned to his hut and said to his eldest son, Ivan: "Go, my dear son, sit under the bridge and listen to what the good people say in passing: Have we done our work well or not?" Obeying his father, Ivan went and hid himself under the bridge.

Two old men came walking over the wooden bridge, speaking to one another: "Whoever built this bridge and cleared this road— whatever he asks of the Lord, may it be granted to him." As soon as Ivan heard these words, he came out from under the bridge. "I built this bridge, together with my father and brothers." "And what do you ask of the Lord?" asked the old men. "May the Lord give me money for a lifetime." "Very well, go out into the open field and there you will find an oak tree; under this oak is a deep vault and in this vault you will find much gold, silver, and precious stones. Take a shovel and dig—the Lord will give you money to last a lifetime." Ivan went out into the open field, dug out much gold, silver, and precious stones from under the oak tree and took them home. "Well, dear son," said the poor old man, "have you seen anyone walking or riding over the bridge, and what did they say about us?" Ivan told his father about the two old men and how they had rewarded him for the whole of his life.

Next day the old man sent out his middle son, Vasiliy. Vasiliy sat under the bridge and listened. Two old men came walking over the bridge; as they neared his hiding place, they said: "Whoever built this bridge—whatever he asks of the Lord, may it be granted to him." No sooner had Vasiliy heard these words then he went out to the old men and said: "I built this bridge, together with my father and brothers." "And what do you ask of God?" "May the Lord give me bread for my whole life." "Very well, go home, stake out a piece of fresh land and sow it. The Lord will give you bread for your whole life!" Vasiliy went home, told his father all that had happened, staked out a piece of fresh land and sowed it.

On the third day the old man sent out his youngest son. Semën, the young lad, sat under the bridge and listened. Two old men came walking over the bridge; as they reached the place where he sat hidden, they said: "Whoever built this bridge—whatever he asks of the Lord, may it be granted to him." Semën, the young lad, heard these words, came out to the old men and said: "I built this bridge, together with my father and brothers." "And what do you ask of God?" "I ask for His grace to serve as soldier to the great sovereign." "Ask for something else. A soldier's service is hard; should you become a soldier, you will fall captive to the sea tsar and shed many tears." "Oh, you old people, you know well yourselves: whoever doesn't cry in this world, will cry in the next." "Very well," said the old men, "if you truly want to serve the tsar, we will give you our blessing." They laid their hands on Semën and turned him into a swift-footed stag. The stag ran to Semën's house; his father and brothers saw him out of the window and rushed out to catch him. The stag turned and ran back to the old men; they turned him into a hare. The hare darted back to the house; Semën's father and brothers saw him and rushed out to catch him but he turned back again. The hare returned to the two old men; they turned him into a little bird with a golden head. The bird flew home and sat at the open window; the father and his two sons scrambled to catch it but the bird flew back to the two old men. They returned it to its human form and said: "Now, Semën, young lad, go into the tsar's service. If you should ever need to get somewhere fast, you can turn into a stag, a hare, and a golden-headed bird, as we have taught you."

Semën, the young lad, came home and began to ask his father to let him enter the tsar's service. "How can you go?" said the old man. "You are young and foolish!" "No, father, let me go; it is God's will." The poor man gave his consent; Semën, the young lad, prepared for his journey, took leave of his father and brothers, and set out on his way.

After a long or a short time, Semën arrived at the tsar's court; he went straight to the tsar and said: "Your Royal Majesty, do not execute me, let me speak." "Speak, Semën, young lad!" "Your Majesty, take me into military service." "How can that be? You are young and foolish; how can you serve?" "Though I may be young and foolish, I will serve no worse than the others. I put my trust in God." The tsar consented, took him as a soldier and kept him near his person. After some time, a certain king declared a cruel war against the tsar. The tsar began to prepare for battle; at the appointed time his whole army stood ready. Semën, the young lad, asked to be taken to war. The tsar could not refuse; he took him along and set out to war.

The tsar marched for a long, long time with his troops; he left many lands behind him. The enemy was now very close; the battle would be starting in three days. At that moment the tsar realized that he was missing his battle mace and his sharp sword. He had forgotten them in the palace and now he had nothing to defend himself with, to repulse the enemy forces. The tsar issued a call to all his troops: Who could return speedily to the palace and bring him his battle mace and sharp sword? He promised his daughter, Mar'ya Tsarevna, in marriage to whoever would undertake this mission, half his kingdom as dowry and the rest upon his death. Several volunteers presented themselves. One promised to accomplish this task in three years, another in two years, yet another in one year. Then Semën, the young lad, said to the tsar: "I, Your Majesty, can go to the palace and bring back the battle mace and sharp sword in three days." The tsar was delighted, took him by the hand, kissed him on the lips, and immediately wrote a letter to Mar'ya Tsarevna, telling her to trust this messenger and to give him the sword and mace. Semën, the young lad, took the letter from the tsar and set out on his journey.

After he had gone a verst, (about a kilometer), he turned into a swift-footed stag and shot forward like an arrow from a bow. He ran and ran, and when he got tired, he turned from a stag into a hare. Then he raced ahead at a hare's pace. He ran and ran until all his legs hurt, and then turned from a hare into a little bird with a golden head. Now he went even faster; he flew and flew, and in a day and a half he came to the kingdom where Mar'ya Tsarevna lived. Resuming his human form, he walked into the palace and gave the letter to the tsarevna. Mar'ya Tsarevna took it, unsealed and read it; then she said: "But how could you run through so many lands in such a short time?" "Here's how" said the messenger. He turned into a swift-footed stag and ran several times across the tsarevna's chamber. Then he went up to her and put his head in her lap. She took a pair of scissors and cut a tuft of fur from his head. The stag turned into a hare; it hopped around a bit and jumped onto the Tsarevna's lap. She cut a tuft of fur from him too. The hare turned into a little bird with a golden head. The bird flew around the room and perched on the tsarevna's hand. Mar'ya Tsarevna cut some golden feathers from its head; she tied all of this—the stag's fur, the hare's fur and the golden feathers—into a handkerchief and hid it. The bird with the golden head then turned back into the messenger.

The tsarevna gave him provisions to eat and drink, prepared him for the journey and gave him the battle mace and sharp sword. Then they said good-by to one another, kissed heartily in farewell, and Semën, the young lad, made his way back to the tsar. Again he ran as a swift-footed stag, hopped like a slant-eyed hare and flew as a little bird. By the end of the third day, he caught sight of the tsar's camp.

At about three hundred paces from the camp, he lay down by the sea shore near a willow bush to rest from his journey. He laid the battle mace and the sharp sword at his side. From great weariness he soon fell into a deep sleep. Just then one of the generals happened to be passing by the willow bush. He saw the messenger, pushed him into the sea, took the battle mace and the sharp sword, and brought them to the tsar. "Your Majesty! Here are your battle mace and your sharp sword. I fetched them myself; that braggart, Semën, the young lad, will surely take three years to get here!" The tsar thanked the general, engaged the enemy and, in a short time, won a glorious victory.

And in the meantime, Semën, the young lad, fell into the sea. He was immediately seized by the sea tsar and carried into the depths. There he lived for a whole year; his heart was heavy and he cried bitter tears. The sea tsar came to him and asked: "Are you lonesome here, Semën, young lad?" "Yes, I am lonesome, Your Majesty." "Would you like to go up to the Russian world?" "Yes, I would like to, if such is your royal favor." Exactly at midnight, the sea tsar carried him up to the shore and returned to the sea. Semën, the young lad, started to pray: "Send me the sun, oh Lord!" Just before the rising of the red sun, the sea tsar snatched him up and carried him back into the sea depths.

Semën, the young lad, spent another whole year in the sea; his heart was heavy and he cried bitter, bitter tears. "Are you lonesome, asked the sea tsar?" "Yes, I am lonesome." "Would you like to go up to the Russian world?" "Yes, I would, Your Majesty." At midnight, the sea tsar carried him up to the shore and returned to the sea. With tears in his eyes, Semën, the young lad, began to pray: "Send me the sun, oh Lord!" Just as it was beginning to dawn, the sea tsar snatched him up and carried him back into the sea depths. Semën, the young lad, spent a third year in the sea; he was lonesome and he cried bitterly, disconsolately. "Are you lonesome, Semën?" asked the sea tsar. "Would you like to go up to the Russian world?" "Yes, I would, Your Majesty." The sea tsar carried him up onto the shore and returned to the sea.

With tears in his eyes, Semën, the young lad, began to pray: "Send me the sun, oh Lord!" Suddenly the sun rose and lit up the world with its rays, and now the sea tsar could no longer take him into captivity.

Semën, the young lad, set out for his kingdom. First he turned into a stag, then into a hare, and finally into the little golden-headed bird. Soon he was at the tsar's palace. By this time, the tsar had already returned from the war and betrothed his daughter, Mar'ya Tsarevna, to the deceitful general. Semën, the young lad, entered the chamber in which the bridegroom and bride were sitting at table. Mar'ya Tsarevna saw him and said to the tsar: "Sovereign father, do not have me executed, let me speak." "Speak my dear daughter. What is it that you wish?" "Sovereign father, my bridegroom is not the one who is sitting at the table, but the one who has just entered. Show us, Semën, young lad, how you had managed to run so swiftly for the battle mace and the sharp sword." Semën, the young lad, turned into a swift-footed stag, ran several times around the chamber and stopped before the tsarevna. Out from her handkerchief, Mar'ya Tsarevna took the bit of fur she had cut from the stag, showed the tsar the spot where she had clipped it, and said: "Take a look, father; here is my proof." The stag turned into a hare; it hopped about the chamber and came to the tsarevna. Mar'ya Tsarevna took the hare's fur out of her handkerchief. The hare turned into a little bird with a golden head. The little bird flew about the chamber and sat on the tsarevna's lap. Mar'ya Tsarevna untied the third knot in her handkerchief and showed the golden feathers. Then the tsar learned the whole truth. He ordered the general executed, married Mar'ya Tsarevna to Semën, the young lad, and made him his heir.

Alexander Afanas'yev, *Russian Folk Tales*, #259, trans. NB.

INTERPRETATION

"In a certain land, in a certain kingdom..." The tale opens up in the usual way of tales, making it clear from the start that the story has little to do with the concrete world, that it is referring to a different kind of reality—a reality neither connected to any specific land nor to any specific kingdom. Moreover, the tale makes no effort to explain this different reality but takes it for granted that it will be of interest to any audience. It speaks in images and leaves it to the reader or listener to interpret its message at will. This is the world which is now opening up before us.

The first image we are presented with is that of an impassable swamp. It is a swamp of enormous proportions. Traveling fast one needs three years to get around it; traveling slowly, even five are not enough. The earth upon which we live, upon which we build our shelter, grow our crops, move from place to place, this earth sinks from under our feet; even worse, it sucks us in and immobilizes us, it renders us powerless; ultimately it can destroy us. A great amount of energy is needed to avoid its dangers, to circumvent it.

Psychologically, this is an apt image for depression where one has lost all hope of ever getting out of the situation one is in, where no light appears at the end of the tunnel, where every impulse, every attempt at change is swallowed up before it can materialize. No words of support, no encouragement, no diversion is able to lift the cloud of futility and resignation which every new day brings.

There are people in the most desperate situations who fight for their lives and for the lives of their loved ones; others are surrounded with comfort and plenitude and have trouble getting up each morning because life has no meaning for them. This latter situation may have different causes, but the basic psychic condition it mirrors is the absence of energy at the ego's disposal. But, we may ask, if there is no energy in consciousness, where has it gone to? It was Jung's conviction that psychic energy, like all kinds of energy, cannot be destroyed; if it is missing in consciousness, it should be sought in the unconscious.[21]

As the source of all life, the unconscious can be symbolically seen as the mother. Such a loss of energy in consciousness may hence be attributed to the mother complex in its archetypal form. The image of the swamp with which this tale opens is an excellent image for this psychic constellation. All energy is pulled away from life, all movement and adaptation to life is frustrated. The word *stagnation*, from the Latin *stagnum*, refers to standing water, and translates symbolically into life that does not move.

In a letter to Warner McCullen, Jung writes: "One of the main features of a mother complex is the fact that one is too much under the influence of the unconscious ... it then looks, allegorically speaking, as if one had (been) swallowed by the mother."[22] But the fact that every archetype is ambivalent gives us hope. In the case of the swamp, we also know that it is a very fertile place. In ancient Egypt the warm mud of the Nile was held to be the source of all life. Mother goddesses have often been connected with the swamp, for example, the Egyptian goddess Helena who lived on a swamp island, or Isis who was honored by the singing of frogs from the Lycian swamp.[23] In his *Zarathustra Seminars*, Jung speaks of the swamp as "an exceedingly fertile place, teeming with low life... [and therefore] an excellent image of the collective unconscious...."[24] The ambivalence of the swamp image, like every other image of the mother archetype, lies in its being both the source of life and the cause of death.

We note that in this initial image there is no mention of a wife or mother. The mother appears only on the vegetative level in the image of the swamp. Viewed psychologically, we can say that the experience of the personal mother is overshadowed by the archetypal mother. Such a situation may also affect a whole culture. Here, the individual has little chance of making an impact upon the society in which they live; no change, no improvement, no strengthening of the ego can take place.

---

21 Jung, *Structure and Dynamics*, CW 8.
22 Jung, *Letters 2*, 305.
23 von Beit, *Symbolik des Märchens*, 128.
24 Jung, *Nietzsche's Zarathustra 2*, 1417.

Totalitarian societies often have such a disabling effect upon human development. Life becomes restricted to survival, and that often leads to regression.

And yet, the fertility of the swamp shows that even in the most hopeless regression there is always the seed of hope, the possibility of a breakthrough. Paradoxically, this seed is provided by the swamp itself, by that very same unconscious which is responsible for the regression. Heroes in fairy tales surprise us again and again by accomplishing the most humanly impossible deeds. This is because, psychologically, the hero represents that part of the personality which has a connection to the Self and which allows itself to be guided by Its impulses.[25]

There are, however, many people who are swallowed up by the mother archetype and who never become heroes. This shows that there is another important component to this figure. The hero must not only be receptive to the unconscious but must also have a strong enough ego to carry this *seed* back to consciousness and integrate it into life. This is the test that the witch often subjects the hero to; she needs to be convinced that he is worthy of being allowed entrance into this other world and being introduced to its secrets.

We can assume that the poor old man did not move to this lucrative location recently, but that he lived by the side of the swamp for a very long time. It is therefore highly significant that our tale begins with his decision to "...clear the swamps, to lay a straight road for travelers on foot and travelers on horseback, and to build white hazel wood bridges over the streams, so that a man on foot could pass through the swamps in three weeks and rider on horseback in three days."

How can one explain this sudden influx of energy? What has taken place that such thoughts could even have arisen in him? The only additional information we have is that the old man accomplished all this with the help of his three sons. If we see the sons as the old man's future, his gradual development, we might say that no solution to this problem could have been found without a substantial increase in the masculine, that is, in the spirit. In the case at hand, it is only after the masculine element has been raised to four that the old man is capable of even imagining such a solution to this problem.

---

25 von Franz, *Redemption Motifs*, 16, 19.

Our usual understanding of the quaternion is wholeness, completion. It is also a function of orientation, as in a compass which allows us to get our bearings in an unknown place. The quaternary system of Jung's typology provides orientation within the psychic structure. In *Archetypal Dimensions of the Psyche,* von Franz interprets the quaternion as representing a hitherto unconscious content which is now *becoming potentially conscious,* adding that this is the result of an inner dynamic process which aims at a broadening of consciousness.[26] Note the tentative formulation in the italicized text; it does not say that the quaternion indicates consciousness, but only the potential thereof.

These two complementary meanings of the quaternion suggest that the unconscious may provide the opportunity for attaining wholeness, but that it is up to the ego to take advantage of this outstretched hand. Indirectly, this also implies that, if the moment is not seized, these contents may sink back into the unconscious. If the apple is ripe, it should be eaten or cooked, made into apple sauce, baked in a pie ... otherwise it will fall off the tree, rot and return to the earth.

Such is the image of *kairos* with which our tale opens. The number four, constellated by the poor old man and his three sons, signals a readiness on the part of the unconscious to support a progressive development. At the same time, it speaks of the man's three sons, thereby showing that something dynamic has entered the picture, for every odd number carries this attribute in number symbolism. Three is also our way of determining the passage of time (past, present, future) and represents the dimensions by means of which we experience the concrete world (height, length, and breadth). Within the rich amplification of the number three we also find the trinary nature of the goddesses of fate. The Greek Moirai were believed to spin the thread of life, measure its length, and determine the time of death by cutting it off.

In light of these different amplifications, we can see the initial situation in our tale as heralding a potential transformation in the masculine psyche. The disabling influence of the swamp, seen as the backward pull of the unconscious, now gives way to the possibility of a more active participation in life. The ego is strengthened by the gradual growth of spirit, enabling such a development.

---

26 von Franz, "The Cosmic Man," in *Archetypal Dimensions,* 142.

Note that the swamp is not eradicated or dried out; it continues to exist, but the old man has found a way of coping with the problem it presents. He has, so to speak, learned to get around it. This shows how difficult it is to deal with an archetype and how naive and arrogant to think that the ego can overcome it by will power alone. There is always an element of *deo concedente*, that favorite expression of the alchemists: God willing.

As should be obvious from the above, I will be taking this fairy tale from the perspective of masculine psychology, that is, I will be seeing the problems encountered, as well as the solutions arrived at, as descriptive of the masculine, rather than the feminine, psyche.

In "The Speedy Messenger," the old way of doing things is represented by the poor man living by the side of the swamp; the transition to a new way of life, the poor man's development out of this original stagnation, is represented by his sons and particularly by his third son, Semën, the young lad. This epithet is used throughout the tale and probably has the same function, though not quite the same meaning, as the fool in other tales.

The fool is usually looked down upon and not taken seriously because he is considered naive, lazy, dimwitted. At the end, however, we realize that this is not so, rather that he is judged in such a way because his values are not recognized by the collective.

Initially, this also happens to Semën: When the lad seeks his father's blessing to go into the service of the tsar, the father answers: "Why should you go ... you are young and foolish!" The tsar responds in like manner: "Impossible! You are young and foolish. How can you serve?" Since we never see Semën acting foolishly, we must assume that the reservations against him are based exclusively upon this youth. In both cases, the decision is reversed after Semën's confident and courageous reply. It may be that the symbolic meaning of the *child* with its creative potential and spontaneity are not sufficiently acknowledged in this collective, and that it is the hero's task to prove that he is able to stand up for his values. We need to keep an eye open for these special values that set Semën apart from the others because they will provide the answer to the problem constellated in this fairy tale.

Clearing the swamps, laying straight roads and building bridges over the streams must have been a Herculean task for the old man and his sons. It required concentrated effort and perseverance. Such traits are often lacking in a man with a mother complex.

But what to do, now that the great work has been accomplished? Perhaps the father senses the need to come out of his one-sided introversion and to make contact with his environment. He bids each of his sons to sit under a bridge and hear what others say about the work they have done. This can be interpreted psychologically as opening up to the world, including the extraversion so badly needed for the flow of energy in the psyche.

Typology is concerned with individuation and hence with wholeness. It is, however, often misused as an excuse for not doing what is difficult. For an extravert, any introverted activity requires an effort; for an introvert, the same holds true for extraversion. We have all heard statements like: "Oh, I can't run for this office. That's much too extraverted for me." Or "How can you sit alone all day with your heartache? Come on, let's go out to a party. I'll introduce you to a whole lot of interesting people!"

It is equally difficult for introverts as well as extraverts to accept the fact that both attitudes are necessary to keep libido (psychic energy) flowing. Jung writes in *Psychological Types*:

> The concept of energy implies that of polarity, since a current of energy necessarily presupposes two different states or poles, without which there can be no current. Every energetic phenomenon ... consists of pairs of opposites: beginning and end, above and below, hot and cold, earlier and later, cause and effect, etc. The inseparability of the energy concept from that of polarity also applies to the concept of libido.[27]

As so often happens in fairy tales, when the hero has done his best and cannot proceed any further, a wise old man or an animal comes to his help. Once again, the archetype of the spirit steps in to support the forward movement. This is what now happens. We see the cyclical process operating in the tale: the hard work on the swamp was impossible without an increase in the masculine element (spirit). Now, after

---

27   Jung, *Psychological Types*, CW 6, § 337.

the four have done their part, the unconscious gives another push to keep the process going. This is the kind of work we do when working on dreams or in active imagination.

The impulse given by the wise old man in fairy tales is usually of a double nature: He makes the hero more conscious of his situation by asking questions or by warning him of possible dangers; he likewise bestows magical gifts upon him.[28] We see this clearly in the case of Semën, the young lad. In answer to his wish to go into the service of the tsar, Semën is told that this will bring him much hardship and suffering, and that it will lead to his falling into the hands of the sea king. This warning doesn't diminish Semën's resolve: "Oh, you old people," he tells the two old men whom he meets on the bridge, "you know well yourselves: Whoever doesn't cry in this world, will cry in the next." Semën's words leave no doubt of his courage and wisdom, and he receives their blessing and their gifts.

Semën is the hero in this tale. Seeing the hero as "...an archetypal model and pattern for the right kind of behavior"[29] implies that the solution he brings will be that of the unconscious. This would be different from any solution coming from the conscious part of the psyche.

When a negative archetypal content is constellated—here the negative mother archetype—the solution is often not to eliminate it, for example, to burn the witch, but to induce it to turn its other face. Fairy tales are rich with such examples: The hero or heroine knows how to speak with the witch, knows what to say and, sometimes, what to avoid saying. "Vasilisa the Beautiful" is a good example of this. By respecting the witch's secrets, Vasilisa wins the witch's approval and gains her favor. We see the opposite in "Mother Trudy" (Grimm 43). Here the heroine doesn't realize that some things are better left unsaid, nor does she possess the wisdom to fear and avoid certain situations. As we know, this maiden pays with her life for such a naive attitude toward evil.

Respecting the witch's secrets is not the only way of inducing the witch to turn her other face; sometimes one needs to show that one can stand up for oneself. When the hero in the Russian version of "The

28   Jung, *Archetypes*, CW 9i, § 404.
29   von Franz, *Redemption Motifs*, 19.

Water of Life" comes to the witch's hut, and when the latter tries to intimidate him by asking if he comes "fleeing duty or seeking it," he answers: "Oh, you old hag, you! You've neither fed me nor given me to drink, but are already questioning me." After these words the witch satisfies his hunger and thirst, gives him one of her own steeds and sends him off with a "God be with you!" [sic].

So too in analysis: By working truthfully and respectfully on the negative aspect of any archetypal constellation, we may gradually come to see a shift taking place toward its positive pole.

In volume 9i of the Collected Works, Jung speaks mostly of the negative aspects of the mother complex, but also of its positive manifestations. Among others, he mentions: "...a finely differentiated Eros ... a great capacity for friendship ... feeling for history ... wealth of religious feelings ... ambitious striving after the highest goals; opposition to all stupidity, narrow-mindedness, injustice, and laziness; willingness to make sacrifices for what is regarded as right ... perseverance, inflexibility and toughness of will..."[30] (NB: The German original for the last two traits, "... Unbeugsamkeit und Zähigkeit des Willens...," may perhaps be rendered more positively as: *an uncompromising and tenacious will...*).

When answering the two old men, Semën displays several of these positive traits. He is not allowing the negative mother to use him for her mouthpiece but is mirroring some of the archetype's positive aspects. In an analytical situation, we would do well to keep these positive aspects in mind and to put as much energy into them as we can whenever they appear in the analysand's material.

We spoke above of the appearance of the wise old man in fairy tales, but in our tale, there are two where one would seem to have been enough. One of the interpretations of the number *two* is the splitting of the original wholeness into the opposites. In the unconscious, opposites coexist. Only when an unconscious content crosses the threshold does the discriminating function of consciousness cause it to break up into opposites. There is an earlier stage, however, when such contents approach the threshold but have not yet crossed it. Here the opposites are not yet manifest, the ego is only capable of perceiving their double nature. As

---

30 Jung, *Archetypes*, CW 9i, § 164 f.

one can imagine, this bespeaks a very tentative and fragile stage of development and, in truth, such impulses can just as easily slip back into the unconscious. This we often experience with dream images.

This twin symbolism of the number two alerts us to the possibilities for development arising from the unconscious, and to the need of putting one's energy into taking such creative impulses on board. There are indeed many myths and fairy tales which lead to a negative lysis because the ego is too weak to perform this supportive role.[31] In the case at hand, the appearance of two old men would indicate that something new from the realm of the spirit was approaching consciousness and, moreover, that these contents could prove helpful to the hero if he responded to them properly.

In order to better understand Semën's response to the two old men, we need to compare it with that of his elder brothers. We saw the father as exemplifying the old attitude and his three sons as the gradual transition into a new way of life. Psychologically, this is an illustration for overcoming the negative mother complex, pictured in our tale by the image of the swamp.

After the tremendous effort of making the swamp passable, the father bids each of his sons in turn to sit under one of the bridges and listen to the comments of those who pass by. The two wise men appear to all three brothers, praise them for their work and offer to fulfill their wishes as reward for their efforts.

The first son, Ivan, asks to be rich for the rest of his life. He is told to look for a chest full of gold, silver, and precious stones. From the context, we can infer that these riches can be equated with money, or psychologically with libido or psychic energy. Ivan only needs to dig up the chest to be rich for the rest of his life. This does not involve too much effort, but, when we consider that all the energy of a man with a mother complex is in the unconscious, in the power of the mother archetype, we can understand that the very first thing he needs is enough libido to counteract the archetype's backward pull.

The second son, Vasiliy, asks to be given bread for the rest of his life. He is told what to do to acquire it. After a man has the necessary

---

31   von Beit, "Die göttliche Zwillinge," *Gegensatz und Erneuerung.*

libido (the libido that Ivan received), he is able to begin doing things for himself. It is worthy of note that the two old men do not simply provide Vasiliy with bread for the rest of his life: they tell him how to work for it. It is difficult to imagine that a peasant would not know how to grow grain and make flour. Rather it seems that, for lack of libido, this had not been possible before, that is, he had not been able to nour-ish himself.

It is now Semën's turn to sit under the bridge. His wish is to go into the service of the tsar. This is a further step in the development of the ego and signals a readiness to go beyond one's own needs, to be of service to others. We are reminded of the initiation rites of indigenous peoples where a similar shift is made away from the immediate family to the clan.

The first son asks for riches; he is given gold, silver, and precious stones. The second son asks for bread; he is provided with the means of obtaining it. In bestowing the ability to transform into a stag, a hare, and a little bird with a golden head upon the third son, the two old men offer gifts whose connection to Semën's wish is not immediately apparent.

For a man with a mother complex the instinctual sphere is often disturbed. It is, therefore, most appropriate that Semën's first two gifts enable him to transform into two animals, the stag and the hare.

The stag is an image of powerful masculine energy. During the rutting season in fall, males begin roaring, thus announcing their inter-est to females and warning other males not to come near. Such a stag might gather up to fifty female deer around him.[32] It is perhaps for this reason that ancient peoples connected the stag with the invincible sun. For the alchemists, the stag's fleeting nature associated it with Mercury; indeed, one of Mercury's epithets was *cervus fugitivus* (the fugitive stag).

The hare is also known for its fleeting movement. It doesn't run so much as it hops, and its path is often zig-zagged, which is the way of nature. The hare is sensitive to outer stimuli and has a nose for the unpredict-able.[33] Typologically, this would refer to the function of intuition.

32 *Grzimek's Animal Life Encyclopedia*, vol. 13, 154.
33 Birkhäuser-Oeri, *The Mother*, 149.

Both the stag and the hare are symbols for Mercury and are hence apt images for the individuation process. The associations with alchemy are interesting because of the title of the tale; after all, Mercury was known as the messenger of the gods, and he was swift-footed thanks to his winged cap and sandals.

In *Psychology and Alchemy*, we find a seventeenth century print where the hare, representing Mercury, shows the alchemist the entrance to "The Mountain of the Adepts" with the Temple of the Wise inside it. This temple is lit by the sun and moon, and stands on seven steps, the seven stages of the alchemical opus. Above is the phoenix, as a symbol of rebirth. That the temple itself is hidden inside the mountain indicates that the philosopher's stone lies buried within the earth. At the bottom, we see two figures depicting the alchemist who is blind until he learns to follow his natural instinct, symbolized by the hare.[34]

The hare is, moreover, a very fertile animal. It is because of its fecundity that it was an attribute of love gods such as Aphrodite and Bacchus. Its meat was considered an aphrodisiac (from Aphrodite). A rabbit's or hare's foot, now worn for luck, was primarily a love charm. The hare's connection with witches was widespread and may be attributed to the negative value attributed to sexuality in Christianity.

In fairy tales, transformation into an animal often represents regression: "The Beauty and the Beast" (French, 33), "Jorinda and Joringel" (Grimm, 69), and "Snow White and Rose Red" (Grimm, 161) are but three tales in which a human being has been bewitched into animal form and must be redeemed, that is, returned to human shape by the hero or heroine.

Our fairy tale differs from all the above in that Semën, the young lad, receives the ability to turn into an animal and back at his own will. This gift of the two old men in our tale leads to a broadening of consciousness through the experience of the instinctual, but makes this transformation dependent upon ego control.

For Germanic warriors, the wild, ecstatic experience of turning into a raging bear at the battlefield was triggered by exhaustion and loss of consciousness. It amounted to a split in the personality; the warrior lay

---

34   Jung, *Psychology and Alchemy*, CW 12, § 195.

sleeping in one place, the bear raging in another. The return was also
not self-willed; the berserker had to be called by name to regain his human shape. This freedom from ego control was considered a desirable
and strengthening experience for a warrior. In Semën's case, it would
have been extremely dangerous to give up ego control. Considering the
tremendous effort which went into coping with the swamp, the hero's
primary task at this stage appears to be strengthening his ego and freeing himself from the regressive pull of the unconscious. In Jungian
terminology this refers to the development necessary in the first half
of life.

The third transformation granted to Semën, the young lad, is that
of turning into a little bird with a golden head. In contrast to the stag
and hare, the bird is at home in the air. For a messenger, it would have
the advantage of being able to fly over obstacles that no animal can.
For example, it could perch on a dried out tree in the very middle of a
swamp and not be in danger of being sucked in. That the bird's head
is golden would suggest some spiritual property of the highest value, or
sun quality. For Semën's role as a messenger it might have been enough
to receive this one gift. What can it mean that the little bird only comes
after the stag and the hare?

As in the case of the brothers' wishes, here too, we can discern a
progression in the three gifts granted to Semën by the two old men. Had
he not integrated the qualities of both the stag and the hare, he would not
have been well-grounded in his instinctual masculinity. This would
have made him an easy prey for a renewed attack by the mother archetype.
Had he only been taught to change into a bird, his sole means of escaping
the mother would have been into the world of the spirit. This is a common reaction of the man with a mother complex; he flees into a realm
where the mother cannot follow. Who knows if Semën's meeting with
Mar'ya Tsarevna would have taken the same course, or if he would have
wanted so badly to leave the sea kingdom had he not experienced the
stag and the hare in himself. That the gift of the bird comes last and
that the bird's head is golden adds a valuable spiritual component to
his development. We note, furthermore, that the three gifts are complementary to one another. Remaining in the stag or hare phase would
have led to a one-sided instinctual development, whereas the ability to

transform into a bird would restrict one's development to the realm of the spirit.

Having said this, we need to realize that the symbolism of the stag and the hare is broader than the instinctual manifestation of these animals. In "The Phenomenology of the Spirit in Fairy Tales," Jung devotes a whole chapter to the theriomorphic symbolism of the spirit.[35] It may seem strange to place animals in the category of the spirit. Jung shows, however, that the appearance of animals in unconscious material merely signifies that the contents they represent are outside the human sphere. They may be below as well as above it: below, as the purely instinctual; above, as demonic or superhuman, that is, spiritual.[36] The conscious mind experiences these two aspects as polarities, but in the unconscious they are one. This emphasizes the importance of always keeping both aspects in mind when amplifying such symbols.

It is easy for us to see animals as instincts, but more difficult to see these instincts as divine; this is probably due to the influence of Christianity on our experience of life. Instincts have fallen into the shadow and are mostly perceived in their negative aspects. That this has not always been the case can be seen in such examples as the Germanic berserkers, the ecstatic rites of the Dionysian mysteries, or the initiation rites of shamans, to name just a few. Helping animals in fairy tales attest to this double aspect; animals that speak, that give advice, and that direct the hero or heroine to their goal all testify to a wisdom and knowledge inaccessible to the ego.

There is yet another way in which animals are superior to humans, namely, in that they remain true to their nature. The human ego which has raised man so high above the animal, has often perverted him.[37] This is the reason why the appearance of animal helpers in fairy tales always indicates a return to man's psychic roots, a psychic grounding. This has a stabilizing effect upon the hero and neutralizes the warping of his consciousness.

The contents of the gifts received by Semën from the two old men bear strong resemblance to the initiation rites of indigenous peoples in

---

35 Jung, *Archetypes*, CW 9i, §§ 419-435.
36 Jung, *Archetypes*, CW 9i, § 419.
37 Jung, *Archetypes*, CW 9i, § 420.

that they further his instinctual as well as spiritual development. He now has the attributes of the stag, the hare, and the little bird with the golden head at his command. They have become part of him to use as he sees fit. The freedom to decide when to use them has also strengthened his ego; furthermore, it has made him responsible for not abusing their power.

Another aspect of Semën's experience with the two old men which is suggestive of initiation is that of secrecy. Semën's secret is that of his transformations. Upon receiving these gifts, he tries them out on his family but he never tells them that the animals they see and try to catch are he himself. This is in contrast to his brothers who tell their father everything that happened and how they were rewarded by the two old men. Semën, the young lad, only asks his father's permission to go into the tsar's service. And later on in the tale, when Semën sets out to fetch the tsar's weapons, he is careful to put some distance between himself and the army before turning into a stag. The first person to whom he divulges his secret is Mar'ya Tsarevna, the tsar's daughter.

The keeping of a secret requires ego strength and is, therefore, ego-building. This is perhaps the reason why man has always experienced a need for secrecy. A secret sets one apart. It separates one from the masses. Initiation prevents man from becoming dissolved in the collective.[38] The initiate is "he who knows" about matters that are not accessible to the community at large.[39] We often recognize this ego-building function in the secrets of children, especially in their games and special relationships.

There is yet another aspect of the secret which bears looking into, for the experience of the unconscious, the breaking through of unconscious contents into consciousness, often becomes a personal secret because it is so difficult to transmit to others.[40] Who among us has not felt cut off from friends and colleagues because the inner experience of analysis could not be shared, or the precious gift of dreams could not be understood? Who has not had the experience of recounting a dream and being confronted with a blank stare or, even worse, with

38   von Beit, *Symbolik des Märchens*, 306.
39   Eliade, *Sacred and the Profane*, 188 f.
40   Jung, *Psychology and Alchemy*, CW 12, § 61.

ridicule? Such experiences isolate us; they keep us from sharing what is most important to us. But they have another effect as well for, if the energy is kept from going out, it flows inward and activates the unconscious. Our dreams become stronger, more meaningful; we register synchronicities where earlier we might have considered them meaningless coincidences. At times contents which had been successfully repressed for a long time break through into consciousness. This may not always be easy, but it is cathartic; it makes us aware of hitherto unrealized aspects of our personality and allows us to work on them. In short, the dialogue is no longer primarily between the ego and the outside world, but increasingly between the ego and the unconscious. This is a shift which normally takes place in the second half of life. It should, therefore, not surprise us that Jung saw individuation as modern man's version of initiation rites.

The betrayal of a secret is a well-known motif in fairy tales. It may disclose a weakness of the ego or indicate a lack of trust in the secret content.[41] We find this in the Grimm tale of "The Golden Children" where the old fisherman cannot refrain from disclosing the source of their sudden wealth to his wife, whereupon the riches bestowed upon them by the golden fish suddenly disappear. In a German parallel to "The Speedy Messenger," a shadow figure is responsible for the betrayal. The hero doesn't realize that he is being followed by a comrade with evil intentions; the man witnesses the hero's transformation, kills him and takes credit for delivering the vital object—in this case, a ring—to the king.[42]

In contrast to the above examples, the secret is kept in "Cinderella" (Grimm, 21) and "The Six Swans" (Grimm, 4); as a matter of fact, the positive lysis in such tales depends upon this being so. The same holds true for "The Speedy Messenger." Here the secret is not divulged until the right moment when the kairos has become constellated; this happens after a bond has been established between Semën and Mar'ya Tsarevna, the tsar's daughter.

At the start of the tale, nothing happens until the old man has three adult sons with whom to take measures against the swamp.

---

41   von Beit, *Symbolik des Märchens*, 399.
42   "Der schnelle Soldat," *Deutsche Märchen seit Grimm*, § 28

Psychologically, we saw this as a strengthening of the spirit, without which such a task could not even have been contemplated by a man with a mother complex. We recognized further development in the wishes of the three brothers and finally in the three gifts received by Semën. The repetition of the number three underscores the dynamic nature of this process. Figuratively speaking, Semën, the young lad, is propelled out of the swamp and made ready for the tasks which lie before him.

That Semën receives his gifts in answer to his wish "to serve as soldier to the great sovereign" may be interpreted as reward for this noble intention. Although, at this point, the reader has no idea where Semën's path will lead, the two old men appear to have this knowledge because they warn him about the difficulties ahead. We can only say with certainty that, unlike for his brothers, his development will go beyond the purely personal, that it will have collective repercussions.

And so our hero takes leave of his father and brothers, and makes his way to the tsar's court. He is no longer living passively by the side of the swamp; he now has a goal. He is still referred to as the young lad, but he is on his way to becoming a man. Going into the tsar's service implies subordinating himself to the collective values of his time and, if necessary, fighting for them. Military service has always been a maturing experience for a man with a mother complex because it teaches him discipline and makes him realize that he is a man like any other.

A man with a mother complex often thinks himself somehow special, privileged. On an individual level this could be ascribed to the exaggerated expectations of his personal mother; on an archetypal level it is the Great Mother, or the mother archetype, which instills such fantasies in him. If he is a real hero, he must prove it with his deeds, like Hercules; if he is not, he will only live a heroic fantasy life and feel unappreciated and misunderstood by the world. Instead of fighting he will then seek solace in the mother's embrace and succumb anew to the backward pull of the swamp.

Such a man often *has* potential, he may indeed be endowed with special gifts, but it is usually hard for him to do the work necessary to bring these gifts to fruition. He takes shortcuts, he procrastinates; consciously or unconsciously, he considers it below his dignity to do simple, menial work, the things that every one of us must, at times, do. He avoids making a decision because this narrows his choices. He is, after all, the son of the Great Mother and he expects the world to appreciate this even if he has nothing to show for it.

In the nineteenth century, a Russian writer by the name of Ivan Goncharov wrote a novel under the title of *Oblomov*. This is a brilliant account of a person with such a psychic disposition. The novel at once became a best seller because the public realized that its hero, Il'ya Oblomov, was to be found throughout Russian society. A word *Oblomovshchina* (Oblomovism) was coined to express this phenomenon and remains in the Russian vocabulary to this day. Incidentally, the novel takes place in St. Petersburg, a city built by Peter the Great upon a great swamp.

Our tale needs to be seen against this cultural background. Semën, the young lad, serves as a perfect illustration for our definition of the hero as a model ego. Despite the fact that he grows up at the edge of an enormous swamp, he doesn't become infected by this national phenomenon; on the contrary, he shows the way out of it.

We left our hero as he was setting out toward the tsar's court. What awaits him there? What sort of tsar will he be confronted with? Today any monarch has, by and large, only symbolic significance; in earlier days the tsar had sole responsibility for his subjects. In fairy tale interpretation, he is considered the collective dominant of his land. He serves as an example for his people and, in Jungian terminology, symbolizes the incarnation of the Self. His duties can be summarized as follows:

1. To make laws

2. To serve as a judge

3. To wage war

4. To mediate between man and God

5. To guarantee the fertility of the land

As we follow Semën, the young lad, on this new part of his journey, we will have occasion to measure the tsar of our tale against the above and see how well he fulfills the expectations of his office.

We remember that, initially, the tsar had rejected Semën's request to serve him. He treated the hero by collective standards and did not have the wisdom to look beyond them. It is only after Semën's courageous and confident reply that the tsar changes his mind. This episode bears similarity to the response of the Baba Yaga in other tales; as the mighty hero enters her hut, the Baba Yaga tests his resolve and courage. After he stands up to her and shows that he will not be intimidated, she changes her tone and later even helps him. Something of the kind may also be heard in the tsar's depreciatory words to Semën, the young lad, at their initial encounter; here too, it is Semën's response which discloses his heroic nature and results in his being accepted into the tsar's service.

This scene reveals something important about the tsar. His speaking to Semën in such a belittling way suggests that he, too, may have such a Baba Yaga in his psyche, that is, that he is under the influence of the negative mother complex but, being unconscious of it, projects it onto Semën.

Whatever the reasons for the tsar's reply, it doesn't speak well for his faculty of judgement (#2). In the *Old Testament*, King Solomon's response to the two harlots who approach him with a child serves as a classic example of judgement which includes wisdom and empathy.[43] From a typological perspective, this would refer to the feeling function, that is, judgement based on value.

Shortly after the above episode, we learn that a "terrible war" has been declared against the tsar. Assembling his army he sets out to confront the enemy. The distance which the tsar's army must travel is especially emphasized: "For a long, long time the tsar marched with his troops. He left many, many lands behind him..." This is an interesting detail to which we will shortly return, but first we must take note of another strange incident. When the troops are only three days' march from the enemy, the tsar suddenly realizes that he has forgotten his weapons in the palace. He is completely unprepared to engage with the enemy, to protect his own life and the lives of his people. We might well say that he is helpless in the face of aggression. This, too, is a characteristic of a man with a mother complex. In the case of a tsar, this would mean that he is incapable of waging war, #3 on the list of a tsar's responsibilities.

But why must he himself fight when he has a whole army at his command; why can't he support his troops by just being with them?

---

43   1 Kings 3, §§ 16-27.

This doesn't appear to be an option; the tsar must go into battle, and now we learn that he has forgotten his weapons.

And what might this enemy be? We only know that the tsar has been challenged to fight "a terrible war" and that the field of battle is very far from his own land. Later we learn by inference that the battle is to take place close to the sea. Symbolically, this implies that the enemy is coming from the unconscious, or indeed that it is the unconscious itself which the tsar must now confront.

The fact that the unconscious appears in such a threatening form should give us thought. Has the tsar been neglecting this part of his psyche or, even worse, has he been living against it? As ruler of his land, the tsar is an image of the Self; he exemplifies unity and totality.[44] Jung even described the Self as a "God-image."[45] The fourth duty on the above list stipulates that the tsar mediate between his people and God; it hardly speaks well of the tsar's relationship to the divine that the present *mediation* is announced as a "terrible war."

We turn now to #5 on the list of a ruler's responsibilities, to that of guaranteeing the fertility of the land. This requirement has always been dependent upon the tsar himself providing offspring; but no man can be fruitful without a feminine counterpart. This is true both concretely and symbolically; in the latter case, the woman in question would be the anima, the inner woman. She is the one who would make him whole and capable of being creative.

We learn that the tsar has a daughter, but there is no mention of a tsaritsa, a queen. This indicates that, at one time, he did have a relationship with the feminine and that this relationship was a fruitful one, at least physically. Symbolically, the absence of a tsaritsa implies that the tsar is no longer united with the feminine part of his psyche and that he is ruling in a one-sided masculine way.

We remember that there was also no female being at beginning of the tale. The feminine only existed in the form of a swamp, an image of the all-devouring mother. In such a situation, a man remains in the role of a son; he cannot get a foothold in life and he is unable to relate

---

44   Jung, *Aion*, CW 9ii, § 64.
45   Jung, *Aion*, CW 9ii, § 42.

to a woman as partner. The task of our hero is to find a way out of this dilemma and break away from this perilous backward pull of the unconscious.

Returning to the tsar, we note that he takes no action toward eradicating or otherwise coping with the swamp. In practice, this would require giving orders or passing laws to improve travel and communication in his kingdom, a responsibility falling under #1. That the task falls to the common man may show that the psychological problem represented by the swamp, the mother complex, is a common one in this kingdom and, moreover, that the tsar is either not concerned about the welfare of his subjects or is unable to deal with it. On an inner level, working on the mother complex must be seen as a psychological matter; it belongs under task #4, for it requires of a ruler that he act as a bridge between the physical and spiritual reality of the psyche.

We have found the tsar wanting in all five points listed above. As the anointed one, as one who is expected to have a special relationship to the divine and to carry the responsibility for his people, the tsar is not scoring well. Might this be the reason for the "terrible war" which is now launched against him? The unconscious turns a vengeful face upon those who do not meet their obligations. The more power one has, the greater is one's responsibility to do the right thing with it.

Faced with a perilous situation, the tsar tries desperately to find someone to fetch his weapons in time; he promises his daughter in marriage with half his kingdom as dowry and the rest upon his death. Today it would be considered unworthy and cowardly of the ruler to sacrifice his daughter in such a way. Viewed symbolically, it witnesses to the insufficient estimation of the feminine in general; in the case of the tsar, it points to a lack of respect toward the young feminine within his own psyche.

Remembering the long journey to the scene of battle, it does not surprise us to learn that the first three volunteers offer to accomplish this task in one to three years. It is only Semën, the young lad, who is able to fetch the weapons in three days. This would never have been possible without the gifts he received from the two wise men.

Semën's return to the tsar's court has additional consequences, for it introduces the young lad to Mar'ya Tsarevna. A young woman, an anima figure, now appears on the scene. She is the same age as Semën and one senses an immediate affinity between them. After Semën explains his mission, Mar'ya Tsarevna asks how he managed to make the journey from her father in only one and a half days. Semën, the young lad, who had never divulged his secret to anyone, now demonstrates his ability to change into a stag, a hare, and a little bird with the golden head. Mar'ya Tsarevna takes a tuft of fur from the stag and the hare, and a feather from the bird for safekeeping; she ties them up into a handkerchief and hides them on her person. Later we see how invaluable this is, for it serves as proof of Semën's being the one to whom she gave the weapons.

The tsarevna feeds Semën, the young lad, and gives him to drink; she prepares him for his return journey and gives him her father's battle mace and sharp sword. "Then they said good-by to one another, kissed heartily in farewell, and Semën, the young lad, made his way back to the tsar." Fairy tales are economical in expressing feelings but we can imagine that this meeting, and especially this farewell, did not leave our lad untouched.

Leaving Mar'ya Tsarevna, Semën sets out on his return journey. Changing from stag to hare to a little bird with the golden head, Semën hastens to complete his mission. At the end of the third day, espying the king's troops but 300 paces away, he lays down by the side of sea to rest from his journey. He is careful to keep the sword and mace at his side, but so great is his fatigue that he quickly falls into a deep sleep.

Such last-minute slackening of the hero's attention is a familiar motif in fairy tales. This regression sometimes occurs as the hero, equipped with the treasure he has obtained from the unconscious, is re-entering the profane world, for example, in "The Water of Life." This is clearly not the case in our tale. Semën, the young lad, is not entering the profane world; his standing on the sea shore rather positions him on the threshold to the unconscious.

In the Grimm fairy tale of "The Two Brothers" the hero sleeps from exhaustion after fighting a seven-headed dragon. There, sleep is the result of the great effort involved in confronting the unconscious in its negative aspect. This is also not Semën's case. Semën is understandably tired from his long journey, but he has fought no dragon; on the contrary, he has just returned from a very pleasant meeting with Mar'ya Tsarevna.

Semën's fatigue may rather be seen as an *abaissement du niveau mental* (Janet) resulting from his meeting with the tsarevna, for, as the anima, she opens the door to the unconscious. In his essay "On the Psychology of the Unconscious," Jung writes the following about the possible effects of love: "Love can summon forth unsuspected powers in the soul for which we had better be prepared..."[46] This can be explained by the combination of two factors: firstly, because emotions arise in the unconscious; one cannot will an emotion, or if one can, it is only because the unconscious feels the same way; secondly, because all unconscious contents are contaminated with one another. Consequently, whatever triggers a romantic emotion may also bring up a complex that is connected to it. We have all experienced the feeling of helplessness in the face of love and the unpredictability of our reactions. We just never know what will *take possession of us*.

The *abaissement du niveau mental* to which Semën, the young lad, is now subjected is immediately followed by the appearance of the general. The general with his evil intentions may be seen as Semën's shadow, compensating the hero's naiveté and modesty. But the shadow may also have positive characteristics; a general must have knowledge of warfare; he must be able to take on the responsibility to lead and to delegate. If he is a good general, he cares for his troops and motivates them. These are all traits that Semën never had the opportunity to develop; they are important not only for a general but also for a future tsar.

As a subordinate of the tsar, however, the general can also be seen as part of the tsar's shadow. On a personal level such a shadow may reflect the tsar's unconscious resistance to giving up his daughter to another man, especially to a commoner. Because the tsar promised his daughter and, ultimately, the throne, to whoever retrieves his weapons in time, this has collective implications as well. It may represent an insufficient respect for the principle of Eros and a power complex which often accompanies such an attitude.[47] We have already noted that the

---

46 Jung, *Two Essays*, CW 7, § 164.
47 "Where love reigns, there is no will to power; and where the will to power is paramount, love is lacking. The one is but the shadow of the other." Jung, *Two Essays*, CW 7, § 78.

power granted to the tsar is contingent upon his being responsible to his subjects and to God. Without satisfying this condition, no ruler can reign legitimately (p. 70).

However we interpret the general, the hero—the new potential for development—is now being threatened by a dishonest and power-hungry aspect of the psyche; furthermore, we realize that this has personal as well as collective implications.

Had Semën been awake, that is, had he been conscious of such a potential shadow, he would surely have dealt differently with the danger presented by the general; he might have escaped by changing into the hare or the little bird, or confronted the general in the form of a stag. He would not have been quite so naive about life and he would surely have known to deliver the weapons needed for this very important battle before taking a nap.

This emphasizes the importance of working on the shadow, for we never know when it will blind or trip us. We learn that this is the first task in the individuation process, and we now realize that Semën skipped this stage. All the positive developments at the beginning of the tale were brought about by the two wise men in acknowledgement of the work done by the father and the three brothers. We have seen this as the masculine, spiritual aspect of the unconscious, supporting their tremendous effort in containing the influence of the archetypal mother. This enabled the hero to free himself from the swamp, and to strengthen his masculinity (stag and hare) and spirit (little bird with the golden head); most importantly, it propelled him into the world. This is an apt image for the initiation of the first half of life, an initiation whose goal it is to anchor one in outer reality.

Semën's falling asleep by the sea leads to a critical moment in his development. Not having learned to deal with the personal shadow, Semën now plunges headlong into the collective one. Confronting the collective shadow is ultimately every hero's task; here it is clearly linked to his ignorance of the personal one. But what does it mean that he is now confronted with the collective shadow?

In this tale we hear of three tsars: the one in whose service Semën stands; the sea tsar under whose power he falls; and the third tsar who declared a "terrible war" against the first. In all probability, the last two are the same and there being three of them points to the dynamism that has now been set into motion. If the first tsar represents the dominant of collective consciousness, the second and third tsars must both be seen as his shadows. As shadows of the tsar they are automatically also collective shadows, and as such affect the entire kingdom. We have seen how wanting our tsar was, how poorly he fulfilled the requirements of his office. The two malevolent tsars may hence be seen as the unconscious compensation to the ruling principle in consciousness.

The general, who comes upon the sleeping hero, steals the tsar's weapons and pushes Semën into the sea. Here the hero is held captive for three years by the sea tsar. He is treated in the most heartless way, and endures much hardship and suffering.

We know from mythology that a reigning monarch who is incapable of fulfilling his duties is killed, concretely or symbolically; if the latter, he must be symbolically reborn or give up his throne to one who satisfies the requirements of this office.

In the present tale, Semen's night-sea-journey is forced upon him by a power-hungry general who wants to marry Mar'ya Tsarevna and succeed to the throne. This definitely places him into the role of the tsar's shadow; he represents that part of the tsar's psyche that wants to hold on to power and is incapable of transformation.

This is recognizable in the present world where those with power are, all too often, blinded by its might and forgetful of the responsibilities which it carries. Fairy tales speak to such situations; they emphasize the gravity if this problem and show that only a hero is capable of solving it. But heroes can be kings or peasants, old or young, rich or poor; heroes can even be heroines... What they all have in common is a connection to the Self and a readiness to accept Its guidance.

This is well illustrated in the Russian tale of "Vasilisa the Beautiful." Here, the heroine must not only deal with her stepmother (negative mother) and stepsisters (shadow) but is forced by them to confront the Baba Yaga. This witch is a nature goddess of archetypal dimensions, an unconscious compensation to the devaluation of woman and disrespect of nature in a patriarchal world order. Whether positive or negative, she is a goddess and, as such, she must be treated with respect. We can see that Vasilisa knows to do this.

Baba Yaga is evil and destructive but she is indirectly instrumental in shaping Vasilisa for her role as queen. Through her initiation in the forest, Vasilisa learns to unite the negative and positive aspects of the feminine into a new holistic Eros principle.

Similarly to Vasilisa, Semën, the young lad, retains his humility and respectful behavior in the sea kingdom. We also note that, whereas before he was active and confident, now he becomes passive; he suffers and weeps, he longs for the world. These are all expressions of Eros, and one wonders whether Semën would have shown so much feeling had he not met Mar'ya Tsarevna, had he not experienced the anima.

Semën's intention had been to bring the weapons to the tsar, but fate would have it otherwise. He had to take a detour and spend three years in the realm of the sea tsar. From this we must deduce that this experience was necessary in his becoming heir to the throne and, subsequently, tsar of this land.

The hero who finally returns to the world will have experienced suffering. As tsar, he will be compassionate to his subjects. He will know that he is responsible for his actions to God; he will not become inflated by the power of his office because he has learned that the sea tsar is a reality that cannot be ignored. Semën has now gone through a new initiation. This one is into the second half of life where the focus of the psyche shifts toward the values of the inner world.[48]

Because the task of fetching the tsar's weapons is of such consequence for the tale, we need to take a closer at the symbolic meaning of the sharp sword and the mace. As any cutting instrument, the sword dissects and separates; in a figurative sense, this can be seen as differentiation or judgement, decision-making as in Alexander the Great's cutting of the Gordian knot. It is a function of the intellect, but also of the heart.

The sword is, moreover, a weapon of strength and power, and serves to overcome hostile forces, to kill and to wound. Swords were often decorated with precious stones and inscriptions which, it was believed, increased their magical power. Like horses on the animal level, swords were experienced as part of their owner. Sometimes they were even given names, for example, Excalibur, the sword of King Arthur.

---

48   Jung, *Structure and Dynamics*, CW 8, § 773.

Because the knight used his sword in confronting the outer world, it can also be seen as an ego-building tool. From early childhood the ego begins to separate itself out from a *participation mystique*[49] with its surroundings and learns to stand independently. NB: This same ego strength is later necessary in confronting the inner world.[50]

The amplifications above confirm the symbolic importance of the sword for any ruler. He must be able to judge wisely and to execute his decisions with authority; figuratively speaking, the sword must become a part of him. Then he will gain the respect and support of his people, and the enemy will have cause to fear his power and wrath. This explains why it was absolutely imperative for the tsar to have his weapons when going to war, and why his army could not engage the enemy without him.

Here again, we touch upon the question of power and its abuse. As mentioned earlier, the tsar's legitimacy in using power is based upon his being an intermediary between man and God. If he loses his connection to God, his use of power will depend exclusively upon his will. What is true of a tsar is true for any man or woman. In Jungian terms we would say that the use of power is the responsibility of the ego, but of an ego which is in harmony with the Self. This is why we work with dreams, do active imagination, consult the I Ching. The responsibility always rests with the ego, but we need to be aware of the unconscious position at all times, that is, we need to be as whole as possible in exercising our ego's decisions.

Another important consideration in the question of power is the ability to differentiate between the voice of the Self and that of the shadow. This is why, while seeing the sword as an ego-building function is significant, it should also be seen as a symbol for individuation. In *Grail Legend* we read: "The sword signifies that life-urge which leads to the recognition of the Self..."[51]

---

49   Jung, *Visions 2*, 1193; *Visions I*, 220, 540 and 624f. *Participation mystique* is a term coined by Levy Brühl and applied exclusively to primitive mentality. Jung believed the essence of this condition to be a state of unconsciousness experienced by modern man as well, especially in relationships.This is the sense in which I will use the term in what follows.

50   Emma Jung and M.-L. von Franz, *Grail Legend*, 79 f.

51   Emma Jung and M.-L. von Franz, *Grail Legend*, 89.

The second weapon which Semën, the young lad, brings back from the tsar's palace is a mace. This is a club-like weapon, with a flanged or spiked metal head. It is a weapon of brute force and often appears in paintings of the Russian heroic epics, the *byliny*, for example, in those of Viktor Vasnetsov.

In Greek mythology Hercules pulled out a wild olive tree from the ground and made himself such a club. It later became an inseparable companion in all his exploits.[52] This Greek hero provides interesting amplification for our tale because he is a classic example for overcoming the mother complex.[53] The ten tasks imposed upon him by Hera were an act of vengeance against Zeus's infidelity with the mortal queen Alcmene, Hercules's natural mother. Hercules's super-human feats of strength and his courage in fulfilling Hera's demands resulted in his attaining immortality and gaining acceptance into the midst of the Olympian gods.[54]

A mace or club symbolizes the brute force of instinctive aggression, a characteristic often found lacking in a man with a mother complex. Here again, personifying the unconscious, we can say that the mother archetype keeps such a man weak because, should he ever become strong, he might think of challenging her. As the tale shows, however, such instinctive aggression needs to be balanced by a sharp intellectual discrimination and courageous decision making, symbolized by the sword.

The above descriptions of the sword and mace demonstrate the symbolic importance of these two weapons for masculine individuation. We recall how our tsar set out to meet the challenge of a "terrible war," forgetting his weapons at home. No sooner were they in his possession, than he won "a brilliant victory" over the enemy. The ego-building function of these two symbols is essential both in the first half of life, as well as in the second; in the latter case, it is one of the prerequisites for a successful confrontation with the negative aspect of the unconscious.

After the sleeping Semën gets pushed into the sea, he falls into the hands of the sea tsar and is carried down to the very depths. Here he

---

52 Kerényi, *Heroes*, 137.
53 Sager, *Die Überwindung der Mutter*, 135.
54 Kerényi, *Heroes*, 140-182; Jung, *Symbols of Transformation* CW 5, § 451, FN 60.

is held captive for three years. The number three indicates that something has been set into motion in the unconscious, and this despite the seemingly hopeless predicament from the perspective of consciousness.

As a year goes by, the sea tsar asks Semën if he is lonely, if he wants to return to the world. He is brought up to the shore at midnight, only to be pulled back before the break of day. Midnight is the threshold to another day. The sea tsar awakens the hero's hopes but then, just before sunrise, just before that promised new day breaks, the sea tsar snatches him away for another year. We may consider the sea tsar sadistic, teasing Semën, or intimidating him with a demonstration of his power. We may also consider this ambivalent attitude of the sea tsar as a typical unconscious reaction; it wants to become conscious, but it experiences what Jung calls a *horror vacui* upon relinquishing a part of itself to consciousness.[55] In this case, it would refer to Semën's leaving the sea realm and continuing his journey to the throne; psychologically, to his becoming the dominant of collective consciousness and a new symbol of the Self.

Semën's three attempts at leaving the sea realm remind us of how difficult it sometimes is to escape the backward pull of the unconscious. For so-called "primitive man" (the term used by Jung), whose ego is weak and always in danger of being swept away by the unconscious, such experiences are known as "perils of the soul."[56] The same holds true for the undeveloped in man today, for example, where the inferior function is concerned.

The hero exemplifies what is called for in any given situation. In this instance, we see Semën, the young lad, showing humility, but also perseverance. He is very sad and weeps bitter tears but he does not despair, nor does he show disrespect to the sea tsar. He acknowledges the sea tsar's power and accepts his own powerlessness. It is possible that it took three years for Semën to realize what this experience really meant. Perhaps the repeated regressions and accompanying suffering were necessary to make him truly conscious of what he was going through. The rising of the sun would then be a suitable image for the final birth of this insight.

---

55 Jung, *Archetypes*, CW 9i, § 426.
56 Jung, *Archetypes*, CW 9i, § 47.

Often we get some partial understanding of a problem, and then begin to believe that we can cope with it. But shortly thereafter, we again fall into the same pattern, making the same mistakes, needing to suffer again; this makes us realize that the problem has not really been solved. If we do not give up or despair, if we do not try to avoid the suffering involved, if we are open to the possibility of there being a reason or need for this repeated trial, in short if we accept the final (as opposed to causal) aspect of our problem, then one day the sun may make it over the horizon for us as well.

Jung described a very impressive ritual among the Elgon tribe of East Africa which illustrates this psychic phenomenon: At daybreak, he observed these people spit onto their palms and stretch their hands toward the sun. Because their word for *god* and for *sun* was the same, Jung interpreted this gesture as an expression of sun worship. This was strongly denied. A tribal chief later explained that the sun up in the sky was not god; it was god only at the moment when it first appeared on the horizon. This witnesses to the tremendous relief experienced by these people as the night with all its demons gave way to the light of day.[57]

On the third try, this also happens to Semën, the young lad: "Suddenly the sun shone with his bright rays and now the sea tsar could no longer take him into captivity." This salvation was completely out of Semën's hands. All three times, he besought God with the same words: "My Lord, give me some sun!" The first two times, the sea tsar brought him up to the shore at midnight and snatched him back just before the sun rose. There is no information to explain this turn of events, and so we must assume that it was kairos, that the time was ripe for this to happen.

Escaping from his captivity in the sea realm, Semën, the young lad, loses no time to ponder his good fortune but immediately sets out for his kingdom. Changing into a stag, a hare and, finally, into a little bird with a golden head, he arrives at the castle to find Mar'ya Tsarevna betrothed to the deceitful general. Seeing Semën enter the hall, Mar'ya Tsarevna addresses her father; she tells him what really happened, and

---

57 Jung, *Structure and Dynamics*, CW 8, § 329.

supports her statements by showing him the tufts of fur she had cut from the stag and the hare, and the feather from the little bird with the golden head. Semën transforms himself accordingly, further confirming her evidence. We note the perfect coordination between the two; even more importantly, we see Mar'ya Tsarevna taking the active role. She doesn't wait for Semën or anyone else to speak. The anima which had earlier appeared passive and subservient now stands up for herself and for Semën. Whereas Semën had to learn about Eros, Mar'ya Tsarevna now takes the initiative and shows spirit. Both are becoming more whole and this will allow them to unite in a more meaningful way. Seen on the inner level, this illustrates the psychic development within the hero. Through his trials, he has become more related, and this has freed his anima to take a more active part in his life.

I would now like to address the question of religious language in this tale. If one reads the text carefully, one cannot help noticing that, in contrast to the other characters, the two old men, as well as Semën and his brothers usually express themselves in pious language. Here are a few examples:

Marveling at the great changes in the swamp, the two old men exclaim: "Whoever built this bridge and laid this road—whatever he ask of the Lord, may it be granted to him."

These two old men are referred to as "venerable hermits." This is a translation of the Russian word *startsy*, the plural of *starets*. In a general sense, this word was used to refer to old men, but more particularly to old *monks* who served as spiritual fathers to both monks and lay persons. This second meaning definitely puts the two old men within the Christian tradition. In answer to the old men's question of what the brothers would ask of the Lord, they reply accordingly:

"That the Lord make me rich for the rest of my life!" is the request of the eldest, Ivan.

"That the Lord give me bread for the rest of my life." asks Vasiliy, the middle brother.

When it is Semën's turn to make a wish, he says: "I ask for His grace to serve as soldier to the great sovereign."

After Semën receives the old men's gifts, he asks his father's blessing to go to the tsar's court. His wish is initially denied: "How can you go? You are young and foolish!" To this Semën says: "No, father, let me go; it is God's will."

Later, when Semën, the young lad, asks the tsar to take him into his service, he is once again refused: "How can that be? You are young and foolish; how can you serve?" Here Semën answers: "Though I may be young and foolish, I will serve no worse than the others. I put my trust in God." This echoes the *deo concedente* of the alchemists.

And finally, each time the sea tsar brings Semën up to the shore, Semën prays: "Send me the sun, oh Lord!"

M.-L. von Franz describes the hero as "...that aspect of the Self which is concerned with the building up of the ego, with keeping it going and enlarging it ... an archetypal model and pattern for the right kind of behavior."[58]

From the above examples of religious language, it appears that the proper attitude toward the divine/unconscious is an important aspect of this "right kind of behavior." It is, on the one hand, a respectful, humble acknowledgement of a power superior to that of the ego; on the other, it expresses the ability to stand one's ground and bravely face the unknown.

Let us return for a moment to the incident of the sea tsar bringing Semën, the young lad, up from the depths and leaving him on the shore. Semën is still too weak from his sojourn in the sea, that is, the unconscious; he is unable to move, he cannot save himself. The only thing he can do is pray. And his choice of words is somewhat ambiguous: "Send me the sun, oh Lord!" Is it the Christian Lord who will save Semën from the sea king, or the sun? Semën might have phrased his prayer differently. He could have said: "Save me from the sea king, oh Lord!" The wording Semën is using is rather confusing. Is he directing his plea to the Christian Lord, expecting Him to influence the sun's rising? Or is his old, pagan worship of the sun still contaminated with Christian belief?

From a Jungian perspective, this can be seen as a plea for consciousness which would free Semën from the backward pull of the unconscious; in this sense, it doesn't really matter who Semën is addressing in

---

58   von Franz, *Redemption Motifs,* 19.

his prayer. Historically, however, the second possibility is more probable because Russia went through many centuries of a double or dual faith.

Christianity became the official religion in Russia in 988. The capital city was then Kiev and Vladimir was the ruler responsible for Russia's conversion. In folk tradition Vladimir carried the epithet of *the red sun*. It is, likewise, worthy of note that in Old Russian *red* referred to *beautiful*. The careful reader will have noticed that the first time the sun is mentioned in this episode, the text reads "Just before the rising of the red sun the sea king snatched him up and carried him back into the sea depths." Until the eighteenth century only the clergy were literate and, consequently, any written documents from this time presented the position of the Church. This was, understandably, intent upon suppressing the old pagan faith. In an indirect way, however, these documents demonstrate the fact that the common people did not give up their pagan faith easily and that the two faiths continued to exist side by side for a very long time. Epic poems, the *byliny*, and fairy tales, both of which were handed down in oral tradition, provide valuable insight into this historical period.

By far the most famous and best loved epic hero was Il'ya Muromets. We learn that he was lamed in both hands and feet for the first thirty years of his life. The term used to designate such a person was *siden,'* from the verb *sidet,'* to sit. It referred to a person with amputated legs, to paralyzed or sick persons, to stay-at-homes. When the Russian hero is presented in this mode, he typically never leaves the stove, a suitable image of the warm, nourishing, protective mother. In a figurative sense, the term *siden'* came to mean an inactive, passive, or idle person.

Such was the fate of Il'ya Muromets for the first thirty years of his life. Then one day, he was visited by two or three (depending upon the versions) old men and miraculously healed of his lameness. Receiving this gift of life, Il'ya Muromets immediately decided to go into Vladimir's service. He asked his parents' blessing and set off for Kiev. This marked the beginning of his heroic career. In his many exploits, Il'ya Muromets always championed the common people. He was not only esteemed for his strength but for his courage and moral integrity. He could not be bribed by power, nor was he vain or ambitious.[59]

---

59 Il'ya Muromets, 393 ff.

We recognize the similarity with our tale: the long period of stagnation; the gifts of transformation bestowed upon Semën by the two wise men, paralleling the magical healing in the case of Il'ya Muromets, the hero's wish to serve the tsar, and his moral integrity. From the archetypal perspective, both our tales speak of the mother complex in man.

This psychic phenomenon is not restricted to the Russian people. There are many nationalities which exhibit the same archetypal constellation. Sometimes one can outgrow the initial stage of stagnation and become active and creative. This is not an easy accomplishment and, as the two examples above indicate, it requires magic, that is, the support of the unconscious. Thus we can say that any positive development, any healing can only take place if both parts of the psyche are involved. If this is not the case, the person remains stuck and unable to develop his inborn potential, psychologically, to individuate.

One such example of the latter is the already-mentioned figure of Ivan Goncharov's *Oblomov* (p. 67). Oblomov was just such a *siden'* and it is conceivable that Goncharov consciously juxtaposed his Il'ya to the mythical hero. Il'ya Oblomov was unable to get away from the mother even to the extent of marrying a simple woman with a good heart who accepted and loved him as he was, one who shielded him from all confrontation with life.

From the start I was intrigued by the names of the three brothers. The first two disappear after the initial challenge of the swamp and are never heard of again. Why are they given names when their role in this psychic drama is so short-lived? Incidentally, it will be noted that, in this tale, it is only the three brothers and the tsarevna who have personal names. This may be accidental, but still, it is worth considering symbolically.

As we can see from the example of the Egyptian myth of Isis and Re[60], or as the fairy tale "Rumpelstiltskin" (Grimm 55) so vividly demonstrates, knowing someone's name gives one power over them. This stems from the old belief that there is a connection between a person's name and his soul. In such societies, a newborn child was given an ancestral name so

---

60   Jung, *Symbols of Transformation*, CW 5, § 451 f.

that this ancestor could reincarnate. Jung understood this to mean that ego-consciousness (here, the name) was equated with the soul.[61]

In the context of the present fairy tale this suggests that the ultimate union of the hero with the anima must also include the two shadow figures. This is an interesting nuance, because usually they are excluded, even killed, when such a *coniunctio* takes place. Is there something in the nature of these shadow figures that would explain this irregularity? In contrast to most shadow figures, Ivan and Vasiliy are both positive; furthermore, being older than Semën, they represent the initial steps in meeting the challenge of the mother complex, that is, they pave the way for his further development. As a matter of fact, Semën could not have accomplished what he did, had they not done their part. Their inclusion in the quaternion of figures with names emphasizes their contribution to the wholeness of the personality and the need for the hero to remain conscious of them throughout his further development.

The uneven ratio of the masculine to the feminine in this quaternion is a warning of the danger for a man with a mother complex to fall back into the power of the mother archetype, succumbing to the subhuman, vegetative pull of the swamp.

Let us now take a closer look at the names given to each of the three brothers and to see whether they can add further to the understanding of the tale. Ivan is the name of the eldest brother. This is the Russian diminutive of John, and John the Baptist is one of several St. Johns commemorated in Russia. In the Christian tradition he is the last of the Old Testament prophets and forerunner of Jesus. He is a herald, a messenger, one who goes before and announces the approach of another.

In Russia, as in many other Christianized lands, his day of birth, the twenty-fourth of June, was merged with the pagan festivals of the summer solstice. In the pagan imagination, this day and particularly the eve of this day, became transformed into a magical world; it was believed that the sun, the sky, the earth, water, plants and animals all opened up to man, revealing secrets which remained hidden the rest of the year. On this day and night flowers and plants were gathered for

---

61 Jung, *Structure and Dynamics*, CW 8, § 665.

medicinal purposes and for divination; people bathed in the rivers and lakes until the morning hours, lit fires and jumped over them. There were common meals and a lot of singing and dancing. This night was also filled with erotic escapades not permitted at any other time of year. Such practices continued into the twentieth century and echoed old pagan festivals honoring the sun in its moment of greatness.[62]

The second son was Vasiliy; this is the Russian form of Basil. In the original Greek, this referred to royal or kingly. We find the same name in the tale of "Vasilisa the Beautiful." St. Basil, Archbishop of Caesarea, lived in the fourth century (329-379). He was a theologian and Church scholar of great renown. An inspiring preacher and prolific writer, he was famous for his works on monasticism. He was also well known for his care of the poor and underprivileged.

In Russia, St. Basil was commemorated on the first of January, the day of his death. This day fell within the two-week pagan festivities in honor of the invincible sun. Celebrations included caroling, divination, and ritual meals. Because in folk tradition St. Basil was patron of pigs, one such ritual meal was the eating of the *Caesarean* pig. At this meal, prayers were said to St. Basil for the welfare of family and livestock, and for a good harvest. These sacrificial relics of paganism are a living example of the double faith. Because the pig was considered an unclean animal, this feast was preceded by the following prayer: "Fire will clean, St. Basil will bless."[63]

It was Peter the Great who, seeking to open Russia up to Europe as well as to weaken the power of the Church, changed the date of the New Year to the first of January. Prior to that, following the Church calendar, the New Year was celebrated on the first of September. As a consequence of this historic event, St. Basil's day was not only contaminated with pagan rites of the winter solstice, but also with New Year's rituals.[64]

And now we come to the third son, Semën. The name of our hero, Semën, is the peasant version of Simeon. St. Simeon the Stylite was the son of a peasant, born in northern Syria (390 to 459 B.C.). At eighteen,

---

62   Shangina, *Russkiye traditsionnyye prazdniki*, 170 ff.
63   Shangina, *Russkiye traditsionnyye prazdniki*, 51.
64   Shangina, *Russkiye traditsionnyye prazdniki*, 49 f.

he took the monk's vows and lived a severe ascetic life. He spent the last thirty-seven years of his life in a small cell on top of a high pillar, a practice other saints were later to follow. He became well known for his piety, and many sought his prayer and his counsel.

In the Eastern Church, St. Simeon's feast is commemorated on the first of September, coinciding, until 1699, with the Church New Year. In Moscow, this day was celebrated with pomp and ceremony. At midnight, the Kremlin canon and church bells heralded the New Year; the next day, services were held in the Cathedral of the Assumption. Icons of Christ, the Mother of God, and St. Simeon were placed in the Red Square where the tsar and the patriarch, surrounded by royalty and clergy, welcomed the New Year. On this day, the poor received alms from the government treasury.

Because of the original contamination with the New Year, in folk tradition St. Simeon became a Janus figure,[65] and received the epithet of *the year's escort* (*Semën letoprovodets*). Even after Peter's calendar reform, the celebration of St. Simeon's day retained many apotropaic rituals which it had in common with the New Year. These were directed toward purging the land of evil and safeguarding against the devil, for example, plowing around fields and villages, reading of prayers and carrying out magic charms.[66]

The above provides a short description of the three saints who might have served as patron saints of the three brothers. The only Christian connection that mirrors the situation in "The Speedy Messenger" is St. John the Baptist's role as herald, for being Semën's older brother, Ivan would have come before him. As noted above, psychologically, he would have represented that part of the shadow which initiated the development out of the mother complex.

Apart from this amplification, the real interest in speaking of these three saints lies not so much in their Christian tradition as in the way the common man adapted them into his (still) deeply pagan experience of life.

---

65 Janus was a Roman solar deity, patron of beginnings and endings and guardian of gates. The first month of the year, January, was named after him and he is often represented with two heads pointing in opposite directions. *Bulfinch's Mythology*, 917.
66 *Bulfinch's Mythology*, 194 ff.

In the people's pagan view of the world, St. John the Baptist and St. Basil the Great were both connected with the solstice: St. John with the moment of the sun's greatest expansion and influence, St. Basil's with the sun's birth. We have seen that Semën, the young lad, is saved from the grasp of the sea tsar by the timely rising of the sun. The sun symbolism is also echoed in the image of the stag and the golden head of the little bird.

The sun heralds the new day; it furthers life in general, and consciousness in particular. The number three which runs through the whole tale speaks for the dynamism which propels the action toward the day when Semën, the young lad, will reign together with Mar'ya Tsarevna. And here we must remember that both St. Basil and St. Simeon were celebrated in connection with the New Year, with a new beginning in time.

This long tale spans the development of a male psyche through both the first as well as the second half of life. The presenting psychic constellation is that of the mother complex. There are two initiations. Psychologically, the clearing of the swamp belongs to the first half of life because it frees the hero from the paralyzing inertia of the mother archetype and enables him to take his position in the collective of which he is a part. This is initiation into the first half of life.

Semën's sojourn in the kingdom of the sea tsar represents an initiation into the second half of life. Here he experiences a dangerous regression into the unconscious realm, a return to the mother. We already noted his passivity and total helplessness at the hands of the sea tsar. This is aptly demonstrated in his being carried up to the shore like a baby, as well as his inability to get up and distance himself from the sea when brought to land.

Two things save Semën, the young lad: his ardent prayer to God for light and his commitment to life. Both stand for consciousness. He has now experienced the reality of the unconscious and will not be naive about its dangers; moreover, he has learned about Eros in a way that only suffering can teach. It is his longing and his persistent plea to return to the outer world that motivates the sea tsar to comply with his wish.

Earlier we spoke of the sea tsar's ambivalent response to the hero's pleas: three times he pulls Semën down into the depths, three times he brings him back to land. It is symptomatic of the unconscious to make its contents available to consciousness and then to take them back again (p. 78).

In the case at hand, however, we may also consider a more causal explanation of this occurrence. We remember that it was implicitly the sea tsar who challenged the tsar to a "terrible war"; we had seen this as a compensatory reaction on the part of the unconscious to the ruling principle in consciousness. Our tsar was, indeed, deficient in the execution of his duties; moreover, we have traced all of these deficiencies to the influence of the negative aspect of the mother archetype. This is *the* problem in our tale, one with which our hero contends throughout the tale. By his respectful and humble conduct in the sea realm, Semën brings about a more conciliatory reaction of the unconscious. The sea tsar's acceding to Semën's wish to be brought on land may hence be seen as the beginning of a normalization of the relationship between the two parts of the psyche.

III. The Feather of Finist, the Bright Falcon

There once lived an old man, who had three daughters: the two elder ones were fond of frills and ornaments; the youngest was only concerned with household tasks. One day the father made ready to go to town and asked his daughters what they wanted him to buy for them. The eldest said, "Buy me cloth for a dress." The second said the same thing. "And what shall I buy for you, my beloved daughter?" the father asked the youngest. "My dear father, buy me a feather of Finist the Bright Falcon." The father said farewell to them and went to town. He bought cloth for his two elder daughters, but nowhere could he find a feather of Finist the Bright Falcon. His elder daughters were overjoyed with the new cloth he bought for them. "I could not find a feather of Finist the Bright Falcon for you," he said to the youngest. "So be it," she said, "perhaps next time you will have better luck." The elder sisters cut their cloth, made themselves dresses, and made fun of their younger sister, but she said nothing. The father again made ready to go to town and asked: "Well, my daughters, what shall I buy for you?" The first and second each asked for a kerchief, but the youngest said, "Buy me a feather of Finist the Bright Falcon." The father went to town, bought two kerchiefs, but could not find the feather. He returned home and said, "Ach, my daughter, again I could not find a feather of Finist the Bright Falcon." "Never mind, father, perhaps you will have better luck next time."

The father made ready to ride to town yet a third time and asked his daughters what he should buy for them. The elder ones said, "Buy us earrings." But the youngest again asked for a feather of Finist the Bright Falcon. The father bought two pairs of gold earrings and began to look for the feather, but no one had even heard of it. He became sad and left town. No sooner had he passed through the gates than he met an old man carrying a little box. "What are you carrying, old man?" "A feather of Finist the Bright Falcon." "What do you want for it?" "Give me a thousand." The father paid him and galloped home with the little box. His daughters came out to meet him. "Well, my beloved daughter," he said to the youngest, "at last I also have a present for you. Here, take it." The youngest almost jumped for joy; she took the box, began to kiss and fondle it, and pressed it tightly to her bosom.

After supper they all retired to their rooms to sleep; the youngest daughter also went to her room. She opened the box, and the feather of Finist the Bright Falcon flew out instantly; it struck the floor and a handsome tsarevich appeared before the maiden. They began to speak in sweet and loving words with each other. The elder sisters overheard them and asked, "Little sister with whom are you talking?" "I am talking with myself," said the lovely maiden. "Well then, open the door." The tsarevich struck the floor and turned into a feather; the maiden put the feather back in the box and opened the door. The sisters looked in all the corners but found no one. As soon as they had left, the lovely maiden opened the window, took out the feather and said, "Fly, my feather, into the open field and stay there till the right time." The feather turned into a bright falcon and flew into the open field.

The next night Finist the Bright Falcon came flying to his maiden, and they began to talk merrily. The sisters overheard them and ran straightaway to their father. "Father, someone visits our sister at night; even now he is there, talking with her." The father arose and went to his youngest daughter's room, but the tsarevich had long since turned into the feather and lay in the little box. "Oh, you malicious girls," the father scolded his elder daughters, "why do you accuse her falsely? Better mind your own business."

The next day the sisters hit upon a ruse. In the evening, when it was dark, they put up a ladder, gathered sharp knives and needles, and stuck them in the lovely maiden's window. At night Finist the Bright Falcon flew to the lovely maiden's window. He struggled and struggled, but could not get into the room; he just cut his wings. "Farewell, lovely maiden," he said, "if you want to find me, you will have to look beyond thrice nine lands, in the thrice tenth kingdom. Before finding me, the brave youth, you will wear out three pairs of iron shoes, break three cast-iron staves, and gnaw away three stone wafers." But the maiden slept on; she heard these unkind words in her sleep, but she was unable to awaken and get up.

In the morning she awoke and saw knives and needles stuck in her window, with blood trickling from them. She threw up her hands: "Oh, my God! My sisters must have killed my beloved!" Straightaway she made ready and left home. She ran to the smithy, forged three pairs of iron shoes and three cast-iron staves for herself, took along three stone wafers, and set out to seek Finist the Bright Falcon.

She walked and walked; she wore out a pair of shoes, broke a cast-iron staff, and gnawed away a stone wafer. She came to a hut and knocked at the door: "Host and hostess, shelter me from the dark night!" An old woman answered, "You are welcome, lovely maiden! Whither are you going little dove?" "Ach, grandmother, I am going in search of Finist, the Bright Falcon." "You have a long way to go, lovely maiden." Next morning the old woman said to her: "Go now to my middle sister, she will tell you what to do. And here is my gift to you—a silver spinning wheel and a golden spindle. When you start to spin flax, you will draw a golden thread." Then she took a ball, rolled it on the road, and told the maiden to follow the ball wherever it went. The maiden thanked the old woman and followed the ball.

After a long time or a short time, the second pair of shoes was worn out, the second staff—broken, another stone wafer gnawed away. Finally, the ball rolled up to a little hut. The maiden knocked at the door: "My good hosts, shelter a lovely maiden from the dark night!" "You are welcome," answered an old woman. "Whither are you going, lovely maiden?" "Grandmother, I am going in search of Finist, the Bright Falcon." "You have a long way to go," said the old woman. In the morning, she gave the lovely maiden a silver dish and a golden egg and sent her to her older sister. "She will know where to find Finist the Bright Falcon."

The lovely maiden said farewell to the old woman and set out on her way. She walked and walked; the third pair of shoes was worn out, the third staff was broken, and the last wafer gnawed away. The ball rolled up to a little hut. The traveler knocked at the door and said, "My good hosts, shelter a lovely maiden from the dark night." Again an old woman came out: "Come in, little dove, you are welcome! Whence do you come and whither are you going?" "Oh, grandmother, I am searching for Finist, the Bright Falcon." "It will be hard, very hard to find him! He is now living in such and such a town and is married to the wafer baker's daughter." In the morning the old woman said to the lovely maiden: "Here is a gift for you—a golden embroidery frame and a needle; just hold the frame and the needle will embroider by itself. Go now and may God speed you; ask the wafer baker to hire you as her serving maid."

The lovely maiden did as she was bidden. She came to the wafer baker's house and became a servant; she worked very diligently, heating the stove, carrying water, cooking the dinner. The wafer baker looked on and was delighted. "Thank God," she said to her daughter, "we now have a servant who is both helpful and kind; she does everything without being told." And the lovely maiden, having done all the housework, took her silver loom and her golden spindle and sat down to spin; the threads she spun were no ordinary ones but of pure gold. The wafer baker's daughter saw this and said, "Oh, lovely maiden, won't you sell me your plaything?" "I might." "And what is your price?" "Let me to spend the night with your husband." The wafer baker's daughter consented. "There is no harm in it," she thought. "After all, I can give him a sleeping potion, and that spindle will make my mother and me rich."

At the time, Finist the Bright Falcon was not at home. All day long he soared in the skies, and only returned by nightfall. They sat down to supper; the lovely maiden served the meal and kept looking at him, but he, the goodly youth, did not recognize her. The wafer baker's daughter added a sleeping potion to his drink, put him to bed and said to the servant: "Go now to his room and chase away the flies." The lovely maiden chased away the flies and shed bitter tears. "Awake, Finist, Bright Falcon! I, the lovely maiden, have come to you. I have broken three cast-iron staves, worn out three pairs of iron shoes, and gnawed three stone wafers, all the time seeking you, my beloved." But Finist slept and heard nothing. Thus the night went by.

The next day, the maid took the silver dish and rolled the gold egg on it, and many a golden egg did she roll out. The wafer baker's daughter saw this and said, "Sell me your plaything!" "Buy it." "And what is the price?" "Let me to spend another night with your husband." "Very well, I agree." Finist the Bright Falcon again spent all day soaring in the skies, and flew back home only at nightfall. They sat down to supper; the lovely maiden served the meal and kept looking at him, but it was as if he had never known her. Again the wafer baker's daughter drugged him with a sleeping potion, put him to bed, and sent the servant to chase away the flies. And this time as well, no matter how much the lovely maiden wept and tried to rouse him, he slept through till morning and heard nothing.

On the third day, the lovely maiden sat holding the golden em-broidery frame, and the needle embroidered by itself, and what wondrous designs it made! The wafer baker's daughter could not keep her eyes off this work and said, "Lovely maiden, sell me your plaything!" "Buy it." "And what is the price?" "Let me to spend a third night with your husband." "Very well, I agree." In the evening Finist the Bright Falcon came home. His wife gave him a sleeping potion, put him to bed, and sent the servant in to chase the flies away. The lovely maiden chased away the flies and implored him tearfully, "Awake, Finist, Bright Falcon! I, the lovely maiden, have come to you. I have broken three cast-iron staves, worn out three pairs of iron shoes, and gnawed away three stone wafers, and all the time I have been seeking you, my beloved." But Finist the Bright Falcon was sound asleep and felt nothing.

The maiden wept a long time, she spoke to him a long time. Suddenly, one of her tears fell on his cheek and he awoke instantly. "Ach," he said, "something burned me." "Finist, Bright Falcon," answered the lovely maiden, "I have come to you. I have broken three cast-iron staves, worn out three pairs of iron shoes, and gnawed away three stone wafers, and all the time I have been seeking you! This is the third night that I stand beside you while you sleep and do not respond to my pleas!" Only now did Finist the Bright Falcon recognize her, and he was overjoyed beyond words. They formed a plan and left the wafer baker's house. In the morning the wafer baker's daughter found her husband gone, along with the servant. She complained to her mother, who ordered the horses harnessed and rushed after them. She drove all around and stopped at the houses of the three old women, but could not overtake Finist the Bright Falcon; all trace of him had long since disappeared.

Finist and his destined bride arrived at her father's house. Finist struck the damp earth and turned into a feather; the lovely maiden took it, hid it in her bosom and went to her father. "Oh, my beloved daughter, I thought you had perished! Where have you been for so long?" "I went to pray to God." It was just then Holy Week. The father and the elder daughters made ready to go to matins. "Well, my dear daughter," he said to the youngest, "make ready and come with us; this is such a joyful day." "Father, I have nothing to wear." "Put on our dresses," said the elder sisters. "Ah, sisters, your dresses won't fit me; I'd rather stay home."

The father with his two daughters went to matins. When they left, the lovely maiden took out the feather. It struck the floor and turned into a handsome tsarevich. The tsarevich whistled out the window and straightaway there appeared dresses and ornaments, and a golden carriage. They dressed, got into the carriage and went to church. Upon entering, they stood in front of the congregation, and the people marveled at the appearance of the unfamiliar tsarevich and tsarevna. When the service was over they left before everyone else and drove home; the carriage and the splendid raiment disappeared, and the tsarevich turned into a feather. The father and the two elder daughters also returned. "Oh, sister," they said, "you did not come to church with us, and missed seeing the handsome tsarevich and beautiful tsarevna" "Never mind, sisters! Since you have told me all about it, it is as though I had been there myself." The next day, the same happened all over again. On the third day, as the tsarevich was getting into the carriage with the lovely maiden, the father went out of the church and watched with his own eyes as the carriage drove up to his house and vanished. The father came home and began to question his youngest daughter. "There's nothing to be done," said the heroine, "I must confess everything." She took out the feather. The feather struck the floor and turned into the tsarevich. They were married at once, and the wedding was a magnificent one! I, too, was present at this wedding; I drank wine and it rolled down my whiskers, past my mouth. They donned me with a cap and began pushing me around; they put a basket over my head and told me to be on my way.

Alexander Afanas'yev, *Russian Folk Tales*, #234, trans. NB.

INTERPRETATION

The interpretation of this tale differs from all the others in this collection in that it will be considered from the standpoint of feminine psychology, that is, from the perspective of the woman or anima. An old man's youngest daughter is the heroine of this tale; she represents that part of the feminine psyche which the unconscious is putting forth as a model ego.

As in the foregoing tale, this heroine also has no name; she is referred to as daughter, sister, lovely maiden, servant, destined bride. Whereas all important characters in the first tale belonged to the royal class, here this is not the case. This indicates that her experiences and development are not restricted to the higher class but are common to all feminine beings. The names she is given throughout the tale witness to a certain progression, leading to the transformation of a maiden into an adult woman; it can, therefore, be seen as a more general account of feminine initiation.

The curtain rises on a father and his three daughters. This is a foursome, a *quaternion*, which usually signifies wholeness in number symbolism. It is, however, a different wholeness from that of two heterogeneous couples, for the latter can potentially be fruitful, whereas in our tale no further life can come from a father who has no wife but three unmarried daughters. The presenting situation is rather one of a standstill.

The quaternion with which our tale begins can best be understood as signaling completion rather than wholeness. It shows that a certain phase of life is coming to an end, thereby making room for further development. In the absence of a mother, the father has managed to give his daughters containment and safety until that time when they will go out into the world and take their position as adult women. But here the absence of the mother becomes sorely felt, for the maidens lack the guidance of an older woman; nor are they exposed to an adult relationship between a woman and a man.

The very next sentence tells us, however, that the father is making ready to go to town. Going to town opens the familial setting up to new experiences and ideas of a more collective nature. The father is fulfilling the archetypal expectation of his role in introducing his daughters to the outside world. It is an example of the dynamic nature of the masculine, breaking through stagnation, and furthering new development.

The feminine in this tale is in the majority and the number three indicates a readiness for change, but nothing happens until the father makes three trips to town, each time asking his daughters what they would like him to bring back. He is including them in the process and giving each the freedom to make their own choices.

The situation can be compared with Grimm's tale "All Fur," where the father won't let his daughter go, or with "King Thrushbeard," where the daughter rejects all her father's attempts at introducing her to a suitable partner. Different as these two examples are, they both refer to the growing need for a daughter to expand her experience of the masculine beyond that of the father. The transition often goes through the brother who, although still a blood relation, is closer to her in age. The developing sexuality colors all such impulses, for it is different when a four-year old speaks of marrying her father than when this is even implied in connection with a maiden of marriageable age. Such is the case in "King Thrushbeard," for if no suitable man is found for the princess, she won't have to leave the father.

The implication of incest in such situations can be understood concretely only in an objective interpretation; viewed subjectively, it refers to the inability on the part of either the father or the daughter to move on to the next phase of life. For a man, this requires turning his attention to the inner woman, to the anima, for this would relativize the one-sided masculinity of his ego and contribute to his psychic wholeness. In the case of the daughter, it necessitates a shift from the dependency of a child to the independence of an adult woman, to a woman who is capable of differentiating between her own views and those of her father.

In the present tale there is a readiness for such a transition on the part of both parties. Riding into town, the father does his best to satisfy his daughters' wishes. By their choices the two elder sisters show that the beautiful dresses, kerchiefs, and earrings will be worn for special occasions; whether they wear them to church or to a dance, their aim will be to impress others and to experience themselves as beautiful women. It is certainly true that in managing the household the youngest has taken over the mother's role, but her wish for the feather of Finist, the Bright Falcon, makes it clear that her interest in the masculine is not focused on the father.

The number three occurs frequently in this tale. As any odd number, it carries a dynamic symbolism and hence represents spirit. But as an archetype, it also contains the opposite, in this case, the material. Our three-dimensional notions of time (past, present, future) and of space (length, depth, and height) serve to orient us in our human existence. It is the tension between these two poles that provides the energy which results in the appearance of something new. This is supported by the triadic form of many gods and goddesses, and signifies the fateful breakthrough of the divine into our lives.

On the first two of his trips to town, the father is only able to satisfy the wishes of his elder daughters. It is not until he returns from his third trip with the feather for the youngest that the story gets into motion. The father spares no expense in obtaining this feather. One can easily imagine that 1,000 rubles was a huge sum for this old man. In another version, the father wonders what can be so special in a simple gray feather. Not so in the present version; here he doesn't question the feather's worth, but is ready to pay whatever price is asked in order to fulfill his daughter's wish. Interpreting money as psychic energy, we can appreciate the father's readiness to support his daughter's choice. This youngest daughter, whose wish had till now remained unfulfilled, rejoices at the gift, and later welcomes the young tsarevich (prince) into her room. Psychologically, this indicates a shift in the masculine energy away from the father toward the animus.

A small detail deepens the understanding of this important transition. As already mentioned, the father had tried to find the feather of Finist the Bright Falcon on each of his three trips to town. The third time he returned home with the feather, but even then he didn't get it in town, that is, in the collective sphere. The text says explicitly that the old man with the little box comes toward the father just as he passes the town gates. The father is hence helped by an outsider who is neither connected with the family nor with the town. In a variant of this tale the old man discloses himself as Finist's father and says that whoever possesses the feather will be a bride to his son, the tsarevich, that is, a member of the royalty. Although it is not expressly stated, we can assume that the original family is of peasant origin. The feather would hence connect the heroine with a man from the royal class, a suitable image for the animus.

It is likewise worthy of note that an impersonal father figure comes to the help of the personal father after the latter has twice unsuccessfully attempted to find the wished-for feather. What we subsequently learn of this feather confirms that the old man with the little box represents a deeper, more archetypal image of the father. This meeting shifts the tale onto another level; furthermore, it supports the psychological fact that it is through the personal father that a woman finds access to the world of the spirit. Therein lies the father's double role in shaping his daughter's character: he introduces her both to the world of concrete reality as well as to that of the spirit.

But what about the mother? She is nowhere to be seen and never even mentioned. We can only say that the mother is absent at a time when the young feminine stands on the threshold of adulthood. Beyond that, we can infer from the heroine's able management of the household that this is something she must have learned from her mother.

However, being an adult woman is not restricted to being a good mother. This echoes the opening situation of such tales as "Vasilisa the Beautiful" or "Cinderella" in which it is the task of the heroine to reactivate the dormant aspects of the feminine archetype. Her way of doing this is not based on rational considerations but on instinct for, as a heroine, she represents that part of the psyche which allows itself to be guided by the Self.

As in the case of the hero, the heroine's task begins with a confrontation with the shadow. We have seen that the two elder sisters are indeed very different from the heroine. Their interest in clothes and ornaments is juxtaposed with her concern for the household. Both are parts of the feminine psyche, although here they are not contained within one person but appear as different figures. From the perspective of the heroine, the two elder sisters would, therefore, represent her split-off, unconscious shadow.

Most often we think of the shadow as something negative; we project it unconsciously onto others because we are unable to see it or to accept it. Because the shadow is an integral part of our psyche, however, it needs to be acknowledged and confronted when it appears in dreams or any other unconscious material; it then becomes the ego's responsibility to differentiate between the various aspects of the shadow and to decide which of them can be lived, which must be rejected.

In the case at hand, the interest in beautiful clothes and ornaments might very well be thought frivolous and superficial, especially by an introvert. If we look deeper, however, we realize that such traits belong to the Aphrodite in every woman. In ancient Greece the most frequent epithet of this goddess was *golden* which meant beautiful. As a goddess of love, her main focus was directed toward her partner and to the relationship between them. Jean Shinoda Bolan calls her, very appropriately, the alchemical goddess, for Aphrodite brings people together with force and compelling desire.[67] Psychologically, this translates into an urge for wholeness within the feminine nature of the heroine.

In an essay entitled *Structural Forms of the Feminine Psyche*, Toni Wolff follows the pattern of Jung's typology in describing four different aspects of the feminine.[68] She calls this Aphrodite aspect, the *hetaera*. For this type of woman, beauty colors all aspects of a relationship. This structural form is diametrically opposed to that of the *mother* and, as with the psychological functions, it is the least accessible to consciousness in the actual mother type.

In contrast to the hetaera, the relatedness of the mother is directed toward the child and the family. Our heroine's concern for household duties can be likened to a bird building its nest; its tireless, often self-sacrificing labors are aimed at insuring the well-being of its off-

---

67   Bolan, *Goddesses in Every Woman*, 233.
68   Toni Wolff, *Structural Forms*. NB: This is not restricted to the female psyche but also applies to the man's anima.

spring. Interestingly enough, it is rare that the mother bird appears in a colorful dress.

Summing up, we can say that the elder sisters represent the structural form which is furthest away from the heroine's consciousness and, consequently, the most difficult to integrate. At the same time, it connects her to the creative and healing aspect of her psyche because it comes from the deepest layers of the unconscious.

Through the suffering and hardships of her quest for Finist, the heroine begins to integrate the essence of this hetaera in herself. Finding Finist becomes the goal of her long and perilous journey, and winning him back requires great sacrifices. At the end of the tale she is portrayed as a beautiful tsarevna (princess), riding together with Finist to church for the Easter service. "When they entered, they stood before everyone and the people marveled to see that a tsarevich and tsarevna had come."

We have jumped to the end of our tale here to shed some light on the initial constellation of the three sisters, and to show the heroine's psychic development through the integration of her hetaera shadow. But let us return now to the moment when the father brings home the little box with the feather and gives it to his youngest daughter. She is overjoyed to receive it: "...she took the box, began to kiss and fondle it, and pressed it tightly to her bosom." After supper she takes the little box to her room; it is worthy of note that it is only here that she opens it. The feather immediately flies out, strikes the floor and turns into a handsome tsarevich.

Our heroine is surely an introvert and a dreamer, perhaps intuitive as well. How else could she have known what was in the little box; why else did she want to keep her relationship secret? The whole notion of having a friend who is a bird points to a rich fantasy life and a reluctance to reveal this experience to the world. Even at the very end, had she not been forced by her father to reveal the nature of her relationship with Finist, she would probably have continued in this clandestine way.

If the heroine is such an introvert, it should not surprise us to find her shadow sisters responding in an extraverted fashion. Their interest in dresses and beautiful objects is indeed a one-sided, extraverted manifestation of the hetaera, totally foreign to the heroine. In this tale, as in so many others, the heroine succumbs to her sisters because she doesn't acknowledge their legitimacy. This split could possibly be traced to the absent mother who might have shown by her example that the two aspects can and should be brought together.

Returning to the tale, we learn that on the third evening, when darkness fell, the sisters "...took a ladder, gathered sharp knives and needles, and stuck them in the lovely maiden's window." In other versions, it is sharp pieces of glass or rusty nails. Upon waking in the morning, the heroine sees blood trickling from the sharp knives and needles in her window.

Interpreted objectively, this may refer to the initiatory aspect of this image, for women's initiation began with the first menstruation. Symbolically, the knives and needles would symbolize sharp, cutting, and hurting remarks. It is likewise noteworthy that the sisters placed these objects in the window through which Finist flew in and out to visit the lovely maiden. Subjectively, this window would symbolize a passage between the inner and outer world, that is, it enabled the heroine to escape into her fantasy at will.

Finist's nightly visits were, beyond doubt, a deeply emotional experience for the heroine. After the masculine energy became transferred from the father to Finist, she became free to love as an adult woman loves, even if this was only in her fantasy.

Fantasy is a double-edged sword. In as much as it replaces human relationships, it robs one of contact with life and makes adaptation more difficult. In this respect it is regressive, for by letting go, by imagining all sorts of wishful experiences, one lays oneself open to the unchecked influence of the unconsciousness precisely at the moment when one imagines oneself to be the creator of these same experiences. Even if unpleasantness is avoided, as it usually is in fantasy, it is amply experienced upon *re-entry*, for then the painful discrepancies between reality and fantasy become apparent. This usually results either in depression, or rejection of the real world in favor of the fantasy world, or repression of the fantasy itself.

Having said this, we must also realize that, precisely because fantasy allows the unconscious to flow freely into consciousness, it potentially furthers the realization of such contents. What is experienced and understood at first objectively—because that is the language into which consciousness translates the unconscious content—has a deeper significance of a symbolic nature. It is the aim of all in-depth interpretation to penetrate into the subjective meaning of a fantasy and thereby to enrich one's understanding with its psychic content.

Even if a fantasy is not lived concretely, it may still be viewed positively because of the fascination that it exerts on the ego. It attaches libido (psychic energy) to the images arising from the unconscious; we remember them, we return to them, we want to experience them over and over again. This is clearly the case in our tale, where the initial experience of Finist makes such a strong impression upon the heroine that she is able to go through much hardship in order to find him again.

Let us take a step back now and return for a moment to the sister aspects of the heroine's shadow. We note that there are two of them and that there are no differences between them, even to the point that they both ask the father to buy them the same things at the market. In short, the tale gives no reason why the shadow could not have been portrayed by one sister. This is another example of the threshold phenomenon which we encountered in the foregoing tale (p. 58). Psychologically, this implies that the shadow, represented by the two sisters, is approaching consciousness. Previously, this might have been experienced unconsciously, for example, in dreams or fantasies, but now it has begun to impact the heroine's waking life. As she awakens and sees the blood on her window, she realizes that this is the work of her sisters.

When the father first went to town, his elder daughters asked him to bring them cloth for dresses. They set about cutting and sewing, and they teased their sister, for whom the father had been unable to find the feather of Finist, the Bright Falcon. However, the maiden did not react, she just kept silent. On his third trip to town, the father was able to find the feather, and she was full of joy upon receiving it, but she kept it to herself; she didn't even open the little box until she got into her room. There the feather turned into a handsome tsarevich and they began to speak with one another "in sweet and loving words." This was overheard by the sisters and reported to the father, but he stood up for her. She, however, did not complain or defend herself; the only thing she did was to protect Finist by telling him to stay away for a while. Somewhere inside, she must have suspected her sisters' maliciousness but, most likely, she did not take it seriously enough. One cannot help wondering whether this had been her mother's response to life.

It was only after the sisters planted sharp objects in the maiden's window, wounding Finist as he tried to fly into her room, that she realized just how dangerous they were. Her emotional response to this tragedy was so great that she immediately left the house and went out in search of him. Remaining faithful to her experience, she followed the instructions she had heard from him in her sleep.

Before we follow the heroine upon her journey, let us take a closer look at this special friend of hers. Any flying bird, because it is not bound to the earth but can fly about at will, symbolizes spirit, ideas, intuitions, fantasies. The particular bird in this tale, the falcon, is a fast-flying bird of prey which spirals its way to incredible heights and swoops down upon its victim at a speed of 100-250 miles per hour.[69] It kills its victim instantly with a special projection in its beak, known as the *falcon's tooth*.[70] The *Encyclopedia Britannica* calls the falcon the most powerful flying bird for its size, and claims that its courage is as great as its power.

The falcon's eyes are one of its distinguishing features. It has extremely sharp vision, 2.6 times more acute than that of man, and a piercing gaze. It is interesting to note that in one variant of the tale the heroine is described as having "sable eyes, the eyes of a falcon."[71] This supports seeing Finist as a part of the heroine's animus.

Due to the falcon's intelligence and hunting abilities, the traditional art of falconry has developed. The fact that the falcon can be trained shows the bird's capacity for forming a relationship with man and, under the proper conditions, of subordinating itself to him. This potential for Eros is also witnessed in its relationship with its mate; many falcons mate for life, hunt together and share in the care of their young.[72]

The etymology of Finist, the falcon's name in our fairy tale, suggests a connection with an old art of decorating principally gold, but also silver, bronze, and copper artifacts. Along with other aspects of Byzantine cul-

---

69 Caspari, *Animal Life*, 102.
70 *Grzimek's Animal Life Encylopedia*, vol. 7, 338, 419.
71 Shandler, *Russian Folk Tales*, 26-36.
72 *Grzimek's Animal Life Encylopedia*, v.7, 339.

ture, this art appeared in Russia at or about the time of the country's conversion to Christianity (988). It consisted of pouring liquid enamel of various colors into different sections of a design. These sections were separated by thin ribs of metal, usually gold. When all the colors had been poured, the object was baked, then polished, producing a flat, even finish. Vibrancy of effect was achieved by the exclusive use of pure colors and by the shining lineation of the design.

Because this art was brought to Russia together with Christianity from Byzantium, most of the artefacts were initially produced for the Church. Later, its application became more widespread, and included decoration of court and military regalia, dishes, jewelry, and other art objects. With time, the art evolved from purely religious to secular, whereby secular subjects often included folklore motifs. The principal themes of this art, which flourished in the twelfth century, were images of saints, fantastical birds, and different designs prevalent at the time.[73] The Old Russian word for enamel, borrowed from the Greek, was *finift'*. In dialectal use this term became changed to *finist*.[74] This derivation of Finist from finift' is corroborated by one of the versions of our tale which bears the title: "The Tale of the Finift' Feather of the Bright Falcon."

Of particular significance for our tale is the fact that "falcon" is an Old Russian term of endearment for a young man. In song and tale, as indeed in the fairy tale at hand, the maiden often calls her lover "bright falcon." *Bright* is a translation of the Russian word *yasnyy*, which conveys the image of clarity and lucidity; this adjective often used in connection with the sky. As the falcon is not particularly brightly colored (its plumage is blackish blue above and white to cream below) the epithet must be of symbolic nature, based on the bird's graceful, soaring flight and on the daring and swiftness which it displays. This contrast between the true coloring of the falcon and the way it is perceived by the heroine is expressly mentioned in a variant of the tale. Here, in obtaining the feather so coveted by the youngest, the father is amazed at how ordinary it looks.[75] This shows that the feather has a special value for the hero-

73   *Russkoye dekorativnoye iskusstvo*, vol. 1, 375 ff.
74   Max Vasmer, *Russisches Etymologisches Wörterbuch*, v.2, 626.
75   Topkov, *Fol'klor Voronezhskoy oblacti*, 197.

ine, that she sees it with different eyes, that is, subjectively. The above characteristics of Finist are an extraordinary image of the heroine's animus: its clarity of vision, its soaring flight, its swiftness on the one hand and, on the other, its ability to relate to man and its devotion to its mate and offspring.

Awakening to find bloody knives and nails in her window the heroine immediately realizes what has taken place, and is deeply grieved. In a variant, she cries and waves the feather to bring back her beloved, but all in vain. Understanding that the fantasy is lost forever, she doesn't lapse into depression, nor does she disown her fantasy. She shows tremendous faith in her experience, which enables her to leave her whole known world and venture into the unknown.

The heroine's deep sleep had prevented her from responding to Finist's plea as he struggled to get through the window and enter her room. However, she remembered his words to look for him "beyond thrice nine lands, in the thrice tenth kingdom," as well as the prophesy of having to wear out three pairs of iron shoes, break three cast-iron staves and gnaw three stone wafers. We note the renewed mention of the number three, signaling time, dynamism, and fate. The fact that she recalls what she heard in her sleep indicates that, even though now awake, the window to the unconscious remains open. Her actions show, moreover, that because of her love for Finist she has now placed her fate in this part of the psyche.

Our heroine leaves home without even saying good-bye to her father. First she runs to the blacksmith and has the iron shoes and cast-iron staves forged for her. In our version she takes along three stone wafers; in others the bread is also of iron. A Russian folklorist, Victor Propp, claims that, according to pagan tradition, shoes, staff, and bread were placed in the grave at burial in order to facilitate the dead person's journey in the other world. Their being of iron, Propp explains, is a later addition, emphasizing the length of the journey.[76] The mention of these objects connected with death is symbolically well understandable, for the realm of death is far from consciousness.

In alchemical symbolism, iron corresponds to the initial *nigredo* stage, which psychologically represents the first realization of the shadow.

---

76   Propp, *Istoricheskiye korni volshebnoy skazki*, 37.

The iron objects are therefore appropriate symbols for the journey which our heroine is now to undertake.

The smith himself, as one who shapes iron with the help of fire, is psychologically an extremely important figure. He is traditionally connected with medicine men and shamans;[77] as such, he often stands for the old pagan faith. Fire, without which the smith cannot even begin his work, is symbolic of purification, of the burning away of all but the indestructible. Moreover, it represents the strong emotion which is indispensable for transformation. Among the many beliefs attributed to the smith is that of patronizing marriages. He is said to weld two people together as he welds two pieces of metal. The Russian language has many proverbs and sayings to this effect, and the image also occurs in courtship and wedding songs. By going to the smithy she connects up with the old pagan tradition. A correspondingly Christian act would have been a special short service for the road, a *naputstvenny moleben'*.

The heroine now sets out on her journey. The present tale only says that "she walked and walked..." In another version the description of her way is much more detailed: "She made her way through dark forests. She walked across deserts and sinking sands. She climbed over high, high mountains. She crossed deep, fast-flowing rivers."

Another striking difference between this tale and other versions is the nature of the three old women she meets along the way. In the present tale they are all kind and friendly, whereas in other variants, it is the terrifying Baba Yaga: "There on the floor lay Baba-Yaga. Her bony legs stretched right to the far corner. Her lips rested on a shelf on the wall. Her nose almost touched the ceiling." Baba Yaga responds to the heroine in her usual way; she recognizes her as coming from a different world and she asks whether the maiden is coming of her own free will or not. In some tales Baba Yaga reveals her cannibalistic nature by saying that the unknown guest is now sitting on a spoon and sliding right into her mouth.[78] This discrepancy warrants looking into. As an archetypal image, the Baba Yaga is ambivalent; most often her

---

77   Eliade, *Shamanism*, 474
78   Chudyakov, *Velikorusskiye Skazki*, 114-117.

conduct depends upon the attitude of her *guest*. It is worthy of note that the Afanas'yev version we are using chooses this rather exceptional positive manifestation of the archetype. Judging from the advice and gifts offered by these three Baba Yagas, we cannot possibly see them simply as kind old women; rather they may be compared to the triadic Greek and Roman goddesses of fate. Viewed psychologically, we can say that this long journey of initiation appears to have the support of the unconscious and that the heroine not only shows the necessary respect and humility, but also steadfastness in pursuing her goal.

An interesting detail, emphasized in other versions, is the harshening of nature as the heroine enters further into this world. Everything around her becomes more threatening, more impenetrable. Against this backdrop, we can better appreciate the gift of a ball of yarn, given to her by the first old woman, a ball to follow as she enters deeper and deeper into the unknown. The ball is one of the chief symbols of the Self. Its ability to roll discloses a capacity for spontaneous movement, a property attributable to divinity.[79] Its being of yarn is an important amplification relating to the goddesses of fate, for they measured out the thread of life and determined its end.

The immense magnitude of the heroine's task can also be measured by her wearing out a pair of iron shoes, breaking the cast-iron staffs and gnawing the stone wafers; this is mentioned each time she approaches one of the old women's huts. These images bear witness to a superhuman effort, one which would be unthinkable without the active participation of the unconscious. It is, indeed, the proverbial *night-sea journey* of the hero, venturing into the non-human part of the psyche in search of answers not available to consciousness.

Apart from the ball, the heroine receives a gift from each of the three old women upon leaving their hut. A notable similarity of these gifts is their being either of silver or gold: a silver spinning wheel and golden spindle, a silver dish and a golden egg, and, finally, a golden embroidery frame and needle. As a symbol of the Self, the Great Mother is para-doxical and ambivalent, and her gifts mirror this fact. It is a holistic initiation which the heroine is now undergoing.

---

79   von Franz, *Interpretations*, 58.

All feminine initiation rites aim at instructing a maiden on her role as adult woman in the community of which she is a part. What is particularly significant in this tale is that both the feminine and masculine are underscored respectively by the silver and golden attributes of these gifts. It points to the psychic breadth of the forthcoming initiation, and acknowledges the development of both the feminine personality as well as the inner masculine component of her psyche, the animus.

In order to better understand the forthcoming initiation, let us consider the symbolic meaning of these gifts. The spinning of the thread of life is a common attribute of all goddesses of fate. Spinning is also closely connected with fantasy, mentioned earlier in the heroine's original relationship with Finist. It can have a life-furthering influence on the surroundings, like the positive fantasy of a pregnant woman toward her unborn child, or like the nourishing fantasy with which a woman envelopes her whole family. On the other hand, it may have the effect of black magic if negative thoughts and feelings are not expressed.[80] This is something a girl must become aware of as she moves into womanhood.

In *Rites and Symbols of Initiation*, Mircea Eliade speaks of "a mystical connection between female initiations, spinning, and sexuality."[81] He refers to a Ukrainian custom, preserved down to the twentieth century which, because of its national origin, is particularly interesting in the case at hand.[82] On certain evenings, girls in the Ukraine and in White Russia gathered together to spin, weave, sew, and so on. After some time, these purely feminine activities were interrupted by the appearance of young men. Singing and dancing ensued, whereby usually no difference was made between the wealthy and poor. As night fell, the young men were chased outdoors. The girls now put straw on the floor and covered it with blankets. The young men then made their way inside again and the couples spent the night together. This apparently licentious behavior revealed its ritual character as the residue of a pagan tradition aimed at the periodic rejuvenation of nature.

---

80   von Franz, *Problems of the Feminine*, 40-42.
81   Eliade, *Rites and Symbols*, 46.
82   For a more detailed account of this custom, see D.K. Zelenin, *Russische (ostslavische) Volkskunde*, Berlin-Leipzig, 1927, 337 ff .

From the second old woman the heroine receives the gift of a golden egg spinning about a silver dish and producing another egg at each round. This gift combines the already discussed symbolism of spinning with the image of fertility contained in the egg. Fertility was always an important feature of women's initiation rites. Because it holds potential for new life as well as everything necessary for this new life within itself, the egg is self-contained or whole and is hence another important symbol of the Self. The egg going around the dish may also be interpreted as a measure of time. Since the dish was round and silver like the moon, it could, moreover, have referred to the moon's twenty-eight-day cycle, paralleled by the woman's menstrual cycle. Significantly enough, the woman's body produces an egg at each cycle.

In many pagan cultures, the birth of the new sun at the winter solstice was an occasion for fortune-telling. In Russia too, the town folk gathered together at this time of year to sing and dance, and to divine what the New Year would bring. The most widespread form of fortune-telling at New Year's was connected with the so called dish songs (bodbliudnye pesni). The participants placed rings or other pieces of jewelry into a dish or bowl provided for this purpose. The dish was filled with water and covered with a piece of cloth. Songs were now sung whose subjects ranged over all possible themes of interest in fortune-telling: health, wealth, success, love, marriage, and so on. One by one, the objects were removed from the dish, determining thereby whose fortune was told by the corresponding part of each song. These dish songs traditionally began with a song entitled *praise of the bread*, indicating that, regardless of what followed, the custom was initially concerned with fertility.[83]

The third gift consists of a golden embroidery frame with a needle that embroiders by itself. Here, once again, we come across the motif of spontaneous motion or action, attributable to the deity. Like spinning and weaving, embroidery is a purely feminine activity. In contrast to the others, however, embroidery is concerned with images. If the embroidered design is seen as a spontaneous image of the unconscious, then this craft may express a greater ability to give such images form, and hence to make them conscious.

---

83 Tschitschetow, *Russische Volksdichtung*, 210-13.

In a monograph on the paganism of the ancient Slavs, Boris Rybakov devotes a lengthy chapter to embroidery, holding that this art contains valuable information on the beliefs of the Slavic peoples. This view is supported by the extensive use of embroidery for objects of pagan ritual. One such example is the elaborately embroidered ritual towels which had long lost their original connection with the everyday towel. Such ritual towels were used for lowering a coffin into the grave; they replaced the reigns of a horse in the wedding procession; they decorated the special corner of the house dedicated to the ancestors, one in which icons were hung with the advent of Christianity. Newlyweds and guests were traditionally welcomed into the house by an offer of bread and salt carried out on just such an embroidered towel. In times of general calamities, the early Slavs were known to erect *common temples* as a sacrifice to the gods. These were built by the whole community in one day. In like manner and under similar circumstances, women of a community gathered together and embroidered a *common towel.* Most significantly for the present tale, this craft played an important role in marriage rites where every possible object was painstakingly decorated with needle and thread. The above are but a few examples of the different religious applications of embroidery by the pagan Slavs. Of particular interest is Rybakov's assertion that the themes of such ritual embroidery focused mainly on the great goddesses of fertility.[84]

The main aspects of feminine initiation mirrored in the above examples center around marriage and childbirth and, in a general sense, on the woman's role in the family. The significance of these rites lies in the fact that these feminine duties or tasks are raised to a sacred level and affect the well-being of the whole community.

In a way, by raising these feminine roles to a sacred level, initiation into the first half of life prepares for the transition into the second half of life, for here the biological demands of life need to be internalized and directed toward a woman's inner development, to the inner *coniunctio* and to creativity in its symbolic sense.

As noted earlier, the heroine's anonymity refers to the common, that is, universal or archetypal, implications of this tale. This is confirmed

---

84   Rybakov, *Yazychestvo drevnich Slavyan,* 495-552.

by her different social positions in variants of this tale: in some versions she is a peasant woman; in others, the daughter of a merchant or noble-man; in still others, as in the tale of "Mar'ya the Wise," she is a princess.

Having worn down three pairs of shoes, broken the third staff and gnawed away the third stone wafer, the heroine leaves the forest and approaches the house where Finist lives. She knows from the third old woman that he is now married to the daughter of a wafer baker. She has reached her destination, and Finist is within reach, but now she must win him back and, as the story shows, this is not an easy matter.

Following the directions of the third old woman, the heroine asks to be taken into the service of the wafer baker. This is a frequent fairy tale motif, meant to test the heroine's humility by accepting serving positions. Here again, "Vasilisa the Beautiful" and "Cinderella" are the typical examples, but also "All Fur." But why does our heroine need to be humbled? She had voluntarily taken on such a serving role in her father's household.

On her journey through the forest the heroine had been guided and supported by three old women; these we saw as the Great Mother in her triadic image, one of the most important manifestations of the Self in feminine psychology. The old women's special status is confirmed by the invaluable gifts they present to the heroine. Such gifts could not have come from an ordinary person. Their value is not exhausted by their being of gold and silver; their magical properties bear witness to their unconscious origin, for, as Jung writes, "magical" means every-thing where unconscious influences are at work."[85]

The humbling which is now required of the heroine must be seen in connection with the *magic* to which she has been exposed on her jour-ney. This exposure to the collective unconscious often poses a danger of inflation. If, for example, we have a dream in which we see an image of the Self and experience Its numinosity, we must beware of attributing these contents to our ego. The heroine needs to realize that these gifts are given to her with a purpose, that she must acknowledge the donor and do the right thing with them. By her actions, the heroine shows that she is aware of this. The same, however, cannot be said of the wafer

---

85   Jung, *Structure and Dynamics*, CW 8, § 725.

baker. She reveals her shadowy nature by not realizing the special value of the objects she covets; instead of putting herself in the service of the Self, she only looks out for her own interests. Her delight over the heroine's diligence and intelligence, as well as her praise for the maiden's doing everything "...without having to be told," likewise shows that she has no insight into what is been played out before her eyes.

After the heroine finishes her household tasks, she takes out the silver loom and golden spindle given to her by the first old woman. As she spins the threads of flax, they turn golden in her hands. This catches the eye of the wafer baker's daughter and she wants to buy the wheel and spindle for herself. The maiden agrees to sell them in return for spending one night with Finist. The perfidious nature of the wafer backer's daughter becomes immediately apparent, for not only is she prepared to drug her husband with a sleeping potion but she justifies her action by the large sum of money she and her mother will make on the sale of these objects; she doesn't even realize their special value, she just wants to profit from selling them in a very mundane way. Psychologically, this as an exploitation of the gifts provided by the Self; it also points to an inability to recognize the symbolic reality behind the concrete one. Such is the nature of the shadow which now stands in the way of a *coniunctio* between the heroine and her animus. Three nights in a row she sits at Finist's bedside, crying and pleading with him to awaken and recognize her. What an interesting complement this is to the falcon's futile attempts to fly through the maiden's window at the start of the tale.

On her journey to find Finist, the heroine went through a major initiation; she was tested on her determination, courage and humility, and richly rewarded both by the benign attitude of the three old women and by their gifts. But now she appears to be confronted with an additional trial; psychologically, this amounts to disengaging the animus from the shadow and achieving a reunion with the ego.

Before going further, we need to take a closer look at the shadow figure with whom the heroine is now confronted. In some versions this woman is referred to simply as the "wife of Finist." In others, she takes on royal dimensions such as queen or sea queen. In our tale, Finist's wife is the daughter of a wafer baker. The latter cannot be ignored because it is so unexpected and so singular.

The wafer referred to is the communion bread in the Orthodox liturgy. We recall the New Year's dish songs mentioned in connection with the gift of the second old woman and the traditional beginning of this pagan ritual with "praise to the bread." We also recall how the heroine went to the blacksmith to prepare herself for the journey rather than ask the local priest for a service for the road. With the appearance of the wafer baker and her daughter, a shift now takes place from pagan to Christian symbolism.

In the Orthodox Church such wafers consist of two separate flat wheat cakes placed one upon the other with a liturgical stamp on the top; the two parts symbolize the double nature of Christ as man and God. During the liturgy, pieces of this top part are cut out and placed into a chalice together with a mixture of wine and water, which is subsequently distributed to the congregation at communion; in other words, it symbolizes the Host. Those who bake the wafers are expected to be faithful members of the Church and morally clean. In monasteries the wafers are baked by the abbot; otherwise the wafer bakers were often widows. Furthermore, this service to the Church was not remunerable, but seen as a privilege for which one did not accept payment.

The wafer baker and her daughter are far from complying with these expectations of moral integrity. The disloyalty and willingness to *sell* Finist for a coveted object definitely positions the daughter as a shadow figure; this parallels the heroine's sisters at the start of the tale. Here, as there, we find egoism, a breach of trust, and a lack of true Eros.

The confrontation with the wafer baker's daughter presents the fourth and final test of the maiden's initiation. Now it is not enough to take on deprivation and exert great effort in attaining her goal, neither is it enough to be respectful and humble toward the unconscious. Instead, she must show that she has incorporated the gifts of the old women and is able to apply them in her life. As we know from dream interpretation and active imagination, this is the very important final step without which no development is possible.

Furthermore, as in every process of individuation, the heroine is now called upon to make a sacrifice; she must give up those very gifts which she received from the unconscious. Psychologically, to hold on to them would be equivalent to seeing them as belonging to the ego, but this is not the case. These objects continue to exhibit magical properties; they are still a part of the unconscious, and connecting them to the ego would amount to inflation. They can best be understood as being on loan to the ego for the purpose of accomplishing the intentions of the Self.

The heroine's ability to do this shows that she has integrated the inner value of these gifts. The gold and silver objects of her initiation remain with her even as she surrenders them to the wife. She has recognized Eros as the essence of these gifts, and will not allow herself to be side-tracked by any other considerations, regardless of their value.

But what do Finist's wife and his mother-in-law represent psychologically? As we are interpreting this tale from the feminine perspective, the two women must be seen as parts of the heroine's psyche. Finist's wife represents another aspect of her shadow; the wafer baker is an image of the mother who has thus far been absent from the tale. The two women are shown to be of like mind; moreover, we note the mother's influence in shaping the daughter's character. Psychologically, this suggests a strong mother complex in Finist's wife.

Furthermore, because of the mother's function as wafer baker, both women are connected to the sacrament of transubstantiation, which, understood psychologically, is transformation. Were it not for their perfidious conduct, this last circumstance might have pointed to a very positive development; as we can see, however, this is far from being so, for they prevent the animus from uniting with the ego.

In amplifying the falcon we noted that in folklore this was a term of endearment for a young man. However, there are no signs of tenderness between Finist and his wife; she doesn't even serve him his supper, but bids the servant do so. This throws doubt upon their relationship and shows that Finist is actually nourished by the heroine, even if he doesn't recognize her.

Our suspicions are further confirmed by Finist's wife drugging him before he goes to sleep. One wonders whether he is so blinded by these two women that he doesn't realize what is going on in his own house. The bond in this household is not within the couple but between the mother and daughter. It is, therefore, the heroine's task not only to confront the shadow, but also to free the animus from the latter's grip. Finist is a bit of a *puer*, flying around all day and returning home in the evening to eat and sleep. This is very much in keeping with the mother complex, which is constellated in this situation.

The heroine's two sisters have been psychologically understood as her personal shadows. However, because of their connection to the Church, the wafer backer and her daughter must be considered collective figures. We have never seen the heroine displaying such corrupt behavior, but we must assume that these traits infiltrated her psyche, for such is the effect of collective phenomena when they remain unconscious.

At the start of the tale, we are given little information on the missing mother; we only know that she was absent at a critical stage in her daughters' lives. She left them no gift, no words of advice that might have helped them in the transition to adulthood. In "Vasilisa the Beautiful," this had been the *blessing* that had saved Vasilisa from peril. In our story, the father appears to have done well by his girls, but, as the story shows, he was unable to replace the mother in this important phase.

As is often the case when some vital development is missing in consciousness, the unconscious steps in to fill the gap. In the present tale, this was provided by the three old women in the forest. Valuable as this experience was however, it did not prepare the maiden for the dark side of the feminine. As noted earlier, this is in contrast to most other variants where the heroine is confronted by three Baba Yagas. To be sure, she had experienced the malice of her sisters, but she did not confront them. Rather, it appears that her individuation lay in following the animus. Had she stayed to challenge them, she may have lost too much of her energy and become entangled in collective life. Hers was a different development and, being a heroine, she trusted her instinct to go after Finist. This demonstrates how individual the process of individuation can be and how the general rule of confronting the shadow before dealing with the animus/anima is not without exceptions. It takes a heroine who is in tune with the Self to be able to set her priorities accordingly. Most importantly, it shows that the problem constellated in this tale cannot be solved by consciousness alone.

Through her initiation in the forest, the heroine became an adult member of the collective of which she is a part. As a heroine, however, she is responsible not only for herself but for the whole collective; she must, consequently, be capable of confronting the collective shadow as well as the personal one. This explains why fairy tale heroines, regardless of their initial social position, often become queens in the lysis, for the queen represents the collective Eros in a society; her example determines the way people relate to one another.

The hero who kills the dragon is not only ridding himself of this destructive force, but saving his whole land. The way the hero goes about achieving his goal is by fighting and killing. This is an illustration of the Logos function, because psychologically it translates into differentiating (cutting apart, separating) between what is desirable from what is not. The heroine resorts to other means—she strives to relate and bring together rather than sever; this is the way of Eros.

As mentioned earlier, in folk tradition the blacksmith was considered the patron of marriages. He was expected to weld a couple together and to purify their relationship by the heat of his fire. In order to *forge* a permanent relationship with the animus, the heroine must now free him from contamination with the collective shadow. Without such catharsis, an animus figure who had been united with the collective shadow would inevitably warp the heroine's spirit and, as the tale clearly shows, stands in the way of a true *coniunctio*.

On the collective level, it is often difficult to detect the influence of an animus in such moral matters because, after all, the Church is very much concerned with the very same issues and sets the standard by which they are usually measured. Therein lays the purpose of the final test to which the heroine is subjected, for her judgement must go beyond collective values.

What is it that finally awakens Finist from his deep sleep? The heroine spends three nights in his room, crying and pleading for him to awake, but all this proves to be in vain. On the third night, however, a tear falls on his cheek, instantly waking him. "Ah," he says, "something burnt me!" This is reminiscent of the drop of oil which burns Amor as

Psyche bends over him with an oil lamp. That the maiden's tear burns Finist, when her words and pleas could not rouse him, emphasizes her suffering but also shows that something has finally touched him in a figurative as well as concrete sense.

A tear is not only a drop of water, it is much more. The biochemists Donald and Judith G. Voet write that those organisms which, in the process of evolution, left the sea and ventured onto dry land, "...still carry the ocean with them," that indeed, the "...composition of their intercellular and extracellular fluids are remarkably similar to that of seawater."[86] As a matter of fact, the body contains an average of eight ounces of salt, and convulsions, paralysis, and even death may result if this level is not maintained.[87]

"Salt requires particularizing," writes James Hillman in *Salt and the Alchemical Soul*.[88] Its success depends upon taking into account the necessary amount to be used. This applies to both medicine and cooking. In the latter case, only the right amount will bring out the fine nuances of a dish, and too much can destroy a good one. In Roman times, the Vestal Virgins, known as Mistresses of the Salt, were entrusted with determining the right amount of salt with which the sacrificial animal was to be sprinkled in order to make it holy.[89]

The alchemists considered salt to be one of the chief symbols for soul. It was argued that, as the world soul permeates everything, so also does salt; moreover, since by permeating it connects everything, salt was seen as the most perfect symbol of Eros.[90]

Salt is also connected with bitterness.[91] The heroine's suffering only gets through to him when a tear touches his cheek; this is what finally makes the vital connection. And here Eros is experienced in its ambivalence, as pleasing and burning at the same time.

We find salt referred to symbolically in the Bible. In the New Testament, both in Matthew 5.13 as well as in Mark 9.50, salt stands for insight, understanding, and wisdom. Jung draws our attention to the

---

86 Voet, *Biochemistry,* 29.
87 Hillman, *Salt,* 162.
88 Hillman, *Salt,* 166.
89 Hillman, *Salt,* 172.
90 Jung, *Mysterium Coniunctionis,* CW 14, § 321 f.
91 Jung, *Mysterium Coniunctionis,* CW 14, §§ 245-255; von Franz, *Alchemy,* 102.

fact that, parallel to the *Sapientia Dei*, the divine wisdom of scripture, the Bible also speaks of a human wisdom—one which needs to be exercised and cultivated. It is clear that for Jung this human wisdom comes from the Self and is archetypally universal while, at the same time, being more individual than Church dogma.[92] Like the wisdom of the I Ching, it mirrors the situation of the given moment and takes into account the individual's role and responsibility within the eternal and transpersonal.

Armed with a rich amplification of *salt*, we return to our heroine as she attempts to free her beloved from the grip of his shadowy wife. Through the latter's symbiotic relationship with the mother, this woman is connected to the making of the liturgical bread, the central-most symbol of the Eucharist, yet we have seen her to be perfidious and egoistic.

Psychologically, the above situation calls for our heroine to free her spirit from contamination with the shadow aspect of the Church. The animus is often the mouthpiece of collective values, and the dogmatic tenets of the Church are an important part of his repertoire. He presents them as universal principles, not to be questioned or challenged. A woman must exercise extreme caution in following his dictates, and she will require all the traits mentioned in connection with salt to achieve this. She will need to have insight into the deeper meaning of the relationship, and she must accept her suffering and the purification involved. Moreover, she must be able to differentiate in a very fine way between what is right and appropriate, independently of collective standards. If this is what the tear falling on Finist's cheek represents, then it is no wonder that it instantly awakens him. Then he is able to hear her litany of the shoes, staffs, and wafers, to learn of her long journey, and to appreciate her perseverance in reclaiming him: "Only now did Finist the Bright Falcon recognize her, and he was overjoyed beyond all words." At this moment, she has redeemed him and connected him to consciousness.

The two plan together and leave the house of the wafer baker. It is the animus who now takes the lead and enables their swift escape. His wife and mother-in-law are unable to overtake them. The joint efforts

---

92   Jung, *Mysterium Coniunctionis*, CW 14, §§ 325-327.

of the conscious and unconscious parts of her psyche have prevailed over the paralyzing effect of these negative aspects.

What awaits them now is re-entry into collective life. Psychologically, this requires finding a way of living the inner experience, of not disowning it, while, at the same time protecting it from those who cannot understand, or who might try to belittle or harm it. At the start of the tale, the heroine loses Finist through her sisters' malice. In retrospect we can see how necessary this experience was, for without it our heroine might well have remained forever in her fantasy. Nonetheless, despite the fact that this led to such a valuable development in her psyche, the knives in her window will not soon be forgotten, and she will rightly be on her guard to avoid losing him again.

As soon as the couple arrive at her father's house, Finist transforms into a feather and the maiden hides the feather in her bosom. Formerly the feather was kept in a box and taken out at the heroine's will. Now it is much closer and more intimately connected to her. Whatever she does, wherever she goes, she feels the feather between her breasts. For a newborn infant, breasts are the nourishing organ of the woman's body; but they are also an important erogenous zone. If we wanted to express this in terms of Toni Wolff's structural types (p. 100), we could say that breasts combine the two opposing aspects of the mother and hetaera. Finist is no longer a fantasy to be activated at will, but an integral part of the heroine's personality. It is interesting to note that at this point in the tale the heroine is first referred to as Finist's *destined bride*.

The father's joy is great as he beholds his long-lost daughter, and he asks her where she had been. Her answer is somewhat cryptic. She tells him that she had gone to pray to God. In a way this is true because, after all, what she went through *was* a religious experience, but is she translating her experience into words her father can understand or is she just giving an explanation that would be acceptable to him? It might be either but, in both cases, she is protecting her secret, she is not exposing it. One might even suspect that she is not yet ready to face up to her experience.

Somewhat later, when the father bids her make ready to go to church, she backs out by saying she has no appropriate dress. Here again, her answer can be understood in one of two ways. Dresses stand for persona, for the way one shows oneself to the world. The persona can also represent the outer form of an inner attitude. If the heroine were to accept the dresses offered by her sisters, she would symbolically also be accepting their attitude. Clearly this is something she doesn't want to do. Despite their friendly manner, she is not so naive as to take them at their word. She is protecting herself and her relationship to Finist. Neither, however, does she confront them about the past; she merely avoids the issue by telling her sisters that their dresses will not fit her.

Marie-Louise von Franz holds that "...evil tends to produce a chain reaction," and that it is therefore wise to detach oneself from it.[93] By not accepting the sisters' dresses, she is doing just that. We witnessed the same in the way the heroine and Finist left the wafer baker's house. They did not wait for morning to confront the two women, nor did they take their revenge in any way. In burying the burning skull, Vasilisa demonstrates the same attitude toward evil.

Let us return to the scene where the heroine refuses her sisters' clothes. As we can see in what follows, this does not mean that she doesn't want to go to church or to be seen in the village; she simply doesn't want to be seen wearing her sisters' clothes. The initiation she has gone through has transformed her into another person. She is no longer the maiden everyone knew, yet she would be at a loss to explain the changes which have taken place in her. In other words, she must now understand and define her new role in the town she grew up in. At this point she may not even know what she wants, only what she doesn't want, and that is to be associated with her sisters. When one has changed, it is always difficult to return to an old situation because one is inevitably seen in one's former role. Here she has returned and it is most important for her to establish and clarify her new position.

As soon as the father and the two elder sisters have left the house, the youngest takes out the feather; striking the floor it transforms into a handsome tsarevich who now takes over. Beautiful clothes and a golden carriage appear at his command, and the couple ride together to church. They take their place at the front of the church as tsarevich and tsarevna, and are admired by the whole congregation. At the end

---

93   von Franz, *Shadow and Evil*, 170.

of the service they leave ahead of the others and make their way to her father's house; here all the magic disappears.

The heroine cannot quite make the necessary step into the outer world. She is split between outer and inner reality, and she is unable to find the right way of bringing the two together. When the going gets rough, she switches into fantasy where everything is made possible by that handsome tsarevich of hers.

This episode is repeated three times, gradually gaining the dynamism and momentum inherent in the symbolism of this number. As in other fairy tales with this motif, something inevitably happens the third time which divulges her secret. The best known example of this is the lost shoe in "Cinderella"; in other tales the heroine forgets to remove a diamond pin or some other object remaining from her royal attire. In our tale, it is not so much the heroine's *fault* or *omission* as her father's suspicion. He catches a glimpse of the disappearing carriage, sees it heading for their home and confronts his daughter upon his return.

> "There's nothing to be done," said the heroine, "I must confess every-thing." She took out the feather. It struck the ground and turned into the tsarevich. They were married at once and what a magnificent wedding it was!

In the space of four short sentences her secret identity is disclosed, and the dilemma is resolved. Had this *coming out* not taken place, she would have lived a double life—part of her would have remained her father's daughter and been subject to his traditional *Weltanschauung*. In this role, she would never have developed into an adult woman, and getting married would not have changed much because her readiness to unconditionally accept her father's views would simply have shifted onto her husband.

There was another part of her, however, that knew of the existence of Finist, the Bright Falcon; this inner fantasy would break into her consciousness whenever her outer life did not satisfy her. This hero-ine had enough courage and perseverance to pursue her fantasy, Finist, and to suffer many hardships in the process of finding him. In the episode with the wafer baker's daughter she came to realize that she had a right to her own view of life; this view was in keeping with the

Self, and ultimately resulted in her union with Finist. That Finist is recognized as a tsarevich speaks for his royal status and makes him a suitable personification of her animus. This makes their union a royal *coniunctio*, the desired conclusion of every alchemical opus and the goal of individuation.

All of this might not have happened had the father not stepped in and challenged his daughter to stand up to her fantasy. Here, at the end of the tale, he plays a decisive role in her development, as he did at the tale's beginning. Back then he was instrumental in ending the stagnation of the initial situation. He had no wife, and his daughters had no husbands; life had no future under such a constellation. By going to town and offering to bring his daughters presents of their choice, the father opened up their lives to new possibilities. The two elder maidens asked for material things: cloth for dresses, kerchiefs, and earrings, which were easily found. The same objects might also be seen symbolically, but from the reaction of the two elder sisters we can assume that such an interpretation could only be considered as a possibility. The third daughter's wish was more difficult to come by. It appeared to have no worldly value, and the first two times the father could not even find it. Despite this, he did not belittle or devalue her request, but showed trust and respect for her choice. As it soon became clear, although her wish had no material value, it had a highly symbolic one. By allowing his daughter to follow her fantasy, the father displayed openness toward the irrational. Moreover, by finally bringing her the wished-for feather, he connected her to the inner world of the spirit.

The father represents the traditional values for his daughter. He provides her with the necessary structure and boundaries while she is growing up, but he likewise has a responsibility for the development of her spirit. Moreover, as a girl's *first man*, he is an example of the opposite sex and of the way a man relates to women. From the way this father treats all three of his daughters, but the youngest in particular, we see that Eros plays an important part in his attitude. Eros is usually a woman's chief concern, but a man cannot be whole if he hasn't developed this function as well. Eros can be seen as concern for the other, a trust in the other's need to develop in his or her own way, and an ability to accept this development even if it does not coincide with one's own views. The heroine received all this from her father in our tale. It gave her courage and confidence in herself as she set out on her long journey through the forest, enabled her to give up the precious gifts she received from the old women for a chance to be close to Finist, and gave her the necessary perseverance in pursuing her goal. But at the very end she still needed her father to give her a little push to bring all this into her everyday experience of life and to leave him for another man. It is not without meaning that this last step takes place at Easter, the feast of the Resurrection, of rebirth, of transformation into another reality.

We spoke above of the woman's need to leave the security provided by the parental home, and to free herself from her father's view of the world. We suggested that, if this was not done, the dependence upon the masculine would simply shift to the partner or husband. This is not meant literally, although it can still be witnessed as such in our day. Moreover, it certainly does not imply that a woman needs to sever all outer connections to the masculine in order to experience the final *coniunctio* with the animus.

The inner component of this constellation is based on the ability of any woman not to experience herself exclusively in connection with the masculine of the outer world. The significance and wisdom of the initiation rites of indigenous people confirm this by making the initiates aware of the very special, religious significance of their role as female beings. In our tale, the heroine's contact with the three old women was essential for her ability to cope with the challenge of Finist's wife and mother-in-law, and later to re-enter the world of everyday life. This was the world she had been born into, and the one she could now return to without giving up the reality of her inner experiences.

IV. The Enchanted Ring

In such and such places, in such and such large villages there lived a peasant; he was neither poor, nor rich. The peasant had a son whom he blessed and left with three hundred rubles upon his coming of age. When the son grew up and reached the age of reason he said to his mother: "I remember that my deceased father blessed me with three hundred rubles; give me at least a hundred." She gave him hundred rubles and he took to the road; along the way he met a peasant leading a flappy-eared dog. "Sell me the dog," he said. The peasant asked for a hundred rubles and he paid him. He brought the dog home and gave him to eat and drink. Then he asked his mother for another hundred rubles. She gave them to him and he took to the road. Again he met a peasant; this time the peasant was leading a little cat with a golden tail. "Sell me the cat," he said. "Buy it," the peasant answered. "What do you ask for it?" "You can have it for a hundred rubles." The son paid him the hundred rubles, took the cat home and gave him to eat and to drink. Then he asked his mother for another hundred rubles. "My dear child," she said, "what are you wasting your money on? These are senseless purchases." "My dear mother, do not worry about the money; someday it will return to us." She gave him the third hundred and he again took to the road.

All very well! In such and such places, in such and such towns, there died a tsarevna. On her hand she wore a golden ring. The good lad wanted very much to take this ring off her finger. He bribed the guards to let him get through to the tsarevna, took the ring off her finger and went back to his mother. No one stopped him.

After a long or a short time, he went out on the porch and switched the ring from one hand to the other; 300 brave youths and

170 strong men jumped out of the ring and said, "What will you have us do?" "Here's what you should do," said the good lad: "First, tear down my old hut and build a stone house in its place; and my mother should know nothing about it." They put up the house in one night. His mother was surprised when she got up in the morning. "Whose house is this?" "My very dear mother," he said, "do not be surprised, but pray to God; this house is ours." After they had lived in this house for a long or a short time, the good lad reached adulthood and began thinking about marriage.

In such and such a kingdom, in such and such a land, a certain tsar had a daughter, and the good lad wanted to woo her. "Go and woo for me, my dear mother! In such and such a kingdom, a certain tsar has a beautiful daughter." "My dear child," the mother said to him, "is it fitting for us to woo a tsarevna?" "Dear mother, you who gave birth to me! Pray to the Savior, drink *kvass* (beer) and go to bed; the morning is wiser than the evening." The good lad walked out on the porch and moved the ring from one hand to the other. Out sprang 300 brave youths and 170 strong men. "What would you have us do?" they asked. "Find me such precious things that even the tsar does not possess, and bring them to me on golden trays. I want to present them to the tsar and tsarevna." His wish was immediately fulfilled and he sent his mother to woo the tsarevna.

The tsar was surprised by the gifts and wanted to know where the old woman had gotten them from. At that moment the tsarevna came in, took a look at the gifts and said, "Well, old woman, tell your son that if he erects a new palace—better than my father's—on the royal sacred meadow, if he connects the two palaces with a crystal bridge, if this bridge is covered with all kinds of embroidered rugs and, moreover, if he does all this in one night, I will marry him; if not, there will be no pardon for him and he will have to lay his arrogant head on the block." The old woman went home in tears and said to her son: "My dear child! Did I not warn you against wooing the tsarevna? She now bids me tell you that if you want to marry her, you must build a new palace on the sacred meadow; this palace must be better than her father's and it must be ready in one night; furthermore, she demands that the two palaces be connected by a crystal bridge, covered with all kinds of embroidered rugs. If you do not fulfill all of her wishes, your arrogant head will lie on the block! What are you going to do about this, my child?" "My very dear mother," he replied, "do not worry, pray to the Savior, drink kvass and go to bed; the morning is wiser than the evening."

The good lad went out on the porch, moved the ring from one hand to another; out sprang 300 hundred brave youths and 170 strong men and asked what there was to do. "My dear friends," he said, "in one night, try to build me a new palace on the royal sacred meadow, a palace better than that of the tsar; and connect the two palaces with a crystal bridge, covered with all kinds of embroidered rugs." In one night, the brave youths and strong men did as they had been ordered. The tsar got up in the morning, looked through his spyglass and was surprised to see a palace, better than his own, standing on his sacred meadows. He sent a messenger to let the good lad know that he could come to ask for the tsarevna's hand, adding that she was willing to marry him. And so the match was made and the wedding was royally celebrated.

After they had lived together for a long time or a short time, the tsarevna asked her husband: "Tell me, please, how you managed to accomplish all this in one night? Now you and I must think together." She flattered him and cajoled him, she offered him different spirits to drink, and when he was dead drunk he disclosed the secret of his ring. She took the ring from the drunkard and moved it from hand to hand; out jumped 300 brave youths and 170 strong men, and asked for her orders. "Here's what you should do: take this drunkard and throw him out on my father's meadow, then carry me with my whole palace beyond thrice nine and three lands, beyond the tenth kingdom to such and such a king." In one night they moved her to where she had told them.

As the tsar arose in the morning and looked through the spyglass at his sacred meadows, there was neither palace nor crystal bridge to be seen; only one man lay sprawled out on the ground. The tsar sent messengers to find out who was lying there. The messengers returned and reported that it was the tsar's son-in law who was sprawled out on the meadow. "Go and bring him to me" said the tsar. When they brought him, the tsar wanted to know what he had done with the tsarevna and the palace. He answered: "Your Royal Highness! I don't know where she is; I lost her as if in a dream." The tsar said, "I give you three months to find out where the tsarevna is, and after that I will execute you." Then he put him into a strong prison.

Then the cat said to the flappy-eared dog: "Would you believe it? Our master is imprisoned. The tsarevna betrayed him; she took the ring off his finger and disappeared beyond the thrice nine lands, beyond the tenth kingdom. We must get the ring back; let's go!" They ran together; whenever they came to a lake or a river, the cat sat on the dog's neck and the dog carried him over to the other side. After a long or a short time, they got beyond the thrice nine lands, beyond the tenth kingdom. Then the cat spoke to the dog: "If anyone in the king's kitchen calls for wood, run and fetch some immediately; I will go to the housekeeper in the cellar; whatever she wants I will fetch for her."

They begin to live in the king's court. Once the housekeeper said to the king: "In the cellar I have I a cat with a golden tail; I just have to think of something and he gets it for me!" The cook says: "And I have a flappy-eared dog; whenever I send the boy for wood, the dog runs headlong and brings it." The king said, "Bring the flappy-eared dog to my bedroom." "And the cat with the golden tail into mine," ordered the tsarevna. The cat and dog now spent day and night in the palace. Before going to sleep, the tsarevna always took the ring into her mouth. During the night a mouse ran into the room, and the cat grabbed her by the neck. The mouse said, "Don't touch me, cat! I know what you are here for; you came for the ring. I will get it for you." The cat let the mouse go. It jumped onto the bed and went straight to the tsarevna; it put its tail into her mouth and wiggled it.

The tsarevna spat and the ring fell out. The cat grabbed it and cried to the flappy-eared dog: "Wake up!"

They jumped right out of the window and made their way home. Over dry land they ran, over water they swam. They returned to their kingdom and went straight to the prison. The cat got into the prison, and the master saw him and began to stroke him. The cat sang songs, then he put the ring into his master's hand. The master was overjoyed. He moved the ring from hand to hand; 300 brave youths and 170 strong men jumped out and asked for orders. "To ease my grief," he said, "let beautiful music resound for a whole day and night." Music began to play. At this time, the tsar sent a messenger to find out if his son-in-law had thought it over, but when the messenger arrived he was captivated by the music. The tsar sent another messenger and the same happened to him; then a third messenger was sent and he too could not stop listening to the music. Now the tsar himself came to his son-in-law, and he too was captivated by the music. As soon as the music stopped playing, the tsar began questioning him. The son-in-law said, "Your Royal Highness! Free me for a single night and I will instantly retrieve your tsarevna."

Then he went out on the porch, moved the ring from hand to hand: the 300 brave youths and 170 strong men appeared and asked what they should do. "Bring back the tsarevna and the whole palace; do this in one night and let everything stand in its former place." In the morning the tsarevna got up and saw that she was back again. She was scared because she didn't know what would happen to her. Her husband went to the tsar: "Your Royal Highness, how will we now judge the tsarevna?" "My dear son-in-law, we will admonish her with words; then may the two of you live well together and prosper."

Alexander Afanas'yev, *Russian Folk Tales*, #190, trans. NB.

INTERPRETATION

This tale starts in a most uncertain way: it speaks of a peasant who was neither rich nor poor, and who lived in some big village in a certain land. Cryptic as it sounds, the ambiguities may indicate that the story refers to any peasant who lives in any big village, in any land. In light of the fact that the peasant's son will later become tsar and, as such, determine the way the kingdom will be run, it emphasizes the potential in what is common and low.

Actually, the word *common* carries a double meaning, for it refers not only to what is low but also to that which applies to the human situation in general; this is true for both Russian and English. According to this play on words, the peasant, who has the lowest rank in society and is hence the most common man in the collective, may represent a part of the psyche that all people have in common. When we speak of the common in this way, we refer to the instinctual and to the archetypal. And this is, in general, the material of fairy tales.

The idea that the fairy tale speaks to a common human situation is supported by the fact that none of the characters have personal names. We read of a peasant, a father, a mother, a tsar or a king, a tsarevna—what takes place in this tale speaks of the human condition, in general.

At this point, I would like to draw attention to the unexplained appearance of both a *tsar* and a *king* in the story. Both terms refer to the ruler of the land and the only difference between them is therefore linguistic. The tsar is the father of the hero's wife and the king is the ruler the kingdom to which she flees. However, the careful reader will notice that the daughter of the tsar, the tsarevna, retains her title in both kingdoms. At first this appears to be a mistake; upon closer scrutiny, however, this points to a small but, psychologically, significant detail. The use of *Russian* in juxtaposition to *non-Russian* refers to that which belongs to the world of consciousness in contrast to that of the unconscious. Psychologically speaking, after stealing the ring from her husband's finger, the tsarevna in the present tale regresses into the unconscious part of the psyche (the realm of the king) from which she is brought back again to the conscious world, that is, to the world of the tsar in the latter part of the story.

Returning now to the beginning of the present tale we learn that the father dies while the hero is still a child. What can it mean for a boy to lose his father? It is from his father that a boy learns the ways of the world. It is he who provides his son with an example of manhood and of relationship to the feminine. Such is the archetypal expectation of a father in the psyche of every boy. If the father dies or fails to fulfill his parental role, the boy is left without such a model of behavior. Often this results in the boy growing up without any structure in life, without guidelines, without knowing a man's role in the society of which he is a part.

But there is another possible consequence of a missing father. The collective values which the father might otherwise have imparted to his son leave an unsatisfied archetypal expectation of a father in the boy's psyche. The absence of the human father, therefore, exposes the boy more directly to the father in its archetypal form. As a result, such a man will be more open to the unconscious and less influenced by collective norms.

The father in this tale dies, but he leaves his son his blessing and 300 rubles for when his son comes of age. As we have seen in the tale of "The Feather of Finist, the Bright Falcon," this *coming of age* is an important threshold in the life of any child, for it marks the beginning of consciousness and responsibility which lead to adult life. A blessing is not a directive on how to live, but rather has a religious connotation of putting someone into God's hands. This is considerably more than the missing mother left her three daughters in the foregoing tale.

For a peasant of those days, three hundred rubles was a large sum. Psychologically, it stands for psychic energy, for libido in the original sense of the word. Here it would represent the necessary masculine psychic energy which the father bequeaths his son so that the latter can live according to the Self (the blessing). It is in this light that we must view the hero's actions in the tale. The decisions he makes are not always in keeping with the expectations of the collective. Why spend a hundred rubles on a dog or cat, when there are any number of such animals running around the village? However, when we consider what these particular animals do for their master at the end of the tale, we cannot but realize that they are worth all the money spent on them.

Psychologically, the animals strengthen his instinct. He makes them his own and nourishes them with food and drink. Befriending animals in fairy tales always brings success. In fact, according to von Franz, that is the only rule without exceptions in fairy tale interpretation.[94] And what about the mother? Her son is clearly the chief concern of her life. This is understandable in her position as widow, for there is no man to protect her and no one to provide for her old age. Such an attitude is the reality of village life in a patriarchal society.

In this situation, we see that she truly does her best by him: She does not stand in his way; neither do we detect any bitterness in her, nor any attempt to compensate the missing father with negative animus. She respects the father's wishes and safeguards the money for her son's use when he comes of age, that is when the son will need more than the holding, nourishing care that she provides. Till then, our hero can develop within the safe matrix of their hut, like an egg under the warm belly of a hen.

However, out of necessity the mother is reality-oriented. At first, she voices no objection to the hero's request for the money bequeathed him by the father, but later, seeing him giving it away for a village dog and a cat, she expresses her dismay at his seemingly reckless spending. What mother wouldn't? Her dismay subsequently turns to horror when she learns of his intention to marry a tsarevna. She is terrified by his audacity as well as the possible danger of his intention, even more so by his asking her to woo the tsarevna for him: "My beloved child," she pleads, "how can such as we get a tsarevna?" One cannot help feeling the anguish in her words. But the son bids her pray to God, drink *kvass* (a Russian form of beer) and go to bed. He ends his admonitions with an old Russian proverb: "The morning is wiser than the evening." We can well appreciate the different realities which govern the perception of these two people.

---

94   von Franz, *Shadow and Evil*, 119 f.

Let us now backtrack and take a closer look at the events which lead to this development. Obtaining the first hundred rubles from his mother, the hero takes to the road. He does not go to the market place, a collective setting where people meet and exchange words, ideas, and goods. There is no indication of his having a goal; seen symbolically, he is leaving home with a lot of psychic energy, and is open to anything that comes his way.

And sure enough, something does come his way—a peasant leading a flappy-eared dog. Without pondering the matter, he asks the peasant to sell him his dog, and is ready to pay a hundred rubles for it. There is nothing outstanding about either the peasant or the dog, nothing to explain why the hero decides to pay a high price for this ordinary village animal. We may, however, be struck by the peasant's *leading* the dog. This might be expected in a city, but is strange on a village road. The only possible explanation for this small detail is that it emphasizes the connection between peasant and animal, owner and dog. Psychologically, this peasant would represent the hero's shadow, an unconscious part of his psyche connected to his masculine instinct. By buying the dog, the hero takes on the responsibility for applying it consciously.

When we speak of the dog as man's best friend, we refer, symbolically, to an instinct which is closest to man's consciousness and easiest to tame and train. A dog accepts man's authority, and is willing to subordinate itself to its master.

A dog has very finely developed senses, so it can serve, for example, as a guard dog and a search and rescue dog; it can follow a scent, detect hidden objects, and find a casualty buried under an avalanche or the rubble of an earthquake. These abilities, together with its relatedness to humans, make it suitable to be trained as a seeing eye dog. Symbolically, this last role is most significant, for it shows that when a human being cannot find their way in the outer world of consciousness, they can rely on instinct to lead them.

In mythology, dogs are often represented as guides to the underworld, or as its guardians. A dog can, therefore, symbolize a capacity to connect with the unconscious part of the psyche, but also to guard against the danger of entering it without justification or preparation. We might see the latter in cases of one-sided ego development or in inflation which often results in a naiveté about the dangers of the unconscious. The same holds true for the casual use of many intoxicants.

Buying something from the shadow would mean giving it the necessary energy to become part of consciousness. This first acquisition will certainly get the hero off to a good start and serve him throughout his journey, provided he earns the animal's trust and takes good care of it. This condition appears to be satisfied, for as we read, upon bringing the dog home the hero gives him food and drink.

Immediately thereafter, the hero asks his mother for another hundred rubles. The situation is repeated; the hero once again takes to the road, seemingly with no apparent purpose. This time the peasant he meets is leading a cat with a golden tail.

It is worth noting that both the dog and the cat in this story are male; they should, consequently, be seen as aspects of the hero's instinctual shadow. We may explain this circumstance by the early death of his father. Growing up to be a man, the hero had no father as a model for adult masculine behavior. Although his father left him his blessing and 300 rubles, the hero never had a close experience of a man and woman interacting with one another on a daily basis.

The two male animals that cross the hero's path may therefore be seen as a necessary compensation to this psychic deficiency. We can better appreciate the importance of this small detail when we consider that, were it not for the animals, the hero would never have succeeded in reclaiming the enchanted ring from his wife, ultimately leading to a positive lysis. It also confirms Jung's assertion that work on the shadow, here the dog and cat, is a prerequisite to work on the anima.

Viewed concretely, the cat's importance for our hero lies in its extraordinary sense of hearing and its ability to see well in the dark. By nature, the cat is less domesticated than the dog and more independent. This implies that it is truer to its own instinct and to what is happening in the unconscious. Barbara Hannah writes of the cat that it possesses an instinct that "...can enter anywhere ... human barriers do not exist for it, it can get to places where we cannot possibly find a way."[95] This suggests the kind of knowledge which Jung refers to as *absolute knowledge* and

---

95   Hannah, *Cat, Dog and Horse Lectures*, 80.

which is not mediated by the sense organs.[96] We have experienced cats knowing that another animal or human is dying, perceiving a presence not registered by the human senses, or anticipating their owner's departure even though the suitcases are carefully hidden behind a closed door.

And what should we make of a cat with a golden tail? Biologically, the cat's tail is vital for its balance. It is an extension of the spinal cord and functions as a counterweight; when a cat looks right, its tail moves in the opposite direction. This increases its maneuverability while in pursuit of prey.

Another function of a cat's tail is to express its feelings. This is important in a cat's social behavior, not only with other cats but also with humans. Because a cat is a very egoistic by nature, it is important to register its emotions and to respond properly to them if one wants to avoid being bitten or scratched. Symbolically, it reminds us to take instinct seriously and not to blindly override it, without at least becoming conscious of what it is telling us.

The fact that the cat's tail is golden brings special attention to these two properties; it attributes the highest value to both equilibrium and instinct in the attainment of one's goal. Psychologically, equilibrium in this context would imply doing justice to both the outer and inner reality; instinct would provide the connection to the archaic roots of all humanity.

As mentioned earlier, there doesn't appear to be any rational purpose in these acquisitions; there is no indication that the hero is following some conscious plan in buying the flappy-eared dog and the cat with the golden tail. This supports seeing the hero as a part of the psyche that is in tune with the unconscious, a part which does things that don't necessarily make sense rationally. It is only the lysis that subsequently justifies the hero's action.

Shortly thereafter, the hero asks his mother for the last hundred rubles. It is at this point that the mother begins to question his *aimless* expenditures, but he bids her not to worry about the money and consoles her by saying: "...somehow, it will come back to us." There is no doubt in him; he appears to have full confidence in what he is doing.

---

96   Jung, *Structure and Dynamics*, CW 8, § 948.

And now, for a third time, the peasant's son takes to the road. Once again, he has no idea what he is looking for, but then he learns that "... in a certain land, in a certain city, a tsarevna died, and on her finger was a golden ring..." The symbolism of the number three gives a sense of urgency to this situation; it also emphasizes the fateful nature of what has now been constellated.

This sudden interest in a tsarevna reveals a new development in the hero's psyche. His earlier purchase of the dog and cat was seen as strengthening his instinctual masculinity. Now his interest turns toward a feminine being and, more specifically, toward the golden ring on her finger.

A ring is something that connects; it is an outward sign of relatedness, of belonging, of committing to another person, idea, or institution. Because of its round shape, it also symbolizes wholeness and, as such, represents a union forged by the Self; moreover, the ring is golden, yet again emphasizing its high value. The fact that a marriage ring is sometimes experienced as a fetter only confirms the ambivalent nature of the archetype.

What can it possibly mean that our hero wants the ring so badly that he is willing to steal it by bribing the guards with the last of his father's hundred rubles? When buying his animals from the peasant, he was acting within the law; here he is ready to commit a crime. Perhaps it is the dog and cat instinct which the hero has now appropriated that enable him to relativize or see beyond the collective values of his day.

We return, once more, to the hero's special position within the psyche, for it is that part of the ego which acts in accordance with the unconscious, or better said, the Self. This becomes evident when there is a discrepancy between the two parts of the psyche, and when the hero is called upon to reestablish the necessary equilibrium. We recall that balancing is one of the chief functions of the cat's tail, and we have already noted that both the tail and the ring are golden.

But why did the tsarevna die? What explanation can we find for her departing from the conscious realm? As an anima figure, she would stand for feminine values, for the Eros which is, all too often, missing from patriarchal society. Might it be that she could not survive in the existing collective situation? Such an interpretation supports the hero's lawless action for, by acquiring the ring, he has made a connection to a part of the feminine which was about to sink into the unconscious. Furthermore, the fact that the hero is not intercepted after stealing the ring would suggest that the unconscious is sanctioning this theft.

As we see from what follows, the main attribute of this ring lies in the fulfillment of the wearer's wishes, regardless of how exorbitant they may be. However, when we first hear of the hero's intention to steal the ring, we are given no reason to think that he is aware of this. We learn that after his return, he lived at home for a while and that it is only after "...a long time or a short time...," that the hero "...went out on the porch and moved the ring from one hand to the other." This resulted in 300 brave youths and 170 strong men jumping out of the ring and offering their services. If we are correct in assuming that the hero was initially ignorant of what his ring was capable of, his moving the ring from one hand to another may be seen as some sort of thoughtless, automatic action with no conscious intent. But it is precisely such action that triggers the unconscious, for the simple reason that the ego is switched off and the unconscious impulse can get through.

This small detail suggests that in order to activate the power of the ring, the hero must move it from one hand to another. The term used in the original Russian is *perebrosit'*, to throw or flip from hand to hand. It has a touch of *to juggle* to it, like in flipping a coin. The hero does this every time he makes a wish, and when his wife gets hold of the ring, she does the same thing. This would suggest that moving the ring from hand to hand is part of the magic ritual.

To do something with the hands, to handle, means to manage, manipulate, direct, and control. *Hand* in Russian is *ruka*; the word *rukovodit'* means literally to direct or guide with the hand, and figuratively to lead, to manage; *rukovodstvo* means instructions. The meanings of this word all symbolize some sort of ego participation. The requirement that the ring be moved from hand to hand must, therefore, mean that both hands must be used, that is, both the right (rational, collective) as well as the left (irrational, feeling). Whether we consider this from a physiological or psychological viewpoint, we need to take it as a condition for making a wish; moreover, we must accept the fact that the result cannot be preempted. This can be compared to consulting the

I Ching, where one needs to consider the question from all sides and then be ready to accept the oracle, whatever the result.

The amplification above discloses the significance of the ring in this tale. It gives the hero great power, but makes this power contingent upon the inclusion of both parts of the psyche. This is the way of the individuation process, which has wholeness as its goal. The ownership of the ring by a tsarevna supports the psychological fact that it is through a woman that a man is introduced to the world of the unconscious. Moreover, she is not just any woman but one of royal status, which speaks for the divine nature of the anima. Summarizing, we can say that the ring, and the way it is meant to connect the two parts of the psyche, is the central symbol of this tale. It should, therefore, not surprise us to find it in the title.

The theft of the ring marks a turning point in this tale. The hero has acquired the ring of a feminine being who, being dead, belongs to the unconscious part of the psyche, to the archetypal world of the anima. He will henceforth be connected with her in all he does. We cannot overlook the fact, however, that no personal relationship has been established between the tsarevna and the hero, nor is there any indication that he is ready to follow her into the unconscious realm. The only thing we know for sure is that from now on the Eros principle will play an important role in his psyche. Let us now follow the hero and see whether this holds true.

The hero's first wish is to replace their old hut with a stone house. He is surely paying his mother back for all the selfless love she gave him; he is likewise satisfying his obligation to provide for her remaining days. There is, however, another explanation which is quite different from the first two and which is especially significant from a psychological perspective. This speaks of the necessity for a son to sever the close ties of childhood in order to become an adult member of his community. In Genesis 24 we read: "Therefore a man leaves his father and his mother and cleaves to his wife, and they become one flesh." To this day, this is echoed in most marriage rituals, as the bride is ritually handed over to the bridegroom by the father.

How are we to understand this symbolic action? For a man, it marks the transition from the mother to the anima. As long as his primary relationship with the feminine is experienced through the mother, he remains a child; this holds true even if he is married and has a family. The mother provides a man's first experience of the feminine, yet she alone does not determine the development of this aspect of his personality, for the collective attitude also plays a role. Depending upon how much the mother herself is influenced by collective values, these may be more or less the same. A third factor in his experience of the feminine is the way in which the archetype itself constellates in his psyche. This is not necessarily the same as in the two foregoing inputs, but it greatly influences his choice of a partner and affects the nature of all his relationships.

The 300 rubles he received from his father started the hero on his way; he returned home after each acquisition and received the next installment from his mother. The ring he acquired with the last hundred rubles opened a very different account in his psychic bank, for it not only gave him access to unlimited power but, as we will presently see, it also enabled him to redirect his allegiance from his mother to a woman outside the family.

This inner transition is now mirrored in the outer story. For a while the hero continued to live with his mother, but upon reaching manhood he began to think about taking a wife. This is a normal biological development and we can imagine that, with the ring at his disposal, his wish would not be difficult to fulfill.

But here the unconscious reenters the scene with another of its ambiguous scenarios: "In such and such a land, in such and such a kingdom, a certain tsar had a daughter...." Of course, this is the woman our hero now decides to marry, and for this he needs his mother to mediate for him. Having someone woo for him would have been the accepted way in the traditions of that time, although the task would probably not have fallen to the mother. Her reluctance to give him away may be attributed at least in part, if not wholly, to a mother's difficulty in cutting the close ties with her son. However, from what was said above, this is precisely what is called for in this stage of development. As he had built a stone house for his mother, so must she now make the contact that will forever change their relationship.

That this is a necessary step is supported by the fact that the son does not allow his mother to go to the tsar's court empty-handed. He appears to realize how risky and dangerous her mission is and he does his part in influencing its outcome. With the help of his ring he provides her with gifts worthy of a tsar. This greatly astonishes the tsar, and his first reaction is to ask where she got them from. He is thinking concretely, and it is indeed difficult to imagine how a peasant woman could honestly have come by such extravagant gifts.

The mother is spared the need of answering the tsar by the arrival of the tsarevna who, upon seeing the precious objects, loses no time in taking advantage of the situation and setting her conditions for marriage. She bids the woman tell her son to build a new palace on her father's sacred meadow, a palace more splendid than her father's. Moreover, she demands a crystal bridge, covered with richly embroidered rugs, to connect the two palaces. All this must be completed in one night. If he complies with her demands, she agrees to marry him; if not, he will have to lay his head on the block.

This first appearance of the tsarevna provides valuable insight into her personality. Although it is the tsar whom the hero's mother addresses, the tsarevna breaks protocol by immediately taking things into her own hands. Without even asking her father's permission to marry this peasant, she presents the old woman with insurmountable conditions and threats of death should they not be met. There is a total lack of relatedness in her, a response which could bespeak a power animus. In the tale of "Mar'ya Morevna," which ends this collection of tales, we will find an example of such a woman; she is under the power of an evil demon.

There is another aspect of the tsarevna's personality that warrants looking into. By demanding the impossible of the hero, she is eliminating him as a husband. This is a familiar motif in fairy tales, one which discloses a girl's reluctance to leave the father. In our tale this is illustrated by her demand that the two palaces be connected with a crystal bridge. There seems to be something immature about her insistence on the one hand that the new palace be bigger than her father's, but on the other that they be connected. Such an attitude is typical for an early developmental stage; if it persists, however, it may result in her remaining forever in the role of a daughter, of relying on her father's values and patterning herself on his view of the world. Most importantly, it results in a daughter's inability to face the responsibilities of being an adult woman. In fairy tale interpretation, this motif is known as psychological incest because it precludes the possibility of the woman uniting with a man outside the family and being fruitful with him. In a literal sense this would imply sterility, childlessness; in a figurative sense, it would stand in the way of a woman uniting with her inner masculine and becoming creative in her own right. The Grimm tale of "King Thrushbeard" is one such example. We recall, however, that our hero also had to separate himself from his mother before uniting with another woman.

But how might we understand the hero's attraction to this immature, strong-headed, and hard-hearted tsarevna? Why the fascination and readiness to stake his life on having her as his wife? Here again, we are given no reason for the hero's motivation; upon hearing of her, he instinctively decides that this is what he wants to do. The nature of the ring, however, and the ritualistic act of moving it from hand to hand may throw some light on this otherwise inexplicable decision, for it prescribes that both parts of the psyche need to be taken into account in any such undertaking (p. 138).

We recall that our hero spent the first two hundred rubles on a dog and a cat. This outlay of energy, as well as the responsibility he took by bringing these two male animals home and nourishing them, strengthened his masculine instinct. He used the last hundred rubles for stealing the ring from the dead tsarevna's hand. Viewed psychologically, in so doing the hero acquired an impersonal or symbolic relationship with the anima. As he now approaches the age of manhood, these acquisitions enable him to unite with a tsarevna who belongs to the outer world. He will then be uniting his symbolic experience of the feminine with a physical one.

We return now to the tsar's court where the tsarevna has just presented the hero's mother with her demands for marrying the son. As can be imagined, the mother is terrified by these conditions. Later, when she shares her feelings with her son, he consoles her with much the same words he had spoken before: "Dear mother, you who gave birth to me! Pray to the Savior, drink kvass, and go to bed. The morning is wiser than the evening." Psychologically, this saying makes tremendous sense, for in sleep we reenter the unconscious, bringing this part of the psyche closer to consciousness and enabling it to influence our response to whatever comes our way in the morning. This is the same expectation we have of dreams when we speak of compensation, for it is such unconscious input which corrects one-sidedness and restores psychic equilibrium. As we have seen above, this is in keeping with the central message of the ring.

The positive constellation of both mother and father, as well as the possession of a ring that grants the fulfillment of his every wish, has thus far spared our hero all unpleasantness in life. And so, full of confidence, he once again calls upon his mighty helpers and bids them to satisfy the tsarevna's wishes. All this comes to pass. Upon awaking, the tsar is dismayed at seeing a splendid palace on his sacred meadow and, moreover, at finding it connected to his own by a crystal bridge. He invites the peasant to seek his daughter's hand in marriage, assuring him in advance that she has agreed to the union. The marriage is celebrated, and the young couple live together "for a long time or a short time," a phrase we are by now familiar with.

As in Grimm's tale of "The Fisherman and His Wife" the tsarevna's curiosity finally gets the better of her. She wants to know how her husband managed to build the palace and crystal bridge all in one night. She tries to extort this information from him by cunning and flattery, and argues that from now on they should *think* together. She then obliterates all possibility of *thinking* by making him dead drunk, pries the secret out of him and steals the ring from his finger.

This scene confirms what was said of this tsarevna earlier—she is power-hungry and manipulative in relationships. These characteristics become even more significant when viewed from an inner perspective, for then this would refer to an unscrupulous aspect of the hero's anima. Whereas Eros is the chief characteristic of the feminine, this anima figure appears to be possessed by its opposite—by power. "Where love reigns," writes Jung, "there is no will to power, and where the will to power is paramount, love is lacking. The one is but the shadow of the other."[97] Till now, it appears that the hero had not really seen through to the negative side of this tsarevna; subjectively, this would imply that he was not conscious of such an unrelated power complex in himself. This lack of insight explains his fascination for the tsarevna and the resulting projection. Such an anima might very well have been responsible for seducing him by the prospect of a rapid rise in social status and the possibility of one day becoming tsar.

Our hero now finds himself in a difficult predicament, for he is confronted with a negative feminine of which he had previously been oblivious. From the point of view of individuation, however, this is a positive development because it broadens his view of life and corrects his one-sidedness. We also note that the tsarevna doesn't kill him, although she could very easily have done so. Is she, perhaps, challenging him to find a solution to this dilemma? If so, it would have to be without the ring, that is, without the *magic* intervention of the unconscious.

Another point to consider is the role of alcohol in this scenario. Alcohol is a spirit, but it also symbolizes spirit. The perfidious tsarevna lames her husband in both mind and body with the wrong kind of spirit, and this causes him to lose consciousness. This shows that consciousness is the sole condition for retaining the power of the ring; a condition which is, moreover, contingent on the understanding that such power is granted by the Self and that it should not be misused for ego purposes.

The ring and its power are now in the hands of the hero's wife and, viewed subjectively, of his anima. At first she bids the 300 brave youths and 170 strong men throw her drunken husband onto the tsar's meadow, then she orders them to bring her and the whole palace to a faraway kingdom. As in all previous cases, this order is carried out overnight, at a time when the unconscious is constellated in the psyche. The tsar awakens to find his meadow empty with only the body of a man sprawled out on the earth. At first he doesn't even recognize his son-in-law. When the latter is brought to him and questioned about the tsarevna, the hero answers: "Your Royal Highness! I do not know; I lost her as if in a dream."

---

97   Jung, *Two Essays*, CW vol 7, § 78.

In contrast to the hero's seemingly fanciful response, the tsar replies in a rather cold and unfeeling way, giving the hero three months to find the tsarevna and promising death if this is not done. Then he locks him up in a strong prison. This is, indeed, a most sobering end to the hero's short-lived marriage with the tsarevna.

The similarity between the tsar's harsh words and the way in which the tsarevna sets her conditions for marriage suggests that the relationship between father and daughter is reciprocal, and that the crystal bridge which was built to connect the two palaces meets with the approval of both.

This mutuality also sheds light on the source of the tsarevna's power complex. There is a parallel between the way the tsar shuts the hero up in a prison, from which he cannot even attempt to comply with the tsar's demands, and the tsarevna's unrealistic demands for a palace and crystal bridge. In both cases this is accompanied by the threat of death should their wishes not be fulfilled; psychologically, this would result in the extinguishing of the ego.

Let us turn for a moment to the symbol of the tsar. He is usually defined as the *dominant of collective consciousness*. In *Mysterium Coniunctionis*, Jung elaborates on this definition by calling it "...a generally accepted principle or a collective conviction or a traditional view...," capable of aging and requiring renewal. Jung adds, moreover, that such renewal usually germinates in the psyche of an individual and may spread to the collective if conditions are favorable.[98] From Jung's extensive amplification of this symbol, it is clear that the principles and ideas he refers to are of a religious nature. Whatever else may have deteriorated or aged in this collective, certainly Eros would be the most critically affected.

We note, for instance, that there is no mention of a tsaritsa (queen), and see that the absence of the ruling feminine principle has impacted both the tsar as well as the tsarevna; here Eros has been replaced by power. The hero, however, has displayed Eros in many ways throughout the tale. He builds a stone house for his mother to ease her last days, and he always speaks kindly to her, even when admonishing her about her fears and inability to accept his decisions. He also attends to his

---

98   Jung, *Mysterium Coniunctionis*, CW 14, § 424.

animals by giving them a home and feeding them properly. This is an example of the kind of individual Jung refers to above; he is the one who is now standing up to the whole collective. Such an impulse is often repressed by force because it is in opposition to the status quo. Had the tale ended with the tsarevna running off with the ring and the hero being incarcerated in the tsar's prison, we would have had to acknowledge that power had won over Eros.

Summarizing, we can say that because of a very physical experience of spirit (vodka) the hero has now lost everything he had previously acquired: his wife, his castle, his crystal bridge, all the wealth and prestige of his new position and, last but not least, his magic ring. For the very first time, the hero finds himself totally helpless.

The impasse at which the hero now finds himself triggers a new and unexpected development—it ushers in the cat and the dog. As we have already noted, like all animals they symbolize the instinctual side of the hero's psyche and the roots common to all human beings; when we have distanced ourselves from these roots, animals reconnect us to universal basic human responses. Here we can appreciate the true significance of the hero being a common man. The animals which the hero bought for the first two hundred rubles at the start of the tale, and whose uneventful appearance at the time was, viewed rationally, rather questionable, now come to his assistance. The way they do this is described in the usual imagery of Russian tales: "...they ran beyond thrice nine lands, beyond the tenth kingdom," a poetic expression of the journey into an unknown world.

We note that it is the cat that now takes over and makes the decisions. This should not surprise us because the cat is the less domesticated of the two animals and, consequently, more familiar with the world of the unconscious. It immediately sends the dog to work in the king's kitchen, and positions itself in the pantry to serve the housekeeper.

This is the realm of the unconscious. From the perspective of consciousness it is the *other world* and, as mentioned in the text (p. 127), its ruler is not a tsar but a king. It is impressive that the fairy tale, which of course was not written by a Jungian, should insist on this small nuance.

Word gets around about these helpful animals and attracts the attention of the king and tsarevna. The king has the dog brought into his bedroom, while the tsarevna takes the cat with the golden tail into hers. The animals stay in the respective bedrooms day and night, take their bearings, and wait to see what comes their way. This is very much the way a cat sits in front of a mouse hole. The cat now learns that the tsarevna always puts the ring in her mouth before going to sleep. This information does not help the cat to get to the ring, so he continues to wait. And then one night a mouse runs across the tsarevna' chamber and the cat snatches it. This is, of course, an instinctive reaction on the part of the cat, and at first we think nothing of it. As it turns out, however, this mouse has knowledge of what is going on in the tsarevna's room, and offers to get the ring in exchange for its life.

This scene provides us with a glimpse into the life of these animals and, psychologically, into the functioning of our instincts. It is not based on moral judgment but on survival; furthermore, it reveals a transmission of information within the unconscious such as we seldom experience in consciousness. This enables the cat and mouse to solve their problems to their mutual advantage; the cat gets the ring and the mouse remains alive, and all of this, notably, without the involvement of the ego. Even more impressive is the fact that the cat and dog would not have been able to retrieve the ring by their own efforts, that is, without the help of the mouse. This leads us to speculate that there had to be something in the unconscious which released the ring, and subsequently returned the tsarevna with her castle and crystal bridge to the conscious world.

A few properties of the mouse may be of interest in this context. One of the important reasons for its widespread use in scientific research is because it shares 95 percent of its genes with humans. Its rapid spread throughout the world is due to its fertility and to its extraordinary adaptability to its environment; in the latter case it is second only to the rat. Moreover, some interesting research from 2012 showed that certain mice are capable of regenerating bites in their ears; this is the same potential for regeneration that exists among salamanders and zebrafish.[99]

Viewed symbolically, the mouse, which played a key role in retrieving the ring, ultimately making it available to the hero, can be interpret-

---

99   Gawriluk, et al., Nature Communications.

ed as a highly adaptive and creative part of the psyche which is capable of regeneration.

Our cat and dog waste no time in pondering such issues; they run at full speed and bring the ring to their master. He is, understandably, overjoyed at this turn of events and, moving the ring from one hand to the other, he now makes a rather extraordinary and unexpected wish: "To ease my grief," he says, "let beautiful music resound for a whole day and night." We might have expected him to wish himself out of the prison, to seek revenge on the wife who shamed and abandoned him, or to punish the tsar for shutting him up in the prison. Why does he now ask for music, and why does he speak of easing his grief when he is once more in possession of the ring with its unlimited power?

As we saw above, the journey to the other world was only experienced by the instinctive part of the hero's psyche—by the cat and the dog—so the hero's ego was only subliminally aware of this process. And yet, because he had been able to establish a relationship with his animals, something had changed in the whole of his psyche. The wish to hear beautiful music for a whole day is not necessarily something we might expect from a peasant. What he now asks for is born of suffering and misery; he longs to be healed and to be shown the way.

In the words of Emma Jung: "...music gives sensuous representation to our deepest associations and most immutable laws. In this sense, music is spirit, spirit leading into obscure distances beyond the reach of consciousness ... music admits us to the depths where spirit and nature are still one—or have again become one."[100] Emma Jung speaks of music as a form of spirit which enables man to fathom the depths of his soul, and yet music is also very much connected with emotion. Physically, music is generated by movement and travels as sound waves; it is not static. Moreover, it not only moves but it also moves *us* when we listen to it or produce it; it produces "e-motion" in us.

We know that archaic man experiences the myths of his people by dancing them, that he cannot go to war and fight the enemy without being brought into a fighting frenzy through war dances. These exam-

---

100   Emma Jung, *Animus und Anima*, 36.

ples confirm that music encompasses both spirit and matter, in this case, the human body.

Any musical instrument is made of matter. It is shaped, fashioned with great care and skill. It must be capable of producing the right tone, of resonating. Regardless of one's skill, one cannot play on just any piece of wood or use any kind of string; the leather on a drum must be taut. In like fashion, every singer must know how to make a properly functioning instrument of their own body. And surely anyone who has sung or played an instrument will experience the emotion which is liberated in the process.

By learning to differentiate and express one's feelings through music, one is better able to give them a form. Emma Jung writes that music objectifies the spirit: "...music can be understood as an objectification of the spirit"[101] and anchors it in matter. Not only does this contribute to the enrichment of others, but it provides a certain protection against the uncontrollable power of the unconscious when released.[102] Grimm's "The Spirit in the Bottle" shows just how dangerous such a spirit can be.

Orpheus is an example of this archetypal constellation; his extraordinary musical skills affected all of nature. When his beloved Eurydice died of a snake bite, he sought to find her and bring her back from the Underworld. "Putting his trust in his lyre, he entered upon the gloomy road to the realm of the dead."[103] This statement underscores the important role of music in Orpheus's undertaking. We read that he charmed and bewitched all who heard his lyre; music allowed him passage into the depths. It even persuaded Persephone, the queen of the Underworld, to release Eurydice against the laws of her own kingdom. As Orpheus led Eurydice out of this world, he turned briefly to look at his wife, and by so doing he erred against another rule of the Underworld which forbade the living to look at the dead. And here we read that "...no looking, only the voice, was allowed in the realm of the departed."[104] This one glance broke the spell of his music and destroyed his chance of retrieving Eurydice from the dead forever. This passage

---

101   Emma Jung, *Animus und Anima*, 36.
102   von Beit, *Symbolik des Märchens*, 516 f.
103   Kerényi, *Heroes of the Greeks*, 282.
104   Kerényi, *Heroes of the Greeks*, 283.

indirectly discloses the amazing power of music for, as Kerényi writes, it is only the voice which is allowed entrance into this realm.

The account of Orpheus's descent into the Underworld reminds us of the tremendous power of the unconscious and juxtaposes it with the relative helplessness of the ego; it warns against the hubris of self-confidence to which the ego too often succumbs by losing sight of this fact. At the same time, it shows the readiness of the unconscious to grant the ego's wishes if they are in keeping with nature.

This is expressed most vividly by Hans Walter Sager. Speaking of the unconscious, he writes: "I find myself confronted by a being before which I must be permanently on my guard, lest it seduce, trick or even tear me apart; one which, on the other hand, I must completely trust and toward which my sole salvation lies in humble obedience and in the acknowledgement of its superior might."[105] In light of these considerations, we can better appreciate the seemingly trivial episode with the mouse. As mentioned above, this proved to be the key to the hero's deliverance and further development. The ring was not taken by force. It was the unconscious itself which set the stage and provided the possibility for the cat to snatch it. This allows us to assume that the return of the ring to consciousness had the support of the unconscious part of the psyche.

Through his marriage with the tsarevna, the tsar's only child, the hero would in all probability one day become the new tsar, the new dominant of collective consciousness. Together with his tsaritsa, he would be in a position to reshape the values of his kingdom. Moreover, being the hero, his actions would by definition be in accord with the Self. This is why the tsar was always considered mediator between his people and God, and why he is one of the symbols of the Self.

In the case of Orpheus, we saw how music provided the means of accessing this other world. In our tale, after the cat has dropped the ring into his master's hand, the hero's first wish is for a musical experience. This differs substantially from all his previous wishes. We sense a longing for something intangible, for contact with some other part of his psyche.

---

105   Sager, *Die Überwindung der Mutter*, 85. The quotation above is my translation.

Tales often show the hero going into the other world in pursuit of his wife, but here it appears that the ego is still unable to do this; it is the instinctual part of the psyche, symbolized by the cat and the dog, which does this for him. The ego itself is still unable to accept the reality of the psyche, and yet something has changed as a result of the animals' journey into this other world. By speaking of his grief he is expressing his emotions, and by asking for music he is rechanneling his wishes into a new direction.

As suggested by the amplification above, music is capable of connecting the hero with the archetypal layers of the psyche. In a letter to Serge Moreau, Jung writes that music "...represents the motion, the development and the transformation in the collective unconscious."[106] We are all too well aware of the constant changes in waking reality, but less so of the changes that take place in the unconscious part of our psyche. According to Jung, it is through music that we can access these layers and give them a voice in the conscious world.

To summarize, we learn that "in his grief," in his frustration over what has befallen him, our hero expresses a need to fathom the deeper layers of the unconscious, layers which cannot be understood rationally but are "...where spirit and nature are one..."[107] The contents of these layers are not static; they represent the eternally moving, developing, and transforming aspects of the unconscious. Their motion creates e-motion, which can be brought to resonate in us through music.

We return now to our tale, and find the tsar deciding to check up on the hero. He sends a messenger to see "... whether his son-in-law has thought it over." Under the circumstances, we might ask what there is to think over. Does the tsar want to put additional pressure on the hero? Is he secretly hoping that the hero will think of a way out of his insoluble problem? If so, is the tsar beginning to consider the possibility of an irrational solution? This would indeed be an important step for a ruler who reigns without a tsaritsa, and who has now lost his only other connection with the feminine. Is he finally becoming aware of his one-sidedness?

---

106   Jung, *Letters 1*, 542.
107   Emma Jung, *Animus und Anima*, 36.

We are not told whether the tsar himself is *thinking it over*; we only know that he sends a messenger to the prison. The text reports that the messenger does not return because he becomes mesmerized by the music. The Russian word *zaslushat'sya* is a special form of the verb *to listen* which implies that one cannot stop listening because what one hears is so very beautiful. What this messenger now experiences is reminiscent of the Orpheus myth.

After the first messenger fails to return, the tsar sends a second messenger, then a third and, after none of these come back, he goes himself. There he hears the music and suffers the same fate. The text says that "his mind was ... darkened by the music." This suggests bewitchment, or falling under a spell, and indeed we learn that he could not speak until after the music had stopped. In answer to the tsar's questions, the hero asks to be freed for one night and promises to return the tsarevna. To our surprise, the tsar believes him. With the ring in his possession, the hero might very well have fled or wrought revenge against the tsar, but he doesn't. Leaving the prison, the hero moves his ring from one hand to the other, 300 brave youths and 170 strong men appear and ask for his orders, and then, in the dark of night, the hero's wish is once again fulfilled. By daybreak, everything is in its place and we find the tsarevna waking up, somewhat concerned about having to face the consequences of her misdeeds. But here the tale takes another unexpected turn. Contrary to the hero's assumption that the tsarevna will now be punished, the tsar answers with empathy and wisdom: "My dear son-in-law, we will admonish her with words; then do you both live well with one another and prosper."

With these words, the tsar is relinquishing his daughter to the hero and stepping in as the father our hero never had. Power has been transformed into Eros and, through music, a stabilizing connection to the psychic roots has been established. In this atmosphere of harmony, the hero would be able to mature and develop the many skills necessary for ruling the kingdom. Moreover, through such a peaceful transition, the hero would acquire a more responsible attitude toward the potentially dangerous power of the ring in his possession. The new tsar would reign together with his tsaritsa, and the old generation would be able to transmit the experience and knowledge it has acquired to the new one. Such is the remarkable lysis to this tale.

But let us backtrack for a moment to the scene where the tsarevna first presents her conditions of marriage. There she appeared as an immature, hard-hearted, and unrelated woman. Later we saw a similarity between her character and her father's cruel punishment of the hero, both of which we ascribed to the absence of a tsaritsa. The missing Eros principle warped their relatedness and replaced it by power.

We return now to two important symbols whose interpretation will add additional depth to this tale. These are the new palace and the crystal bridge which connects it to the palace of the tsar. A palace is a royal residence; it is a collective center of the elite, and a place of culture. If we speak of a tsar's palace symbolically, then we understand this to be the place where the image of the Self is enthroned. Physically and symbolically, it provides structure and protection; it enforces rules and values for those who live within and without its walls. Being collective, however, it runs the risk of being overly influenced by conscious reality and of failing to heed the new flow of libido from the unconscious part of the psyche.

Let us consider the tsarevna's demand that the hero build a new and more splendid palace than her father's. We have interpreted this as the inability of the father to let go of his daughter, or of the daughter to take on the responsibilities of becoming an independent, adult woman. We might, however, also interpret this as the tsarevna's laying the ground for one day reigning together with the hero, and for bringing in a new world order more splendid than the existing one. For this she needs to test his worth. The tsarevna also demanded that the old and new palaces be joined together by a crystal bridge. We ascribed this to the strong bond which still existed between the tsar and his daughter. Alternatively, we could see this bridge as facilitating a transition from one rule to another and, through its extraordinary beauty, promoting a peaceful coexistence between the old and the new.

The bridge is to be built of crystal, a very fine and light substance, transparent like air and very fragile. This is not the usual material for bridges and must, therefore, be considered symbolically as a bridge for the anima in her function as personification of the Eros principle. Its ethereal nature speaks of the spirit, of that which raises one above mundane reality. The richly embroidered rugs covering the bridge introduce the creative aspect of the Great Mother, the weaver of man's fate. In addition, as already mentioned in the tale "The Feather of Finist, the Bright Falcon," embroidery was used in old Russia to depict sacred images of nature and of divine beings.[108]

The amplifications above result in a more archetypal view of the current fairy tale. The tsarevna is not merely the stubborn and power-hungry daughter of the tsar; she is unveiled as the anima who demands the respect and obedience of the hero, and who could rightly be considered a goddess. This perspective does not replace the more concrete one offered earlier; it does, however, encourage collective consciousness to accept the more archetypal dimension of the feminine in every woman.

It is fascinating to follow the role played by the hero because he is so unconscious of the development he initiates. Had he not bought the dog and the cat, he would never have been able to regain the ring. Had he listened to his mother's pleas and given up his wish to marry this hard-hearted tsarevna, he would never have become the tsar's heir. Had he not succumbed to the alcohol, he would not have learned the most important lesson of the tale, namely that consciousness is the only condition for retaining the power of the ring. Had he not experienced the loss of this power, he might never have had to realize that, even as hero, he was still a common man.

Actually, his problems begin soon after he gets married, for his wife is not satisfied with the fulfillment of her original conditions. She wants more from him; in particular, she wants him to tell her how he did it. If we see her as his anima, we can assume that she knows about the ring and that she is testing him to see whether he is truly conscious of the power at his disposal. When he disappoints her with his response, she robs him of all consciousness and leaves him to face the consequences of her father's, that is, of the tsar's, of collective, justice.

We had suggested that the first tsarevna died because she could not survive in this collective (p. 136). The tsarevna-wife does not die, nor does she kill her husband; she leaves the possibility open for the hero to follow her. This is prevented by collective consciousness (the tsar throws him into the prison). Nonetheless, the hero's connection made

---

108   Rybakov, *Yazychesto drevnich Slavyan*, 495-552.

earlier with the dog and cat enables the instinctive part of his psyche to follow his anima into the other world. With the help of the mouse, which we interpreted as a readiness on the part of the unconscious to support this development, the ring is brought back to the hero. This episode might well be seen as the night-sea-journey of the soul. It has a transformative effect on the hero, manifested by his wish to hear "… magnificent music played for a whole day."

The music subsequently also transforms the tsar and leads to a happy ending. It is interesting to see that the lysis is the same in both interpretations, the only difference being the interpretation of the second tsarevna's role in this story. Had we not looked at both, however, we would not have fulfilled the conditions of moving the ring from hand to hand and would not have understood the tale in its wholeness.

V. Two Ivans, Soldier's Sons

In a certain kingdom in a certain land there lived a peasant. The time came for him to be recruited into the army. Bidding farewell to his pregnant wife, he said, "Mind you, wife, live decently, do not become the laughingstock of respectable people, do not ruin our house, but manage it wisely and await my return. God willing, I may be retired and return home. Here are fifty rubles for you; whether you give birth to a daughter or a son, keep the money till the child is of age. Thus you will have a dowry for a daughter, and if God grants us a son, this money will be of no little help to him when he grows up." He took leave of his wife and marched off with his regiment. Three months later, his wife bore twin boys and named them both "Ivan, son of a soldier."

The boys began to grow; like leavened wheat dough they grew taller and taller. When they were ten years old, their mother sent them off to school. Soon they learned to read and write, and were more than a match for the boyar (old Russian nobility) and merchant sons; no one could read or write or answer questions better than they. The boyar and merchant sons started to envy the twins; every day they beat and pinched them. One of the brothers said to the other, "How long will they beat and pinch us? Our mother will never be able to make us enough clothes or buy us enough caps; whatever we put on, our comrades tear to shreds. Let's deal with them in our own way." So they agreed to stand by each other. Next day, as the boyar and merchant sons began to provoke them, instead of bearing this patiently, they fought back; they smashed the eye of one, tore the hand off another, and knocked the head of a third to the side! They beat them all up. The good lads were immediately surrounded by guards, tied up and thrown into jail. The tsar learned of this incident; he summoned the boys, questioned them about everything, and ordered them to be released, saying, "They are not guilty; God always punishes the attackers."

When the two Ivans grew up, they asked their mother, "Mother, did out father leave us any money? If so, let us have it; we will go to the town fair and buy ourselves each a good horse." Their mother gave them fifty rubles, twenty-five to each, and said, "Listen to me, children! As you travel to town, bow to anyone whom you encounter." "Very well, dear mother," said the two Ivans. The brothers went to town, came to the horse market, looked about and saw many horses, but none to suit them. Then one brother said to the other, "Let us go to the other end of the square to see what great crowds are gathered there." They made their way through the crowd and saw two colts fastened with chains to oaken posts—one with six chains, the other with twelve. The horses tugged at their chains, gnawed their bits, and pawed the ground with their hoofs. No one could go near them.

"What do you ask for your colts?" asked Ivan, soldier's son of the owner. "Don't stick your nose into this, brother. These wares are not for the likes of you; there's no point in asking." "How can you judge without knowing? Perhaps we'll buy them, but first we need to have a look at their teeth." The owner smiled. "Go ahead and look if you don't fear for your head!" Straightaway, one of the brothers went to the colt that was tied with six chains, and the other to the one with twelve chains. They tried to look at their teeth, but no way! The colts reared up on their hind legs and snorted. The brothers struck them in the breast with their knees, the chains burst, and the colts were hurled ten yards away, hitting the ground with their legs up. "And this is what you were boasting about! We wouldn't take these jades if you were giving them away." The crowd gasped with amazement at their strength. The owner was almost in tears; his colts had galloped out of the town and begun to wander about in the open field. No one dared to come close to them, and no one knew how to catch them. The two Ivans took pity on the owner; they went out into the open field, shouting loudly and whistling piercingly. The colts came running and stood before them as though rooted to the ground. Then the good youths put the iron chains on them, led them to the oaken posts, and tethered them tightly. When they had done this they went home.

As they walked along the road, they saw a gray old man coming toward them. Forgetting what their mother had told them, they passed by without greeting him. Only later did one of them realize this, "Oh, brother, what have we done? We did not bow to that old man; let us catch up with him and bow." They caught up with the old man, took off their caps, bowed to the waist, and said, "Forgive us, grandfather, for passing you without a greeting. Our mother enjoined us strictly to bow to everyone we meet on our way." "Thank you, good lads! Where has God taken you?" "We went to the fair and wanted to buy us each a good horse, but we could not find any that suited us." "What shall we do? Shall I give you each a little horse?" "Oh, grandfather, if you do, we shall always pray to God for you." "Well, let's go." The old man led them to a big mountain, opened a cast-iron door, and brought out two mighty steeds. "Take these steeds, my good youths. God be with you; may they serve you well." They thanked him, mounted the steeds, and galloped home. They rode into their yard, tied the steeds to a post, and walked into their house. "Well, my children," their mother said, "have you bought yourselves horses?" "We did not buy them, we received them for free." "What have you done with them?" "They are by the side of the house." "Be careful, my children, someone may take them away." "No, mother, not these horses. No one could even come near them, let alone take them away." The mother went out, looked at the mighty steeds, and burst into tears. "Oh, my dear sons," she said, "surely you will not support me in my old age."

Next day the sons asked their mother's leave to go to town and buy themselves swords. "Go, my dear ones," she said. They made ready and went to the smithy. "Make us each a sword," they said to the master. "Why make them when I have ready ones? Take as many as you need." "No, brother, we need swords that weigh a thousand pounds each." "What kind of nonsense is that? Who could wield such a thing? Besides, in the whole world you couldn't find a furnace big enough to forge them." The good youths hung their heads and went home. As they walked along the road, they met the same old man. "Good day, young lads," he said. "Good day, grandfather!" "Where have you been to?" "We went to the town smithy to buy ourselves swords, but there were no suitable ones." "That's unfortunate! Shall I give you each a sword?" "Oh, grandfather, if you do, you will be eternally in our prayers." The old man led them to the big mountain, opened the cast-iron door, and brought out two mighty swords. They took the swords and thanked the old man, and their hearts were full of joy. When the two Ivans came home, their mother asked: "Well, my children have you bought yourselves swords?" "We did not buy them, we received them for free." "What have you done with them?" "We left them standing by the wall." "Be careful, lest someone take them away." "No, mother, no one could carry them; no one could even cart them away." The mother went out to the yard and saw two heavy swords leaning against the wall; the little hut was barely standing. She burst into tears and said: "Ah, my sons, "surely you will not support me in my old age."

In the morning the two Ivans, soldier's sons, saddled their good steeds, took their mighty swords, came into the house, prayed to God, said farewell to their mother and asked for her blessing. "Bless us, dear mother, for the long journey ahead." "May my never ceasing parental blessing be upon you, my children. Go with God, show yourselves, and see people; offend no one without cause, and yield not to evil enemies." "Fear not, mother! We have a motto: 'When I ride, I don't whistle, when I fight, I don't yield.'" And the good youths mounted their steeds and rode off.

After they had gone a short distance or a long distance, after they had traveled a long time or a short time—for quickly is a tale told, but less quickly is a deed done—they came to a crossroads with two posts. On one post they read: "He who goes to the right will become king"; on the other: "He who goes to the left will be slain." The brothers stopped and wondered where each should go. If both took the road to the right, it would not do honor to their mighty strength, their youthful valor. If one went to the left—but who wants to die? There was no way out, and so one brother said to the other, "Well, dear brother, I am stronger than you, so let me take the road to the left and see what it is that can cause my death. But you should go to the right; God be willing, you'll become tsar." They said farewell to each other, exchanged handkerchiefs, and solemnly agreed that each would go his way, put up posts along the road, and leave messages on these posts to mark their way. They promised to wipe their faces with the other's handkerchief each morning; if blood appeared on the handkerchief, they would know that the brother had died. In such an event they would set out in search of the dead.

The good youths parted and rode in different directions. The one who turned his steed to the right came to a glorious kingdom. In that kingdom there lived a tsar with his tsaritsa who had a daughter, Nastas'ya the Beautiful. When the tsar saw Ivan, the soldier's son, he loved him for his heroic valor and, without thinking very long about it, gave him his daughter in marriage. The tsar called him Ivan Tsarevich, and charged him with the rule of the whole kingdom. Ivan Tsarevich lived happily, feasted his eyes upon his wife, gave law and order to the kingdom and amused himself by hunting animals.

One time when he made ready to go hunting and began to harness his steed, he came upon two phials sewn up in the saddle: one with healing water, and the other with the water of life. He looked at these phials and put them back into the saddle. "I shall keep them for the time being," he thought. "Who knows when they might be needed?"

Meanwhile, the brother who had taken the road to the left galloped night and day without rest. A month went by, a second, a third, and Ivan, soldier's son came to an unknown kingdom; he rode right into its capital. There was a great sorrow in this kingdom; the houses were draped with black cloth, the people staggered about as though in sleep. He rented the most humble quarters at a poor woman's house and began to question her. "Tell me, grandmother, why are all the people in your kingdom so grieved, and why are all the houses draped with black cloth?" "Ach, good youth," said the old woman, "a great misfortune has befallen us. Every day a twelve-headed dragon comes forth from the blue sea, from behind a grey stone; each time he devours a human being, and now it is the tsar's turn... He has three beautiful tsarevnas; just now the oldest has been taken to the shore to be devoured by the serpent."

Ivan, the soldier's son, mounted his steed and galloped to the blue sea, to the grey stone. On the shore stood the beautiful tsarevna, bound by an iron chain. She saw him and said, "Go hence, brave youth! Soon the twelve-headed dragon will come. I am doomed, but you too will not escape death; the ferocious serpent will devour you." "Fear not, lovely maiden, he may well choke on me." Ivan, soldier's son, came up to her, seized the chain with his mighty hand, and tore it into little bits as if it were a rotten rope. Then he laid his head on the lovely maiden's knees and said, "Now search through my hair; do not search so much as watch the sea. As soon as a cloud darkens the sky, the winds begin to roar, the sea to surge, rouse me straightaway." The lovely maiden did as he told her; she searched through his hair, but even more she watched the sea.

Suddenly a cloud darkened the sky, the wind began to roar, the sea surged; a serpent emerged from the blue sea and reared himself up. The tsarevna awakened Ivan, soldier's son. No sooner had he gotten up and mounted his steed than the serpent came a flying. "Why have you come here, Ivanushka? This is my territory. Say farewell to the bright world and hasten into my throat of your own accord; it will be easier for you if you do!" "You lie, accursed serpent!" answered the mighty hero, "You won't swallow me, you'll choke on me!" He swung his sharp sword and cut off all twelve of the serpent's heads, then he lifted the gray stone and put the heads under it. He threw the remains of the serpent into the sea and returned home to the old woman. He ate and drank his fill, lay down to sleep, and slept for three days.

At this time the tsar called his water carrier. "Go to the shore, and at least retrieve the tsarevna's bones." The water carrier rode to the blue sea and found the tsarevna alive and well. He put her into his wagon and brought her to a dark forest; he drove her into the forest and began whetting his knife. "What are you going to do?" the tsarevna asked. "I am whetting my knife to slay you." The tsarevna began to weep: "Do not slay me; I have done you no harm." "I will spare you," said the water carrier, "if you tell your father that I have rescued you from the serpent." She had no choice but to consent. They returned to the palace; the tsar was overjoyed and made the water carrier a colonel.

Upon waking up, Ivan, soldier's son called the old woman, gave her money, and said, "Go to the market, grandmother, buy what you need, and listen to what the people are saying. Find out whether there is any news." The old woman went to the market, bought various provisions, listened to the news and returned home. "This is the talk in town," she said. "Our tsar was giving a grand dinner. Princes and ministers, boyars and notables were sitting at the table when a red-hot arrow flew through the window and landed in the middle of the chamber. A letter from another twelve-headed serpent was fastened to this arrow. The serpent wrote, "If you do not send me your middle tsarevna, I will burn your kingdom with fire and scatter its ashes." Already today they will bring the poor maiden to the blue sea, to the grey stone."

Straightway, Ivan, soldier's son saddled his good steed, mounted him and galloped off to the seashore. The tsarevna said to him: "Why you, good youth? My turn may have come to die and to shed my warm blood, but why should you perish?" "Fear not, lovely maiden! Perhaps God will save us." No sooner had he said this than the accursed serpent flew at him, breathing flames and threatening him with death. The hero struck him with his sharp sword and cut off all twelve heads; then he put the heads under the stone and threw the remains into the sea. After that he returned home, ate and drank his fill, and again lay down to sleep for three days and three nights.

The water carrier went down to the shore again, saw that the tsarevna was alive, put her in his cart, drove to the dark forest, and set about whetting his knife. The tsarevna asked him why he was whetting his knife." "I am whetting my knife to slay you. Swear to speak to your father in my favor, and I will spare you." The princess swore to do so and he brought her to the palace. The tsar was overjoyed and promoted the water carrier to general.

Upon awaking on the fourth day, Ivan, soldier's son told the old woman to go to the market and listen to the news. The old woman went to the market, returned, and said, "A third serpent has appeared; he wrote a letter to the tsar demanding that he send the third tsarevna to be devoured." Ivan, soldier's son saddled his good steed, mounted him, and galloped to the blue sea. On the shore stood the beautiful tsarevna, bound to the stone with an iron chain. The hero seized the chain and tore it apart as though it were a rotten rope; then he laid his head on the lovely maiden's knees. "Search through my hair. But do not search so much as watch the sea: as soon as a cloud darkens the sky, the winds begin to roar, and the sea to surge, rouse me straightaway." The tsarevna began to search through his hair...

Suddenly a cloud darkened the sky, the wind began to roar and the sea to surge; a serpent emerged from the blue sea and reared himself up. The tsarevna began to rouse Ivan, soldier's son; she shook him and shook him, but he did not awaken. She burst into tears, and one of those burning tears fell on his cheek. This woke the hero and he ran to his steed; the good steed had already dug up half a yard of earth with his hoofs. The twelve-headed serpent flew toward them, breathing flames. He cast a glance at the hero and cried out, "You are handsome and stately, good youth, but you won't stay alive; I'll devour you down to the last bone." "You lie, accursed serpent! You'll choke on me!"

Instantly they were locked in mortal combat. Ivan, soldier's son swung his sword so fast and with such strength that it grew red hot and he could not hold it in his hand! "Save me, lovely maiden!" he pleaded. "Take off your dear kerchief, wet it in the blue sea, and give it to me to wrap around my sword." The tsarevna immediately wet her kerchief and gave it to the good youth. He wrapped it around his sword and went on battling the serpent. He cut off all twelve of its heads and put them under the stone, then he threw the remains into the sea, galloped home, ate and drank his fill, and lay down to sleep for three days.

Again the tsar sent the water carrier to the seashore. The water carrier took the tsarevna to the dark forest, drew out his knife and began to whet it. "What are you doing?" asked the tsarevna. "I am whetting my knife to slay you. Tell your father that I conquered the serpent, then I will pardon you." He terrified the lovely maiden, and she swore that she would say what he commanded. Now the youngest daughter was the tsar's favorite. When he saw her alive and unharmed, he was even more overjoyed, and to reward the water carrier he gave him this youngest tsarevna in marriage.

Rumor of this ran through the whole kingdom. When Ivan, the soldier's son learned that the tsar was making preparations for a wedding, he went straight to the palace where a feast was in full swing; the guests were eating and drinking, and diverting themselves with various games. The youngest tsarevna saw Ivan, the soldier's son; she recognized her dear kerchief on his sword, sprang out from behind the table, took him by the hand, and brought him to her father. "My dear father and sovereign, here is the one who saved us from the accursed serpent and from undeserved death. All the water carrier did was whet his knife and say: 'I am whetting my knife to slay you.'" The tsar was furious; he immediately ordered the water carrier to be hanged, and married the tsarevna to Ivan, soldier's son. There was great rejoicing, and the young couple began to live together happily and prosperously.

While all that was going on, this is what befell Ivan, soldier's son's brother. One day Ivan Tsarevich went out hunting and came upon a fleet-footed stag. Ivan Tsarevich spurred his horse and took after him; he galloped and galloped and came to a broad meadow. Here the stag vanished. The tsarevich looked around and wondered where he should go now. Then he saw a little stream flowing in the meadow, and on the water two grey ducks were swimming. He took aim with his gun, fired, and killed the pair of ducks; he pulled them out of the water, put them in his bag, and continued on his way. He rode and rode, and soon he came upon a white stone palace. Dismounting, he tied his horse to a post and went into the chambers. They were all empty without a living soul in sight, but in one room he found a stove burning, a pan standing on the hearth, and the table set with a plate, a fork, and a knife. Ivan Tsarevich took the ducks out of his bag, plucked and cleaned them, put them in the pan, and shoved the pan into the oven; he roasted them, put them on the table and began to carve and eat them.

Suddenly out of nowhere a lovely maiden appeared before him, such a fairy tale beauty as neither tongue could tell nor pen describe. "Welcome, Ivan Tsarevich, she said to him. "Welcome, lovely maiden! Won't you sit down and eat with me?" "I would sit down with you, but I am afraid of your magic steed." "No, lovely maiden, you are mistaken. I left my magic steed at home; I have come on an ordinary horse." When the lovely maiden heard this she began to swell up. She swelled up and turned into a terrible lioness, opened her jaws and swallowed the tsarevich whole. She was not an ordinary maiden, but the sister of the three serpents that Ivan, soldier's son had slain.

Ivan, soldier's son got to thinking of his brother; he drew Ivan Tsarevich's handkerchief out of his pocket and wiped his face with it. Lo and behold, the whole handkerchief was drenched with blood. He was deeply grieved. "What can this mean?" he said. "My brother took the road which should have made him tsar, but he has met his death!" He took leave of his wife and father-in-law, and rode his mighty steed in search for his brother, Ivan Tsarevich. After traveling a short or a long distance, a long or short time, he came to the kingdom where his brother lived. He made inquiries and learned that the tsarevich had gone hunting and vanished without a trace. Ivan, soldier's son went hunting along the same road; he too came upon the fleet-footed stag and pursued it through the forest. He rode into a wide meadow and the stag vanished; he saw a little stream flowing through the meadow and two ducks swimming on the water. Ivan, soldier's son shot the ducks, came to the white stone palace, and entered the chambers. It was empty everywhere, with the exception of one room where a fire was burning, and a pan stood on the hearth. He roasted the ducks, took them outside, sat on the porch, carved and ate them.

Suddenly a lovely maiden appeared before him. "Welcome, good youth!" she said. "Why are you eating in the yard?" "I don't like to eat indoors, it is more pleasant outside," replied Ivan. "Sit down with me, lovely maiden." "I would sit down gladly, but I am afraid of your magic steed." "Nonsense, my beauty! I have come on an ordinary horse." She foolishly believed him and began to swell up; she turned into a terrible lioness, but just as she was about to swallow the good youth, his magic steed came running and grabbed her with his mighty legs. Ivan, soldier's son bared his sharp sword and cried in a loud voice, "Wait, accursed one! Didn't you swallow my brother, Ivan Tsarevich? Disgorge him, or I will cut you up into little pieces!" The lioness spat out Ivan Tsarevich, but he was dead and had begun to rot, and the skin on his head had fallen off.

Ivan, soldier's son took two phials from the saddle, one with the healing water and the other with the water of life. He sprinkled his brother with the healing water and the flesh grew together, and when he sprinkled him with the water of life, the tsarevich stood up and said, "Ah, how long have I slept!" Ivan, soldier's son answered, "You would have slept forever were it not for me!" Then he took his sword and wanted to cut off the lioness's head, but she turned into such a beauty as no words can describe. She began to shed tears and beg for forgiveness. Looking on her indescribable beauty, Ivan, the soldier's son took pity on her and let her go free.

The brothers returned to the palace and celebrated with a three-day feast. Then they said goodbye to one another. Ivan Tsarevich remained in his kingdom, and Ivan, soldier's son returned to his wife and began to live with her in love and accord.

After some time, Ivan, soldier's son went for a walk in the open field, and chanced to meet a small child begging for alms. The good youth was moved; he took a gold coin from his pocket and gave it to the boy. The boy took the alms and began to swell up; he turned into a lion and tore the hero into little bits. A few days later, the same thing happened to Ivan Tsarevich. He went to walk in the garden and was met by an old man, who bowed low and begged for alms. The tsarevich gave him a gold piece. The old man took the coin, swelled up and turned into a lion; he seized Ivan Tsarevich and tore him into little bits. Thus perished two mighty heroes at the hands of the serpents' sister!

Aleksandr Afanas'ev, *Russian Folk Tales*, §155, trans. NB.

INTERPRETATION

The psychological understanding of the hero or heroine is of great importance in the interpretation of fairy tales. This figure represents that part of the ego which has a door open to the Self and is, consequently, in harmony with the archetypal roots of consciousness. The hero's actions will be instinctively correct, even if they run against the prevailing attitudes of the day. There may be times when the hero shows a weakness or appears to make a wrong move, but from the final outcome we can see that this was but a detour which leads to deeper psychic development. The fact that this happens, however, suggests that the Self had condoned or even provoked such a *mistake* to test the hero's potential in fulfilling Its goal.

A tale like "Two Ivans, Soldier's Sons," where the heroes are killed in the lysis, therefore surprises and shocks the reader. Such a negative development suggests that something went wrong, or perhaps that the heroes were found wanting from the perspective of the Self. Thus, the question of why this happened will be ever-present in this interpretation.

The initial scene of our tale takes place in a town. A peasant is taking leave of his wife to go off to military service. This is a sad beginning, especially when one considers that up to the end of the nineteenth century military service in Russia lasted twenty-five years. It broke up marriages and destroyed families. Anyone who could financially afford to do so bought himself out by paying another to take his place. It was a tough lot which fell in large part to the lower classes.

One can easily imagine how heart-breaking such a farewell would be, and is therefore somewhat taken aback by the peasant's parting words to his wife: "Mind you, wife, live decently, do not become the laughingstock of respectable people, do not ruin our house, but manage it wisely and await my return. God willing, I may be retired and return home." He does not say "return home soon" but "return home."

Some comfort for the young woman as she faces motherhood! No empathy, no expression of feeling, nothing which would make their common fate easier to bear.

On the other hand, we must also take into account that the man did not willingly leave his family. The text reads: "The time came for him to be recruited into the army." It was fate, the oft bitter and hard lot of the common man, which separated him from his wife at a time when something was beginning to grow between them. They were at the mercy of the collective, and they belonged to the peasantry, the lowest class.

The abolition of serfdom in Russia only took place in 1860. Although Afanas'yev doesn't date this tale, his first serial publications of Russian fairy tales appeared between 1855 and 1864. Hence, the tales in his collection very probably existed at a time when a landowner still had complete power over his serfs, and certainly military service was determined by him. This is the world into which the twin heroes in our tale are born.

Fairy tale heroes often begin life under precarious conditions: abandonment, rejection, persecution, and so on. In our tale the twin heroes are not abandoned or totally orphaned. They receive the care and love of a mother who does an exemplary job of integrating them into the society of which they are part. She sends them to school, and teaches them human values and proper behavior toward others. This is extremely important in view of their tremendous strength, which they might have easily abused. The account of the twins' fight with the merchant and boyar children, and their consideration for the owner of the two wild colts at the town fair are good examples of this.

A further example of their mother's upbringing is her admonition to greet everyone they encounter. As they prepare to go out to buy themselves horses, she says: "Listen to me, children! As you travel to town, bow to anyone whom you encounter." Here we can say that it is not only good manners, but also openness toward the stranger, toward that which one doesn't know or cannot judge; symbolically, this means to the *other* in us, to the unconscious. And this lesson pays off very well for, had the twins not shown respect to the old gray man, they would never have come upon their magic steeds and swords.

It soon becomes clear that this is not just any old man whom the twins encounter on their way but a manifestation of the Self in the guise of the wise old man. Such a fairy tale figure often appears when the hero has done all in his power to reach his goal, but without success. In this particular case, the heroes go off to buy themselves horses at the town fair but are unable to find any to their liking. Since the town fair is a common place for the whole community, psychologically, this would imply that the problem cannot be solved by collective means. In contrast to this, the old man brings the twins to a big mountain. He opens a cast-iron door and leads out two magic horses. Magic is always an indication of unconscious processes,[109] and the mountain, reaching up to the sky where its peak is often obscured by clouds, is proverbially a place where gods descend to speak with men. The juxtaposition of the town fair and of the mountain with its hidden treasure is a striking example of the two levels of psychic experience.

The horse is an animal and, as such, stands for instinct; it is also big and powerful. We see this in the expression *horsepower* which designates the power of an engine. A horse is hence a powerful instinct. Apart from this, it is an animal that carries man, and would therefore symbolize a strong, carrying instinct. Horses are used for transportation, covering much greater distances than any man could manage on foot; they can also be harnessed to perform heavy work and carry loads. Furthermore, horses are intelligent and have very well-developed senses. More importantly, they can sense the unseen, that is, they have strongly developed intuition. There are stories about horses saving their master's life by refusing to go over a bridge which would have collapsed under them, even though it looked safe. Because horses are highly intuitive, they are also easily scared and panicked. They can, therefore, symbolize an instinct which can easily get out of hand. Luckily, horses can be domesticated and taught to subordinate themselves to human will. This, however, can only be achieved if the domestication takes the form of a partnership. A good rider and their horse form a unit. They move as one, and the horse often intuits its rider's wishes, fears, thoughts, feelings and intentions. We can easily see why it is so important for the hero to have such

---

109   Jung, *Structure and Dynamics*, CW 8, § 725.

a trusting relationship with his horse, treating it as a helper and comrade while at the same time bearing the responsibility for its actions. This probably explains why the twin heroes decided against buying the two wild colts at the town fair, for those animals (instincts) could only have been managed with brute force and willpower.

The sword is the second gift of the wise old man. First and foremost, a sword is a weapon. It was used to subdue, to kill, to impose one's will over the enemy. In the Middle Ages it was also a weapon with which a knight fought for his lady. It was hence connected with chivalry, with Eros. Swords were personalities in and of themselves. They were given names and decorated with inscriptions, such as King Arthur's beautifully decorated sword *Excalibur*. Like a horse, the sword, although inanimate, was seen as being connected, even related, to its owner; it became a part of him. This is easy to understand when one considers the function of a sword, which cuts, divides, and separates; symbolically, it differentiates. With it, a man makes decisions and carries them through. Because of this, it can be seen as an ego-building instrument, for in using it, one takes a stand and faces the consequences of one's actions.

As we have seen, the heroes in our tale receive both their horses and swords from the unconscious or, more precisely, from the Self, appearing here in the guise of the wise old man. They are given the means to incorporate the will of the unconscious into life, but they must do this as the men that they are. Moreover, they cannot succeed with power alone, but need to be related and responsible for their actions toward both the outer and the inner world.

We return, for a moment, to the father. He disappears from this tale before the end of the first paragraph, never to return. Interestingly enough, however, just as he provided the seed to initiate the pregnancy, the peasant also leaves his wife fifty rubles for another beginning, for the coming of age of their child. In the tale, he specifically instructs her to keep this money until that time. A peasant woman bringing up twin sons might surely have needed the money earlier, but she honors his wish and keeps it safe for the time he stipulated. The coming of age represents a transition from childhood to manhood, so the father provides his children with a spurt of energy which will start them on their independent journey through life. In the end, it appears that the fifty rubles were never used because the old gray man gave them the horses and swords without payment, but the twins might never have been motivated to go to the town fair if they had no money to buy their horses and swords with. Symbolically this shows that, even though circumstances forced the father to leave his family, it is his energy which supports their transition into manhood. The father's importance in their lives is emphasized in the title of this tale, where they are both referred to as "soldier's sons."

As the episode with the merchant and boyar sons shows, it is not only the old gray man and the personal mother and father who support the twins' development, but the tsar as well. Despite the fact that the twins are repeatedly beaten up and their clothes torn by the village children, they do not misuse their superior strength by retaliating. It is concern for their mother which finally makes them decide to fight back. "How long will they beat and pinch us? Our mother will never be able to make us enough clothes or buy us enough caps; whatever we put on, our comrades tear to shreds..." After they beat up the merchant and boyar children who attacked them, the twins are thrown into jail, but here the tsar intervenes and justifies their action.

The tsar in Russia was always held in high regard by the common people and referred to by an endearing diminutive form of father (tsar batyushka). Here he comes to the assistance of the twins; he judges righteously, even deciding against the children of the upper classes. The father the twins never knew now enters their lives as a collective image in the person of the tsar. This shows that the new impulse, represented by the twins and coming from the sphere of the common man, is acknowledged and supported by the tsar.

Viewed symbolically, the mother and father represent the more personal aspects of the mother and father archetype; the tsar, as the dominant of collective consciousness, and the gray old man, as a Self symbol, also play an important role in preparing the twins for the task ahead. It is truly amazing that so many aspects of the psyche are supportive of this new development.

We should say a few words about the special powers of the twins, for it is clear from the start that these are no ordinary children. They grow faster, they are stronger, and they are more intelligent than other children of their age. The trip to the town fair makes their heroic nature indisputable. No one can even approach the two wild colts at the horse market; the twins use brute force to subdue them and later tame them with their willpower. These are typical characteristics of the hero, which echo the epic heroes of the *byliny*, the Russian epic tales. One such example is Ilya Murometz, Elias from Murom, who begins his heroic life by clearing farmland for his parents by *simply* uprooting a forest of trees.

Before leaving this part of the tale, I would like to draw the reader's attention to a small and seemingly insignificant detail. In the last sentence of the first paragraph we learn that the twins are born three months after the father goes off to military service, so the mother would then have been six months pregnant. This information does not appear to add to the objective interpretation of the tale, but the symbolism of the number six is most revealing.

The number six is to be found in such natural phenomena as snowflakes and honeycombs. The radius of a circle, inscribed on the inside of the circumference, forms a perfect geometrical hexagram, and the six-line hexagrams of the I Ching express the eternally ordered cycles of transformation in life.

Jung presents a particularly interesting amplification of the number six in a quotation from Joannes Lydus in "The Psychology of the Transference."

> The number six is most skilled in begetting, for it is even and uneven ... for which reason the ancients also named it marriage and harmony. For among those that follow the number one, it is the only number perfect in all its parts, being composed of these: its halves of the number three, its thirds of the number two, and its sixths of the number one (6 = 3+2+1). And they say also that it is both male and female... And another says that the number six is soul-producing...because in it the opposites are mingled. It leads to like-mindedness and friendship, giving birth to the body, harmony to songs and music, virtue to the soul, prosperity to the state, and forethought to the universe.[110]

110   Jung, *Practice of Psychotherapy*, CW 16, § 451, FN 8.

In this quote, the relationship between the sexes is given as one example of the polarity so necessary for the harmonious flow of life. For the unborn twins, this psychic process is disrupted by the departure of the father, but at the same time we note that powerful forces are constellated to support their further development: the father leaves them his energy in the form of money, the mother prepares them for life, the tsar shields them from injustice, and the old man's gifts indicate the interest of the Self in their survival. Nonetheless, if we take the above amplification to heart, we will be alerted to the fact that the *soul-producing* element in their psyche has been infringed upon by the absence of the father. However, in the first part of the tale we see no evidence of this—the twins show a heroic development and have prepared themselves for the challenges of adult life; they have also proven themselves to be related, which is a feminine quality.

It is worthy of note that our tale doesn't speak of a hero, but of twin heroes. The twin motif is a special illustration of the symbolism of the number two. Two symbolizes polarity, opposition. If seen as the breaking up of the original unity, it signifies discrimination, consciousness, but also potential conflict. At the same time, it can represent a union of these same opposites, something we often witness at the end of a fairy tale when the prince and princess marry. The original unity from which the two evolves is often described as a pre-conscious state, a state of *participation mystique* (p. 76 FN 49) or symbiosis.

In the original Greek, the term "symbiosis" means "living together." It is best known in its biological sense where it refers to any type of a close and long-term biological interaction between two different biological organisms. Symbiotic relationships can vary from mutually beneficial to mutually harmful, and can either be the same for each of the two organisms or not, for example, beneficial for one and neutral or even harmful for the other. The biological polarities of symbiosis attest to its archetypal nature.

It is interesting to note that the biologist Lynn Margulis challenged Darwin's view on evolution by arguing that it was not so much competition as symbiosis that shaped the Earth's development since life did not take over the globe by combat, but by networking. This implies relating, and therefore a much more feminine view of evolution than

Darwinian "natural selection" through competition. Here "feminine" must also be understood in its archetypal sense, in its positive as well as negative manifestation.

We turn now to the specifically Jungian understanding of symbiosis. Jung extended the above-mentioned biological considerations to the human experience. Furthermore, he held that the growth of consciousness in human beings necessitated an adaptation of such primordial patterns "...to the challenge of the present."[111]

In *Psychological Types* Jung speaks of the deeper implications of the opposition in typological functions. In addition to the conflict they represent, he sees a "reciprocity [...], a community of interest, [...] a *symbiosis* in which the waste products of the one would be the food supply of the other."[112] We see this in the attraction between persons of the opposite type and in the frequent marriages which ensue from this constellation, attesting to the archetypal force of the symbiotic relationship.[113]

Jung also speaks of symbiosis in a collective sense, seeing it as one of the necessary conditions of life. For him society is simply "...a concept for the symbiosis of a group of human beings." Here, we are once again confronted with the ambivalence of the archetypal nature of symbiosis for, just as one relies upon society to survive in the world, so too one can lose one's individuality to the mass mentality.[114] In both examples, we can see that the source of symbiosis is initially unconscious and that the task of human adaptation is realized through consciousness.

We return now to the tale at hand and to this very special phenomenon of the twins motif which is found in fairy tales, dreams, and in all symbolic material. It presents a duality which at first shows no sign of differentiation. In our tale, for instance, until the crossroads scene the brothers are completely identical, not only in their outer appearance but in the way they act. There is nothing to distinguish one from the other; in effect, the mother could have borne one son. Parting at the crossroads, the twins exchange handkerchiefs, promising to wipe their

---

111   Jung, *Civilization in Transition*, CW 10, § 547 f.
112   Jung, *Psychological Types*, CW 6, § 166.
113   Jung, *Two Essays*, CW 7, § 80-88.
114   Jung, *The Practice of Psychotherapy*, CW 16, § 224.

faces with them each day and hastening to the other's side should they find them stained with blood. Their handkerchiefs symbolize the inner connection which remains between them even as they each go their own way.

Psychologically, this twins phenomenon can best be understood as representing the approach of some hitherto unconscious content toward the threshold of consciousness. Unconscious contents are always ambivalent in nature; in approaching consciousness they are first perceived as two identical parts. This is the first intuition of something unknown, which *may* cross the threshold into consciousness, but can as easily fall back into the unconscious, disappearing as a dream image disappears upon waking. Only when we have given it enough libido and secured it in consciousness, for example by writing it down or by painting it, can we be sure that it will not slip away from us. Only then can we consider the symbols therein and try to understand what is coming up from the unconscious.[115]

We find a short and very concise description of the twin motif in *The Grail Legend*: "In itself, the doubling of a symbol ... generally indicates that it is constellated on the threshold of consciousness, but it is not yet realized in its essential nature."[116] This points to the very tentative nature of the twins phenomenon and alerts us to the precariousness of its integration into consciousness. We can, therefore, better appreciate the importance of all the support and guidance the twins receive in the early stages of their development, for without it they would probably never have even made it to the crossroads.

We now return to that moment when the twin heroes have obtained their magic horses and magic swords and make ready to venture out into the world. Their mother's blessing is as warm and intense as their father's words to his wife had been cold and unfeeling. "May my never ceasing parental blessing be upon you, my children," she says. "Go with God, show yourselves, and see people; offend no one without cause, and yield not to evil enemies." These are the words of a loving mother who is ready to part with her children because this is what is demanded of

---

115   Jung, *Children's Dreams*, 139 f.; See also chapter on "Die göttlichen Zwilling" in von Beit, *Gegensatz und Erneuerung*, especially, 279, 282 f., 363.
116   Emma Jung and von Franz, *Grail Legend*, 249.

them in life. She doesn't hold them back with sentimental feelings, nor does she weaken their courage with fearful doubts and premonitions.

After travelling for a while, the twins come to a crossroad with two signposts. One post bears the inscription: "He who goes to the right will become tsar"; the other: "He who goes to the left will be slain." The motif of crossroads and signposts is a common one in Russian tales. The fork or crossing in the road forces the hero to make a choice, and the signpost provides him with alternatives. Often the hero is accompanied (or preceded) by two brothers, but it is always one signpost, regardless of the number of forks in the road. In our tale, this would also have been possible; both directions could have been indicated on the same post. The mention of two signposts therefore places additional emphasis on separation, on splitting. Psychologically, this shows that the unconscious contents represented by the twins are about to cross the threshold into consciousness and become differentiated into two separate, opposite entities.

But what are these two entities? What are the opposites which will now become apparent? Already at the crossroads, one of the brothers decides which way each of them will go. He bids the other take the easier way to the right, saying: "I am stronger than you, so let me take the road to the left and see what it is that can cause my death." Since both brothers have, till now, proven themselves equally strong in a physical sense, this quality must refer to inner strength and, indeed, this is confirmed in the second part of the sentence. By choosing to go in the direction of death this brother is, symbolically, anticipating the possibility of transformation.

Interestingly enough, the other brother does not question this decision. He is happy to take the easier way to the right. Riding into a "glorious kingdom," he is instantly "loved for his heroic valor," given the tsarevna as wife and charged with the ruling of the kingdom. If the way to the right is seen as the direction of consciousness, of the outer world, then it is understandable that the tsar's positive response to him is based on outer appearance. This twin has done nothing to earn the "heroic valor" ascribed to him, yet he accepts the new title of "tsarevich," feasts his eyes upon his wife, takes over the rule of the kingdom as if this were all his due and, because he doesn't find it necessary to question the opinion of the tsar, follows the collective principle. Here we recognize two characteristics of Ivan Tsarevich: firstly, his extraverted attitude, and secondly, his expectation that life will treat him well. The latter is indicative of a positive mother complex, which often helps to constellate a supportive, favorable reaction from others.

We also read that Ivan Tsarevich "amused himself by hunting animals." This is somewhat strange in connection with a former peasant, for it is very much a pastime of the upper classes. The common man hunts for food, he depends upon hunting for his survival. When killing an animal, indigenous hunters apologize to the animal's soul, explaining that this was out of necessity. To hunt for amusement is to show disrespect for animals, forfeiting their lives for man's pleasure. With the emergence of weapons, hunting became an increasingly one-sided confrontation.

In most parts of the world today, man no longer needs to hunt for survival, and yet hunting still exists as a sport. Since animals represent instincts, recreational hunting may be seen as a sport in which man measures himself against his instincts. It explains why even this more supposedly *civilized* form of hunting has retained its archetypal fascination. Man's consciousness is supported by these roots. The more civilized man becomes, the more he is in danger of estranging himself from his instinctual roots, the more his consciousness becomes split off from his instincts, and the more easily they regress into the unconscious. The more they regress, the more potentially dangerous they become because they lose the differentiation of consciousness.

Animals often play this kind of a role in fairy tales. They come to the hero's rescue when the latter finds himself in a dilemma. They reconnect the hero with the instinctual part of his psyche and, thereby, enable unconscious impulses to reach the ego. This is, however, dependent upon the hero having a correct attitude toward them. Von Franz considered this the only unconditional rule in fairy tales; her deep knowledge of fairy tales led her to postulate that whoever acquired the gratitude and help of animals would always be victorious.[117] In light of these considerations, Ivan Tsarevich's hunting for amusement discloses

---

117   von Franz, *Archetypal Dimensions*, 89.

a dangerous flaw in his attitude toward animals and bodes ill for his future development.

The tale now turns to the twin who takes the road to the left. He rides three months without rest, and finally reaches a kingdom completely different from the one in which his brother is living. "There was a great sorrow in this kingdom; the houses were draped with black cloth, the people staggered about as though in sleep." Psychologically, this can be seen as deep depression, a hopeless state of despair. In contrast to his brother, this twin does not go to a palace, but stays with a poor old woman from whom he learns of the great misfortune that has befallen the kingdom. She tells him of the twelve-headed serpent that demands daily sacrifices and threatens to destroy the whole kingdom if his demand is not met.

Why does the second twin not go to the tsar directly? He is as handsome a hero as his brother, he rides a magic horse and he carries a magic sword. Moreover, his response to the old woman shows that he is ready to prove himself by confronting the serpent. But this is not the same reality, and the values of Ivan Tsarevich's world do not apply here. The second twin appears to understand this. He realizes that the tsar is as much a victim of the serpent as are his people. Symbolically, this would mean that the values and power of the collective dominant are weakened or no longer effective. Entering this kingdom, the twin is careful not to expose himself before he gets his bearings. He is wise enough to stay hidden until he has found out all he can about this land. As we learn later on in the tale, it is not only the serpent that poses a danger, but also the tsar's water carrier. In staying at the house of a poor old woman this twin shows caution but also humility. As the son of a peasant he is closest to his roots with her, and he senses that he can learn more about the true situation from the common people. "Go to the market, grandmother, buy what you need, and listen to what the people are saying. Find out whether there is any news."

There is additional significance in Ivan, soldier's son stopping at the house of a poor old woman. Apart from her being of the common class, she is also a mother figure. As we have seen, the mother played a positive role in the life of the twins. Here he seeks the help of a mother figure, but one belonging to an older generation and hence, symbolically, of a more archetypal form of the mother. From his experience of his own mother he is inclined to trust the feminine. And this old woman justifies his trust; she gives him lodgings, feeds him and, most importantly, supplies him with information. By turning to her, he is tapping into the healing source of his psyche; he is connecting up with the unconscious so it can work with and through him in the task ahead. This is in contrast to his brother whose heroic valor is accepted on appearance.

This brother's connection to his roots is further emphasized by his name. In the Russian text he is called Ivan, soldier's son throughout the tale; this discloses his common background because, as already noted, soldiers were recruited primarily from the lower classes. It also emphasizes his connection to the father. There are a few instances where Ivan, soldier's son is referred to as *bogatyr*, the name given to heroes in the Russian epic myths. He is called by this name when confronting the serpent, or when challenged to show his superior strength; otherwise, he is always introduced as "Ivan, soldier's son." Interestingly enough, this holds true even after his marriage to the tsar's daughter when he officially becomes a member of the royal family.

This small detail discloses yet another difference between the twins. We will remember that the first sign of their splitting into two separate beings occurred at the crossroads when Ivan, soldier's son decided to take the road to the left. The difference in their titles now places the twins into different social classes. Furthermore, we note that Ivan Tsarevich is rather passive, whereas Ivan, soldier's son shows character, strength and tremendous courage. All this emphasizes their increasing individuality; psychodynamically, it shows that their symbiosis at the beginning of the tale is weakening; moreover, looked at from the symbolism of the twin phenomenon, it indicates that the new contents have crossed the threshold of consciousness and are becoming more differentiated in their polarity.

And yet, we must not lose sight of the fact that, psychologically, the twins represent one personality and that the differences between them must not only be made conscious but eventually also reconciled within one psyche. The kingdom into which Ivan Tsarevich rides is described as glorious. Everything there is positive; the sun is shining in every corner. The second kingdom is dark and gloomy. Misfortune and grief are everywhere. The tsar in the first kingdom appears to be in command; in the second, he is powerless against the destructive evil which comes from the sea. If we see the twins as a two parts of the hero, then the different worlds they arrive at disclose a dangerous split in their psyche. The outer glorious world is offset by the black depression of a kingdom by the sea.

Despite the differences between the twins, there is one interesting similarity which deserves mention. In discussing the crossroads scene, it was suggested that the twin who chooses the road to the left, toward death, may symbolically be seen as opting for transformation. The name of the tsarevna in the other kingdom is Nastas'ya, a diminutive of Anastasia—*rebirth* in the original Greek. Hence, again symbolically, Ivan Tsarevich is also given the possibility of transformation by uniting with an anima figure through whom he can be reborn.

We return now to the twin who came to the kingdom menaced by the twelve-headed serpent. Learning from the poor old woman that the eldest daughter of the tsar is about to be sacrificed, Ivan, soldier's son mounts his mighty steed and heads for the sea. Here he finds the tsarevna in iron chains. One can feel the tsarevna's despair and resignation as she stands alone on the shore, awaiting her fate. "Go hence, good youth!" She says to Ivan, soldier's son, "Soon the twelve-headed serpent will come. I am doomed, but you, too, will not escape death; the ferocious serpent will devour you." After the repeated onslaughts of the serpent on her kingdom, it is understandable that she may have given up hope of escaping death, but how humiliating it must be for a tsar's daughter to be held fast by chains. Does the tsar not trust her to accept her fate with dignity? Does he fear she will try to run away and thereby endanger the kingdom?

It is true that the tsar himself is at the mercy of the serpent, for it is his responsibility to protect his people from such a destructive force. Many have already been sacrificed to the serpent, and it is now the tsar's turn to provide the sacrificial offering. But even so, must he expose his daughters in such a dishonorable and humiliating way? This situation is even more problematic when viewed subjectively, for what the tsar is sacrificing is his anima or, viewed collectively, the newly emerging Eros. It is no less disturbing that all three tsarevnas do not seem to be in position to question or oppose their father's will.

Earlier we saw that the women in Ivan Tsarevich's kingdom are not very independent. The tsar does not consult them about bringing the young man into the royal family, nor does he consider his daughter's wishes in marrying her to a peasant. Of course, we already know that Ivan Tsarevich is handsome and radiates heroic valor, but nevertheless in other tales, for example, "The Enchanted Ring," the tsarevna sets conditions for marrying the hero. Here, both the tsar's wife and his daughter silently go along with his decision.

The women are voiceless in Ivan Tsarevich's kingdom; worse still, they are passive victims in the kingdom to the left. This gives us insight into the role of women in this tale; Eros is acknowledged and appreciated in the mother, but otherwise held in check and subordinated to man's will. What may look like protection or concern in the kingdom to the right is but the outer expression of a much more repressive attitude toward the feminine in the kingdom to the left.

We also note that the tsaritsa is missing in this kingdom; the tsarevnas have no mother, and the tsar no wife. Had his wife died, the tsar might have remarried, but this has not happened. Symbolically, this means that the tsar is reigning without Eros. We might ask whether the tsaritsa had not been able to survive under the prevailing conditions. What we can say for sure is that, in the tsaritsa's absence, the three tsarevnas are the tsar's only relationship to the feminine. Although the number constellation here is four, the idea of wholeness with which this number is generally identified doesn't make much sense. It may be better understood as completion of a stage, preparing for a new development. This is most likely connected with the tsarevnas reaching marriageable age. They are no longer children, and this calls for a different relationship between the father and his daughters.

What the tale clearly shows, however, is that the tsarevnas are subordinate to the tsar and at his mercy. They do not question his decisions, nor do they express their opinions. This is especially significant in light of the fact they are the only female beings capable of continuing the royal blood line. We can, therefore, assume that the problem of the missing tsaritsa only becomes constellated when the tsarevnas arrive at the threshold of an adult relationship with the opposite sex. In the absence of suitors, this represents a situation which can be seen as sterile or incestuous.

Incest need not necessarily be understood in a literal way. In the case of a father and daughter the man is always in a superior position to the woman. The implication for a woman is that she never becomes an equal partner and an independent adult. Her views are shaped by her father's spirit; even in marriage, she remains her father's daughter. This has grave consequences if applied to the tsar's inner feminine, his anima, for then anything that is connected with Eros will be subordinated to his will.

Since the tsar symbolizes collective consciousness, such an attitude would impact his whole kingdom. This is a very real situation in our world today: Both individual as well as wide-ranging political and economic decisions are made on the basis of greed and self-interest masquerading as rational considerations with no concern for the welfare of others (Eros). The enormous Three Gorges Dam is built on the Yangtze River in China, flooding the homes of thousands of people and destroying towns and villages. Oil spills pollute the waters of our planet, killing innumerable sea life; ski slopes, highways, increased urbanization continuously shrink the habitat of plants and animals worldwide. Whole species of animals are endangered by uncontrolled slaughtering. Animals are raised under unnatural conditions, abused and exploited for greater profit. What happens to animals is also happening to children, to adult men and women, and to nature in general. If we consider that power was originally the prerogative of the gods, we can see that man's use of power is dependent upon his being responsible to the divine, to the creator, to life. Without accepting this responsibility, *use* turns into *abuse*. The examples above illustrate the far-reaching consequences of power without Eros.

In our tale, the tsar sends out his water carrier to collect the remains of his daughters after the serpent's departure. It is noteworthy that he specifically sends out the servant who is responsible for supplying the tsar's court with water, for water is essential for life, both on a physical as well as symbolic level. It must be clean and not contaminated, for it permeates the whole of our being.

The water carrier abuses the tsar's trust and threatens the tsarevnas with death if they do not name him as their champion against the serpent. Overjoyed at seeing his daughters, the tsar rewards the water carrier by making him a colonel after the first time, a general after the second, and finally by promising him the youngest in marriage. He shows himself to be completely unconscious of the servant's treachery. Psychologically, the water carrier can be seen as the tsar's shadow, or as a shadow aspect of the collective. The tsar's gullibility allows the servant to amass more and more power, and finally to secure his way to the throne by marrying the youngest tsarevna. Here we have a fitting illustration of the incest discussed above.

Let us now turn our attention to the twelve-headed monster that rises out of the sea and threatens the tsar with the destruction of his kingdom. This terrifying being is called a serpent in the original Russian version and usually translated as dragon in the English. In most tales these terms are used interchangeably, and they are all traceable to the reptiles which emerged from the waters hundreds of millions of years ago, developed lungs, and adapted to life on land. Today's reptiles are but toy versions of their predecessors, but they are still cold-blooded animals with a cerebrospinal nervous system, devoid of all but the very basic instinctual mechanisms for survival: *self-preservation, nourishment, and procreation.* For this reason, the appearance of a snake in dreams often signals the activation of some basic instinct responding to a vital need or threat to life.[118]

In folklore and mythology, serpents appear as both male and female beings. One of the oldest manifestations of the serpent in its feminine manifestation is the mythological figure of Tiamat. In the Babylonian epic *Enuma Elish* (1750 B.C.) the gods are created by the union of two bodies of water, personified by the freshwater god Apsu and the goddess of the salt sea, Tiamat. In the ensuing conflict, Apsu is killed by his son. Tiamat avenges his death by giving birth to a multitude of monstrous serpents. She herself was often depicted as a dragon. Marduk, Tiamat's grandson, finally subdues the goddess and creates the world from her dismembered body. Through this act Marduk becomes Babylon's

---

118   Jung, *Dream Analysis,* 644-646.

national deity and establishes himself as a creator god. Interpreting this symbolically, we can say that the mother's death results in transformation and creation.

This motif lies at the foundation of many myths where the killing of the mother is a necessary first step on the hero's way. The image symbolizes the need for a man in the first half of life to detach himself from the mother, both outwardly from the influence of the personal mother, and inwardly from the backward pull of the unconscious. In both cases, the goal is that of strengthening the ego and anchoring a man in the outer world.

This is an integral part of masculine initiation rites, in which separation from the mother and from the world of the feminine is a condition for a boy to take his place in the male world. This first initiation, as well as any subsequent ones he may undergo, transforms him from a purely biological member of his family into one who is entrusted with the spiritual heritage of the larger community for which he now also bears responsibility.

The epic tale of "Dobrynia Nikitich and the Serpent" is a Russian illustration of this motif. Ignoring his mother's admonition, this mighty hero invades the female serpent's territory and kills off all her offspring. While refreshing himself in the nearby river he is attacked by a twelve-headed serpent which suddenly comes upon him in a menacing storm. He manages to defend himself and cut off all twelve of the serpent's heads. He then seals a truce with her, designating the river as a boundary between them which neither is to cross. Despite this agreement, the serpent invades Russian territory and steals the ruler's niece. Dobrynya Nikitich is now called upon to rescue the maiden and to save his land from devastation. In that tale, the hero's mother first tries to spare him the danger of a confrontation with the serpent. Not listening to her protective advice is equivalent to taking his life into his own hands and detaching himself from her. The second time he ventures into the serpent's territory, his relationship with his mother has changed. She only suggests that he *sleep on it* and decide in the morning. Furthermore, we note that, just as this motif appears in other cultures, in his final confrontation he pursues the serpent in the interest of his land.

In the nineteenth century, the Russian writer Ivan Goncharov published a novel, *Oblomov*, portraying a man who spends the better part of his days lying on his couch. He is extremely passive and unable to cope with life; he cannot manage his estate or marry the girl he loves, nor does he contribute to the society of which he is a part. The condition was immediately recognized as typically Russian, and the word *Oblomovism* was coined to reflect such an attitude toward life. Psychologically, this is an example of the mother complex in its archetypal manifestation. This condition is by no means restricted to the Russian psyche, but it shows how deeply it is ingrained in Russian culture.[119]

Should such passivity and weakness of ego become prevalent either in an individual or in a whole culture, one would expect a compensatory reaction from the unconscious to emphasize the need for more instinctual male energy, energy capable of holding the regressive forces at bay. It should, therefore, not surprise us to learn that most of the serpents in Russian folklore are male. N.V. Novikov, a Russian folklorist, distinguishes between three types of male serpents: the abductor, the aggressor, and the devourer. There is one female serpent that he adds to this list, and she is always a close relative of the male serpents: a wife, a sister, or a mother. This serpent is a temptress, a cunning, insidious being who can change her appearance at will, and whose main purpose is to avenge the death of her kin.[120] We see this motif in the lovely maiden toward the end of this tale.

It is also worthy of note that in Russia such negative forces were most often interpreted in reference to historical events or personalities. Already in the pre-Christian era, the regions north of the Black Sea had been repeatedly invaded by such nomadic tribes such as the Cimmerians, Sarmatians, and Scythians. Later, in the tenth to thirteenth centuries A.D., Russia was overrun time and again by the Tartars from Mongolia. These historical events left deep scars in the people's memory. The cold-blooded and merciless attacks of serpents in fairy tales were hence often seen as reflecting the brutality and destruction of these invasions.

---

119   Baratoff, *Oblomov*.
120   Novikov, *Obrazy*, 64 f., 189.

Another such historical event was the so-called Dual Faith. Russia officially converted to Christianity in 988 under Prince Vladimir. The size of the country, as well as the unstable political situation, did not facilitate the establishment of a unified religion. The further one went from large cities, the stronger was the influence of paganism. Even in the cities themselves, paganism retained its importance for many centuries, even among the nobility. As can be imagined, this precarious situation was a thorn in the eye of the Orthodox Church, which combated paganism with all the means at its disposal. However, so strong was the attraction of paganism that it continued to exist along side the official doctrine in its beliefs and practices way into the nineteenth century.[121] Any experience which retains its vitality for such a large part of the population, and which is repressed so systematically by a new world order, is bound to amass a great amount of negative libido in the unconscious. Psychologically, it is, therefore, quite understandable that the appearance of serpents and other evil figures in folklore could be seen as compensation to collective consciousness. Needless to say, this is not restricted to Russia and accompanies comparable changes in the worldview of other cultures.

We find an example of this in Greek mythology. In an attempt to establish his rule over the gods and men, Zeus fights and subdues the Titan Typhon, a huge monster that was half man, half snake: "He was so large that his head often knocked against the stars and his arms could extend from sunrise to sunset. From his shoulders, according to Hesiod's account, there reared a hundred serpent heads, all flashing fiery tongues, while flames darted from the many eyes."[122] This account is strikingly similar to the victory of Indra over the cosmic serpent Vritra.[123] In both cases these battles end with the victory of a new generation of gods over an earlier, more archaic order. Interestingly enough, as in the case of our tale, the serpents are male, and therefore support seeing this as a spiritual development.

Such a split can also be seen in our heroes. The pagan faith of the Slavs was much closer to the earth and to nature, and, consequently,

---

121   Rybakov, *Yazychesto drevney Rusi*, 803.
122   Campbell, *Occidental Mythology*, 22; Kerényi, *The Gods of the Greeks*, 26 f.
123   Campbell, *Occidental Mythology*, 23.

spoke more to the common man than did the highly spiritual religion of Byzantium. In our tale we see the twin who took the way to the right immediately moving into the ruling class of society. His position as tsarevich would oblige him to support the official Christian faith. His hunting animals "for amusement" would, therefore, alienate him from nature and instinct. In contrast, the other twin does not affiliate himself with the ruler; he takes up lodgings with an old woman of the common class and combats the three serpents with the help of his horse. As mentioned earlier, this brother retains the epithet of "soldier's son" throughout the tale, whereas the other becomes Ivan Tsarevich. The two brothers, representing two parts of the hero would, therefore, bear witness to this polarization within the Russian soul; and it might, indeed, be one of their tasks to bring these two positions together.

In her excellent article in *Russian Legends, Folk Tales and Fairy Tales*, Ellen Rutten speaks of the continued use of folklore motifs in interpreting historical events in Russia. Because of their archetypal nature, folklore motifs lend themselves well to such interpretation. So, for example, the liberation of the serfs in the 1860s called forth images of the old epic heroes, courageous champions of the common man who performed the most incredible feats of strength for the salvation of their land. At a later time, Koshchey, an immortal villain, was used to personify the tsarist regime from whom the revolutionary *intelligentsia* was striving to save the country. In a political poster from 1914, we see a simple worker swinging a mace, a well-known attribute of the epic heroes, in combat with a huge many-headed serpent with the eyes of tsarist personalities. Interestingly enough, after the revolution of 1917, the tables turned and it was now the revolutionaries, led by Lenin, upon whom the image of Koshchey was projected. In contrast to all these male human and non-human figures, the country of Russia was most often portrayed as a sleeping maiden or as *one awaiting deliverance*.[124] Interpreting this maiden as a collective anima figure, we may say that the Eros principle is passive and awaiting rebirth. How amazingly close this is to the situation in both kingdoms of our tale.

As Ellen Rutten demonstrates in her article, it was not always the

---

124   Rutten, "Koshchey," *Russian Legends*, 51-59.

artist's intention to insinuate such interpretation of their works, but rather that it was often a projection on the part of the people or a conscious attempt of those in power to influence the public. In all probability, the artist was reaching down into the deeper layers of the psyche, in search for a creative solution to the turbulent times in which they lived. The images that surfaced from these depths were symbolic and should not have been used indiscriminately in the service of external aims. That they did make an impression upon the people, however, confirms the importance of the folk tradition in Russia and discloses a strong, perhaps unconscious, conviction that therein lie the roots of the Russian soul.

We now resume our interpretation from the perspective of Jungian psychology. The only information we are given about the serpent is that it is male, comes from the sea and devours a maiden every day. Being male would assign it to the realm of the archaic spirit, and appearing out of the waters would symbolize its unconscious, that is, irrational nature. Therefore, we cannot hope to fully understand the serpent's intentions, but can only try to deduce them from its actions.

In tales with this motif, the serpent's main focus is usually on the maiden; the threat of destruction is the means by which it enforces its intentions. According to Novikov, in some tales the serpent devours the maiden; in others, it takes her as its wife.[125] The latter does not sound like *sex between consenting adults*; it is more like the savage rape and killing of women in war. Much as this speaks to the horrible reality of our day, we must also consider it from the inner perspective. Symbolically, the serpent may then represent an archaic spirit that wants to unite with or incorporate the young collective Eros, and is ready to destroy the whole of collective consciousness for this purpose. Such a view greatly broadens the possible interpretation of this scenario.

As mentioned earlier, the absence of the tsaritsa or any suitors for the tsarevnas indicates an insufficient concern for Eros in this kingdom; it presents a tsar with no suitable partner to counterbalance his masculinity, and a developing feminine with no model for adult relationship. In general, the feminine does not have a voice and is subordinate to

---

125 Novikov, *Obrazy*, 182-4.

the masculine. This is confirmed by the tsar's readiness to sacrifice his daughters for the salvation of his land. However, we might ask what sort of land will this be if Eros is enslaved and contaminated by cold-blooded instinct? As noted above, this is the cause of much wrongdoing in our world today and can be traced to a lack of awareness of the anima as a principle of relatedness and connection to the unconscious. Could it be that this tale is introducing the possibility of a different attitude toward the feminine principle in a patriarchal society?

We had spoken earlier of the symbolic meaning of incest as a tendency to keep the daughter tied to the father, thereby preventing her from becoming an independent woman. We had also considered the water carrier as the tsar's shadow because he was intent upon acquiring the tsarevna and, through her, getting to the throne. As the tsar's shadow, the water carrier does what the tsar cannot allow himself to do; moreover, he does this through power and duplicity.

Might we then see the invasion of such a repressed archaic spirit as compensating the existing imbalance between the two fundamental principles of life—the masculine and the feminine? The distance of the serpent from the human realm emphasizes the depth of this archetypal source, and likewise the ferociousness of its attacks shows the repression to which it has long been subjected.

Because the ego carries a responsibility for what it receives from the unconscious, it must use its powers of discrimination to differentiate between what it can and cannot accept. It is quite clear that the serpent cannot be allowed to violate the feminine, regardless of the circumstances. Till now there has been no one strong and brave enough to confront this cold-blooded being; the tsar himself is powerless against it. He tries to save his kingdom by appeasement, by complying with the serpent's demands, but this is very short sighted because, as already mentioned, he would thereby be sacrificing the future Eros in his kingdom. Suddenly and most miraculously, Ivan, soldier's son appears on the scene, just in time to put an end to this brutality. Magic always suggests the involvement of the unconscious,[126] and here we can see the Self stepping in to avert this calamity.

At this point we must briefly return to the image of the serpent

---

126   Jung, *Structure and Dynamics*, CW 8, § 725.

in Russian folklore, and most importantly to the hero's confrontation with this archaic force. The hero usually fights three serpents. The number three reveals the dynamism which has now become constellated, propelling the action forward. The number of heads emphasizes progression, for it goes from three to six to nine or to twelve. Each serpent is a greater challenge, a further step in the battle with this cold-blooded enemy. Twelve is usually the highest number of heads the serpent has. Here, in our tale, the progression is only symbolized by the number of serpents; the number of heads remains the same and the maximum. This can be likened to a musical piece which has no *crescendo* but heralds each of the three battles with an instant *forte*. It symbolizes the highest tension, the greatest peril, the most critical moment, in all three battles.

Twelve is a number which represents wholeness in time. We have the twelve hours of the day and the night, the twelve months of the year, the twelve signs of the Zodiac. When the twelve hours of the day come to an end, night starts, and when the twelve months pass, a new year begins. The twelve apostles, with Jesus as the thirteenth, likewise signal the beginning of a new spiritual development. The number twelve, like the number four, can therefore symbolize the end of some process or development; a stage has been completed, and the time has come for change. The feeling of urgency is hence transmitted in our tale by the appearance of three twelve-headed serpents.

Such is the psychic constellation in the kingdom on the left; the images there show a kingdom heading for destruction. The people are in despair, and the city shrouded in black. Something terrible is about to happen, and it is clear that the responsible person—the tsar—is unable to turn the tide of events. The terrifying serpent, which may also be seen as a violent instinctual anxiety, has a paralyzing effect upon the inhabitants of this kingdom.[127]

This is where the hero who acts in concordance with the Self becomes a model for the ego. He does not allow himself to become influenced by the depressive attitude of the collective, nor does he make contact with the tsar. Between each of his battles with the serpent he

127   Jung, *Dream Analysis*, 654.

rejuvenates himself by sleeping three days in a row in the old woman's lodgings. Since sleep is an unconscious state, we can see that he is allowing the unconscious to heal and strengthen him before his next battle. He does not allow the praise and admiration of the collective to inflate him, but relies on the support of the unconscious to get him through these trials.

Another reason for the hero's success is his inseparability from his horse. In fact, according to Novikov, it is not the hero himself who poses the greatest danger for such a serpent, but the hero's animal. At the critical moment, it is the animal which comes to the hero's assistance and saves his life.[128] In our tale we can see this on two occasions. As the third serpent rises up out of the sea and the tsarevna is unable to awaken Ivan, soldier's son, we see his mighty speed churning up the earth beneath him in impatience. Later, this same steed comes to the hero's rescue as the lioness is about to devour him. Images such as these show that the hero cannot overcome the serpent with willpower or intellect alone; the battle must also be fought on another level, by that part of the psyche over which the ego has only limited influence. To be sure, this would never have been possible had the ego not previously formed a bond with this instinctual part of himself, for it is such a bond that domesticates instinct and brings it closer to consciousness.

Arriving at the shore, Ivan, soldier's son finds the third tsarevna, the tsar's youngest daughter, in chains, awaiting the approach of the serpent. First he frees her, tearing the chains into little bits as if they were rotten ropes. Then he assures her that she has nothing to fear, that the serpent will not be able to devour him, rather that it will choke on him. This is the familiar rhetoric of the hero as he faces a terrifying opponent. As we have seen in the tale of the "Water of Life," the hero stands up to Baba Yaga in a similar manner. There, Baba Yaga immediately changes her tone and complies with his wishes for a bath, food, drink, and rest. In the end she gives him advice and helps him on his way.

The serpent in our tale does not respond in any such way. It rep-

---

128   Novikov, *Obrazy*, 189.

resents a much deeper, more archaic instinctual force with which no human relationship is possible. It cannot be reasoned with, nor can it be intimidated or tricked. We see the hero taking the only possible action against the serpent by killing it. He has not calculated his chances of winning, nor made any compromises or concessions; he just does what he must do because he instinctively knows what he is dealing with.[129] Fear and panic in the face of the devouring unconscious are normal reactions of the ego. But the hero who, as the model ego, is acting in accordance with the Self, opposes and kills all three serpents with the help of his horse. This shows how dangerous it is to become paralyzed by one's emotions in the face of such negative instinctual energy. It is interesting to note that the cobra does just that to its victims; it mesmerizes them so that they cannot escape.

Before fighting each of the three serpents, however, Ivan, soldier's son does something which, at first glance, is difficult to understand: He puts his head onto the tsarevna's lap and bids her search through his hair while he takes a *power nap*. This almost certainly refers to delousing. Lice are insects and, as such, living creatures which function in a completely automatic way. They crawl out of their eggs, and molt three times before becoming sexually mature adults. Within a limited period of time, they must attach themselves to that part of the human body for which they are suited and drink their host's blood by biting through the skin and injecting their saliva to keep the blood from clotting. Under suitable conditions they spread rapidly, causing itching and potentially infection. Lice infestation has plagued humans and animals throughout history. It should hence not surprise us that such a troublesome situation would be well-known at the time the tale appeared. But what might such a motif contribute to the symbolic understanding of the tale?

If we ask where we experience such automatism in ourselves, then it is surely in the functioning of the sympathetic nervous system[130]; here we need as little control, guidance, and decision-making as a louse.

---

129   Jung, *Dream Analysis*, 326 f.
130   Jung, *Letters* 2, 616 f., FN 2. Jung's basic understanding of the sympathetic nervous system was that of an unconscious form of life. In 1960, however, he wrote the following to Albert Jung: "Originally the whole autonomic-vegetative system was called the sympathetic nervous system. Later it was subdivided into the sympathetic and parasympathetic systems."

On an inner psychic level, this would represent the collective unconscious. It too does not need our attention in order to exist, although we have learned that it is to our advantage to know as much as possible about its functioning so that we can differentiate between what we can accept and what we cannot.

Summarizing, we can say that lice symbolize autonomous parts of our psyche which make themselves felt by causing infection and pain whenever conditions are *favorable* for them to do so. Being blood-suckers, these little vampires rob us of the substance of life (blood), lower our resistance to disease, cause us to fixate on the irritation they have caused, and generally weaken us.

The same holds true for psychic disturbances. Although we usually try to suppress them in the waking state, they often come up in our dreams or otherwise disrupt our well-being in irrational ways. In the tale, we note that the hero falls asleep as soon as the tsarevna begins to delouse him. This enables any such disturbances to rise up to the threshold of consciousness where they can more readily be dealt with. Sometimes doing active imagination or even sharing such painful or embarrassing contents with another makes it easier for us to understand and confront such disturbances. And when we are confronted with some unusually demanding or dangerous task, we would do well to free ourselves of such disturbances and seek the support of the unconscious side of our psyche. Taking an exam is a good illustration of this. Obviously we must prepare ourselves thoroughly for an exam, but equally important is making sure we have a good connection to the unconscious so that it will release all the material we have *saved*, and allow us to react freely and creatively to the examiner's questions. Getting the unconscious on our side also helps in suppressing thoughts such as: "You know, you will never do well. After all these years, you should know more. What will the examiner think of you?" These might be the little lice that start to bite and suck our blood on such an occasion.

The hero's confrontation with the three serpents is just such an existential showdown. In the last moments before the battle he puts his head on the tsarevna's lap, gives up ego control by going to sleep, and asks her to remove any disturbing or distracting impulses which may sap his strength or otherwise undermine him in the ensuing trial.

There is another interesting amplification to delousing based on eating the lice once picked. This practice has been observed in gorillas and many other primates. It is a gesture of friendship, of acceptance, of goodwill. And when we consider that, in eating the lice, one is also assimilating the blood of another, then the jump to the concept of *participation mystique* is not far away.[131] In our tale, the tsarevna does not eat the lice from the head of Ivan, soldier's son, but we should not underestimate the bonding which must have taken place between them from this experience. Symbolically, it would correspond to the hero's revealing a less attractive side of himself to the tsarevna, exposing his complexes, shadow sides, doubts, and weaknesses. What a difference from his heroic persona!

Consider also the tsarevna's frantic attempts to rouse Ivan, soldier's son before the final battle. We read the now familiar signs of the serpent's approach: "...a cloud appeared, the wind began to roar and the sea to surge, and from the blue sea a serpent emerged and reared himself up." No matter how the tsarevna tries to rouse Ivan, soldier's son, she is unable to do so. Realizing the impending calamity, the tsarevna bursts into tears and it is her tear, dropping upon his cheek that awakens him. Her emotional response reveals the bonding between them; it is very different from the resignation of the two preceding tsarevnas.

It is symbolically relevant that in their composition, tears are similar to sea water and that the salt contained in both is essential for life. In alchemy, moreover, salt was seen as one of the chief symbols for the soul, for both are all-permeating. The symbolism of salt was discussed at length in the interpretation of "The Feather of Finist, the Bright Falcon" (p. 118).

As Ivan, soldier's son fights the third serpent, his sword becomes so hot that he cannot hold it. This may be due to a stronger opponent, but it may also emphasize the hero's greater involvement. When we remember that the sword was a weapon with which a knight fought for his lady in the Middle Ages, we can imagine that this battle has now also become a more personal commitment. It motivates the hero to fight

---

131   von Franz, *Creation Myths*, 32 f.; von Beit, *Symbolik des Märchens*, 560.

even harder while, at the same time, making him more vulnerable; he must remain objective and focused in combating the serpent and his hand must remain steady. It is likewise significant that Ivan, soldier's son now asks the tsarevna to wet her kerchief in the sea in order to cool down his sword. For the first time she takes an active part in her redemption; it has now become a common battle.

After killing the third serpent, Ivan, soldier's son rides back to the old woman as he had the first two times but, learning of the impending wedding, he immediately makes his way to the palace. The tsarevna recognizes him when she sees her kerchief tied to his sword; taking him by the hand, she leads him to her father. The bond which had developed between them at the seashore now gives her the courage to speak out against the water carrier, and to credit Ivan, soldier's son for killing the serpent. "My dear father and sovereign," she says, "here is the man who saved us from the fierce serpent, from undeserved death." Incidentally, this is the first time that any of the three tsarevnas opposes their father's will. She not only stands up for the hero but, more importantly, she acknowledges the relationship between them. She is voicing her opinion and her feelings, and thereby positioning herself quite differently in this collective situation. This youngest tsarevna has made the transition from daughter to adult woman, which seems to make everybody in this kingdom happy except, of course, the water carrier who is "hanged on the spot."

With this third battle, the kingdom is saved from devastation, and the three tsarevnas are no longer endangered by the serpent's demands. Ivan, soldier's son is married to the youngest tsarevna and integrated into the royal family. This marriage is not only a union of the new masculine and feminine, it has social implications as well, for it brings together the ruling class with the peasantry.

Such would surely have been the lysis of this tale were we not dealing with the twin phenomenon. Given the fact, however, that Ivan, soldier's son represents only half of the hero, we must realize that his accomplishments will have no durable impact if they are not brought together, in whatever way, with the experiences of Ivan Tsarevich.

And this is precisely what now takes place. Leaving the newly wedded couple to enjoy their honeymoon, the tale turns its attention back to the other brother. Here we learn that Ivan Tsarevich decides to go out hunting. It will be remembered that, after marrying into the royal family, this is something Ivan Tsarevich did "for amusement" (p. 177). In *Children's Dreams* Jung discusses the dream of a seven-year-old boy who goes fishing. Symbolically, to go fishing would be to bring unconscious contents into consciousness. At this age, writes Jung, fishing is still a game where the child experiences different activities in a playful way; the same holds true for hunting. Play is important for a growing child because it acquaints them with skills and experiences that they will be able to apply in later life. Jung goes on to say that many adults continue to use material from the unconscious in a similarly playful way. For example, they relish theoretical and even philosophical discussions, but remain rather superficial because they are not really involved in a personal way. Then one day the unconscious quite suddenly becomes activated, and these people find themselves in the grip of a very different reality.[132] This describes Ivan Tsarevich's experience in the forest. He goes hunting "for amusement," but then he comes upon a fleet-footed stag and pursues it over a great distance through the forest. Suddenly the stag vanishes, and Ivan Tsarevich finds himself in a broad meadow.

Before continuing with his progress, we must take a closer look at this animal which has gotten him into its grip. The stag is an image of powerful masculine energy. He carries his weapons on his forehead for all to see and be impressed. During the rutting season in fall, his deafening roar is meant to attract the hinds, of which he may gather up to fifty, and discourage any rivals from coming too close.[133] Fights between stags are vicious—rarely do the competitors disengage unscathed.[134]

In the mythologies of archaic peoples, the stag was often a symbol of the invincible sun.[135] Von Franz writes that "...the deer symbolizes an unconscious factor which shows the way to a crucial event, either toward rejuvenation ... or into the Beyond ... or even to death."[136] Thus the

---

132   Jung, *Children's Dreams*, 332 f.
133   *Grzimek's Animal Life Encyclopedia*, vol. 13, 154.
134   Federer, *The Animal Within*, 119.
135   Becker, *Encyclopedia of Symbols*, 280; Federer, *The Animal Within*, 120.
136   von Franz, *Interpretation*, 87.

stag can be seen as a *psychopomp*, a guide into the unconscious, to either rebirth or death. As such it is an important symbol of individuation.[137]

The alchemists connected the stag's fleeting nature with mercury. For them, mercury (quicksilver) was the ever-changing, volatile, evasive, irritating, and fascinating element they worked with. One of mercury's by-names was *cervus fugitives*, the fugitive stag.

This powerful, masculine energy now breaks into the quiet, regulated life of Ivan Tsarevich. Whereas hunting had been a matter of "amuse-ment" in which an armed hunter definitely had the upper hand over the animal, now he finds himself gripped and *forced* to pursue the stag into unknown territory. Ivan Tsarevich is confronted with a numinous experience, coming from the instinctual part of the psyche. He never had to prove himself as a stag does, either to win his lady or to fight off competitors. He had never been active in his pursuits; things just fell into his lap and he accepted them as his due. Now, all at once, some-thing overpowers his ego and leads him he knows not where.

According to von Franz's aforementioned amplification of the stag, we expect this to lead Ivan Tsarevich to some crucial event, "either toward rejuvenation...or even to death." It is, therefore, somewhat surprising that the stag disappears upon entering a broad meadow. A meadow is a less dangerous place than a forest. Here one can better orient one-self, and there are no trees to obscure the light or conceal predators. One could imagine that the crucial event in this part of the tale is the impending meeting with the lovely maiden in the white stone palace. Why doesn't the stag lead Ivan Tsarevich directly to her?

In Grimm's tale of "The Golden Children"—also a twin tale— the stag does just that; he leads the hero to the house of a witch. The reader is told that this is a witch, but outwardly the scene is deceptively neutral and even friendly. The hero takes the woman who comes to greet him for a motherly old lady, and must pay with his life for such naiveté. As in our tale, this is the extraverted twin who, guided primarily by the outer object, is unable to see behind the witch's disguise. He doesn't take his bearings in this new situation, and walks into a trap.

Whenever the unconscious is constellated, we become gripped by its energy. We can neither think nor feel clearly. But sooner or later the grip

---

137   von Franz, *Interpretation*, 87.

eases, the ego is once again at the helm, and we return to normal functioning. Then we are faced with the responsibility of understanding what as taken place and, even more importantly, how it might affect our life.

Let us observe Ivan Tsarevich in this new situation. After the disappearance of the stag, our hero has no one to follow; he is no longer driven by that powerful instinct and must rely upon himself. In a way, this situation parallels the crossroads scene because, now as then, his ego must determine his fate. Here, however, there are no signposts, no roads to follow and no brother to decide for him. Ivan Tsarevich catches sight of a little stream. This stream, a body of flowing water, may well represent the flow of his life: a quiet, safe flow of water, not a churning river or a roaring waterfall. Could it be that, after the intense chase, Ivan Tsarevich is meant to sit down, take a rest, lower his adrenalin level, perhaps give some thought to his experience, smoke a pipe, or throw a coin? Such behavior would be foreign to an extravert, so instead, Ivan Tsarevich makes a very practical move. Seeing the ducks on the little stream, he takes aim and shoots them; after all, he had gone out to hunt.

The extravert is good at solving problems, but usually restricts their evaluation of a situation to outer reality. Here, Ivan Tsarevich takes into account that he has been riding for a long time, doesn't know where he is, and hasn't brought any food with him. Coming upon two ducks is a godsend, and he loses no time in providing for his supper. But why is he now drawn to the ducks, swimming in the stream? What role do these ducks play in the story? Are they only there to provide him with a meal? And why are there two ducks? Wouldn't one have been enough to satisfy his hunger?

A duck is a bird with very special properties. It can walk on land, fly in the sky, and swim on water. It is capable of moving about in all three mediums and, consequently, of overcoming obstacles that no man can by his own means. For these reasons von Franz sees the duck as a symbol of the Self and/or of the transcendent function.[138] The transcendent function may be understood as a psychic mechanism that is triggered in moments of deadlock. It also has a uniting function, for it brings together the conscious and unconscious parts of the psyche,

---

138   von Franz, *Shadow and Evil*, 223 f.

bridging the gap between them by means of a symbol. It provides the means by which the split can be healed to enable further development.

This amplification is supported by there being two ducks, for two emphasizes the opposition and polarity in this image. Furthermore, as a threshold phenomenon, it points to the tentative, unclear nature of any hunches, fantasies, or fleeting thoughts that may rise up in him; these might be first impressions of some unknown content approaching consciousness. Dwelling upon such intuitive impulses may have enabled Ivan Tsarevich to see beyond the ducks' objective appearance; by giving them libido he would have strengthened their symbolic meaning, thereby bringing them closer to consciousness. But introspection is foreign to Ivan Tsarevich. He loses no time pondering the situation. "He took aim with his gun, fired, and killed the pair of ducks. He dragged them out of the water, put them in his bag, and continued on his way."

I turn now to further amplification of the duck, this time from Slavic folklore. As in most cultures, a bird's ability to fly places it symbolically into the realm of spirit or soul. In Slavic folklore, especially in its songs and marriage rituals, the duck is often referred to as a maiden or bride.[139] This is supported by a small detail in our tale which describes the ducks as being gray. If it were a pair, the male duck would have colorful plumage. Psychologically, their both being gray suggests that they are a double image of the anima.

In these same cultures, however, the duck was also seen as an unclean spirit. The devil and other folklore figures were believed to transform into a duck.[140] This polarity illustrates the ambivalence of every symbol; moreover, it should alert us to the danger of restricting our interpretation to one aspect of a symbol, or of taking things at face value as the hero did so naively in "The Golden Children."

The amplifications of the duck, given the above, present two different sides of the symbol. Its positive aspect is soul-furthering and bridge-building; its negative one discloses shadow elements of the feminine, accompanied by sudden transformations, which are not always outwardly recognizable. A man might experience the latter in a woman

---

139   Gura, *Symvolika*, 669.
140   Gura, *Symvolika*, 668.

with dubious moral values who is nonetheless capable of exerting an intense sexual fascination on him. If he has never been exposed to such a negative aspect of the feminine, he would be poorly equipped to deal with her.

This is a danger for both twins because their experience of the feminine has been one-sidedly positive so far in the tale. The appearance of the duck may, therefore, be seen as an attempt on the part of the Self to compensate this shortcoming. It could well be compared to a dream image, anticipating the dangers ahead. Needless to say, this insight would hardly have been possible for one who saw the ducks merely as something to fill his stomach with.

We now rejoin Ivan Tsarevich as he approaches the white stone palace. White is a color which can symbolize initiation, transformation. That a bride wears a white gown is not only meant to indicate virginity; it also signals a change of status, a transition into new stage of life. In Eastern cultures, white is the color of death, another transition. In indigenous initiation rites, boys are often painted white and laid into a grave from which they later emerge, reborn to a new role in society; after this they are accepted as adult members of their collective and entrusted with the cultural heritage of their people.

Stone, as a building material, is stronger and more durable than wood, as is vividly shown in the tale of "The Three Little Pigs"; the house of stone could stand up to the wolf's huffing and puffing, whereas those of straw or wood were blow down. What is meant in our tale by "white stone" is probably marble, which is a precious material reserved for prestigious public buildings such as churches, court houses, museums, libraries, and palaces of the nobility.

Earlier in the tale, Ivan, soldier's son combats the serpents as they "...come forth from the sea from behind a gray stone." It is to this stone that the tsarevnas are brought and chained. Here the stone marks the point of entry of the serpents onto human territory. It is a threshold physically between land and sea, and symbolically between the conscious and unconscious parts of the psyche. Might the white stone palace likewise symbolize some such threshold?

A palace is a dwelling place for people with means and influence, for the elite. It is a gathering place for society, a place of culture, of feasts and celebrations. Ordinary people did not have the means to build their homes out of stone, and especially white stone. Nor were they capable of providing such fruits of civilization which distinguish a palace from the home of a simple man. A palace usually needs many servants for its upkeep and for the care of its residents. Why is Ivan Tsarevich not met at the door and welcomed inside by some servant? Might this be an abandoned palace and, if so, who does it belong to and why has it been abandoned?

The amplification above shows that the white stone palace is the dwelling of some very special person, one with power and influence. That this palace stands empty indicates that life has gone out of it, that it no longer enjoys the prestige or commands the respect it once had, and that its many benefits are no longer accessible to man. In a way, it reminds one of "The Sleeping Beauty," in which her life stops for a hundred years until the hero redeems it. But whereas in "The Sleeping Beauty" the prince only needs to kiss the princess, in our tale the task is much more difficult and dangerous.

Entering the white stone palace, Ivan Tsarevich walks through its many chambers until he reaches the room with a hearth. Here a fire is burning and a table is set for one. The hearth was normally built in the innermost part of the house. Its fire provided protection against the cold and heat for the cooking of food; it was a place of warmth and nourishment. Symbolically, it would also stand for transformation because here different raw ingredients would be prepared for human consumption. As in "Hansel and Gretel," however, this turns out to be a trap for one who cannot see beyond outer appearances and is naive in their expectation of life.

And Ivan Tsarevich is just such a person. Not questioning how all this came about, he plucks and roasts his ducks and starts to eat them. Warmth and nourishment! This is just what our tired hero needs after a long day's travel. And if this were not enough, a lovely maiden suddenly appears to keep him company. Why should he doubt his good fortune? Isn't this the way life has always treated him?

But slowly, the scales begin to tip: Ivan Tsarevich invites the lovely maiden to share his meal, but she declines on the pretext of fearing his mighty horse. What she really fears is that the strong masculine instinct and acute intuition, symbolized by the horse, will see through her deception. She is covertly testing him to see if this is the case. But Ivan Tsarevich is flattered and blinded by her feigned helplessness, and tells her that he has left his magic horse at home and come on an ordinary one. He intends to trick her by saying this, but actually he does the very opposite; he gives himself away by falling for her deception. This information inflates the lovely maiden with power. She transforms into a terrible lioness and swallows him whole! It is exactly the sort of a situation which the episode with the ducks might have prepared him for, and Ivan Tsarevich pays dearly for not having been receptive to the unconscious message.

It is precisely at this moment that Ivan, soldier's son remembers his brother and discovers the blood-stained handkerchief. He immediately takes leave of his wife and father-in-law, mounts his mighty steed, and rides out to discover what misfortune has befallen Ivan Tsarevich. Despite their individual development, this reveals how strong the existential bond between the twin heroes still is.

Reaching Ivan Tsarevich's kingdom, Ivan, soldier's son learns that his brother went out hunting and disappeared without a trace. He follows the path taken by his brother, comes upon the stag, rides after him into the forest, arrives at the meadow, shoots the ducks, continues on this way to the white stone palace, makes his way into the room with the hearth, cleans and roasts his ducks and prepares to eat them. He does all this in exactly the same way that Ivan Tsarevich did. Is this just fairy tale language, or can we see any psychological significance in all these similarities?

In a waking life, if I were trying to find someone and had nothing to guide myself by, I would imagine where this person might have gone or what they might have done. I would try, so to speak, to put myself in this person's shoes. The better I knew the person, the better my reasoned guess would be. On the inner level, such a reproduction of one brother's actions by the other would be a fitting example of the *participation mystique* between them.

At the start of the tale, we referred to *participation mystique* as a threshold phenomenon. This was ascribed to the stage where the unconscious contents had not crossed the threshold into consciousness and where the ego could only perceive them as two identical entities. An important development was noted as the twins parted at the crossroads, for there-after their experiences of life became more individual. In alchemy this stage of the alchemical opus was called *separatio*; psychologically it refers the necessary discrimination which shifts such a symbiotic relationship onto a more conscious level.

We see a suggestion of this in the account of Ivan, soldier's son's meeting with the lovely maiden. As already mentioned, Ivan, soldier's son follows in his brother's footsteps almost every step of the way, but in the end he chooses to eat his meal on the porch steps rather than inside the palace. When the lovely maiden tells him that she is afraid of his magic horse, he gives the same answer as his brother had, namely that he came riding on an ordinary horse. Most likely, both brothers lied to the maiden in order to enjoy her company, but Ivan, soldier's son was not as naive as his brother and took this small precaution of sitting on the porch—a precaution which saved his life.

This twin's success in thwarting the lioness's malicious plans may be explained by several factors. Firstly, he had been alerted to danger by the blood on his brother's handkerchief; secondly, he is less inclined to trust outer appearances than his extraverted brother; and thirdly, the battles with the serpents forged a stronger bond between him and his steed. At the critical moment when the maiden transforms into a lioness, the hero's horse comes to his master's rescue, and the tables turn. In the end, it is instinct that saves the day. Actually, it is not the horse itself as much as the bond between it and Ivan, soldier's son that results in a dif-ferent outcome. Here, again, the two work together as they had in the battle with the serpents. Sadly, we read of no such bonding between Ivan Tsarevich and his horse.

We have taken Ivan Tsarevich for an extravert, that is, one who lets the outer world determine his fate and interests. He is a man who enjoys life, who is open to what comes toward him and makes the best of it. There is merit in such an attitude, and his death would signify that all this extraverted openness and ability to adapt to the world would have been lost had Ivan, soldier's son not looked at his brother's handkerchief, hastened to his help and revived him with the phials in his saddle.

Reviving the dead with the water of life is a familiar motif in Russian fairy tales. Sometimes only one phial is mentioned, as in "The Water of Life."

In other tales two kinds of water are used. The present tale belongs to this second category, as does the tale of "Mar'ya Morevna" which ends this volume. In both of these tales, the dismembered body must first be reassembled in the proper order. After being sprinkled with the first of the two waters, which is referred to as "the healing water" in "Two Ivans," and the water of death in "The Water of Life," the pieces grow together but the body is still lifeless. It is only the water of life which now vivifies the body and the person awakens, exclaiming that he had slept for a long time.

This motif is a good illustration of the shift from the first to the second half of life. Whereas in the first half of life adaptation to the outer world is given priority, in the second half of life the psyche shifts its emphasis toward the inner world and insists on the inclusion of all aspects of the personality which have hitherto been neglected. Unaware of this change, people often continue to live in the old way. The new way is experienced as too difficult, too strenuous, it doesn't come *naturally*; and so it is tempting to follow the path of least resistance, the way of life in which one has become proficient.[141]

The twin phenomenon we are dealing with presents us with an excellent example of this inner need to integrate unfamiliar, opposing aspects of the psyche; indirectly, it also raises the question of what happens when this need is not fulfilled.[142]

The transition into the second half of life is often difficult to recognize and even more difficult to accept. We have become accustomed to living life in a certain way and are unprepared for the obstacles which now confront us. Whereas before we have been successful in our endeavors, now we increasingly meet with frustration and failure. What we fail to realize is that we are entering an inner transition, a transition in which our psyche is shifting from a biological to a cultural attitude toward life. Jung speaks of it as an extraordinarily important transition,

---

141   Jung, *Structure and Dynamics*, CW 8, § 772.
142   The Jungian psychiatrist, Heinrich Karl Fierz traced the progressive deterioration of the personality resulting from such one-sidedness in his chapter on "The Clinical Amplifications of Extraversion and Introversion" in *Jungian Psychiatry*.

individual in nature and not enforceable by general rules and maxims.[143]

According to Jung, this transition can only be effected through an understanding of the symbolic.[144] We see this in all indigenous initiation rites, in which the initiates are introduced to the cultural heritage of their community, which is symbolic in nature. They become "those who know," for they are able to see life in two dimensions.[145] Behind the outer world that they knew before their initiation, they are now able to discern the spiritual, non-material aspects of their surroundings. It is as if we were wearing bifocal glasses. With a slight movement of the head we have the possibility of changing our perspective. This is an apt image because it implies an act of consciousness and differentiation; we consciously move our head to see far away, and are hence aware of the difference from seeing near. This is not so obvious when shifting between physical and symbolic vision, and may lead to confusion if we are not aware of the differences in the two perspectives. For the Eastern psyche this is not so difficult because ego consciousness is ascribed less importance and the shift is therefore considerably more fluid.

In his *Zarathustra Seminars*, Jung quotes the following sixteen century Latin text of a Hermetic philosopher: "*In habentibus symbolum facilior est transitus...* For those who have a symbol" or, we might say, for those who are capable of thinking symbolically, "the passing from one side to the other, the transmutation, is easier."[146] It is worthy of note that Jung translates "*transitus*" not as "transition" but as "transmutation," for this latter, which is the essence of alchemy, indicates a "change into another nature, substance, form or condition," hence into another psychic reality.

It should come as no surprise that this inner psychic reality becomes known to us through symbols because, belonging to both worlds, they bridge the gap between the conscious and unconscious parts of the psyche. If someone entering the second half of life is in tune with both parts of their psyche, they may be more inclined to ask why something is happening to them, or to give more credence to irrational feelings

---

143   Jung, *Structure and Dynamics*, CW 8, § 113.
144   Jung, *Structure and Dynamics*, CW 8, § 113.
145   Eliade, *The Sacred and the Profane*, 188 f.
146   Jung, *Zarathustra 2*, 1248.

and ideas.

In the mid-life transition, the rules and regulations of the first half of life need to be modified and differentiated to meet the changing demands of psychic life. The unconscious part of the psyche is changing its course and, if there is no realization of this shift, we will be out of step and split.

In his article "The Stages of Life," Jung very poetically likens the life of a human being to the movement of the sun across the sky. "At the stroke of noon," Jung writes, "the descent begins... After having lavished its rays upon the world, the sun withdraws its rays in order to illuminate itself."[147] Here *illuminating* refers to introspection, to directing our energy toward the inner world. In a general way, we can say that the goal of the second half of life is toward wholeness. For a man this is—first and foremost—toward the anima, for she acts as a bridge to the unconscious part of the psyche. In the hunting scene we noted that Ivan Tsarevich doesn't appreciate what happens in the forest. The stag leads him to the open meadow and vanishes, then two ducks appear, swimming on a stream. He asks no questions, draws no conclusions; he doesn't realize that something new is entering his life, and that the challenge ahead will be connected with the feminine. We note that the episode with the ducks failed to alert Ivan Tsarevich to the danger awaiting him at the white stone palace.

Could it be that Ivan Tsarevich is not ready to make the transition into the second half of life? Jung has shown that the task of coming to terms with one's shadow belongs to the first half of life and, moreover, that a man cannot successfully deal with the anima without having first integrated his shadow. By killing the three twelve-headed serpents and frustrating the designs of the evil water carrier, Ivan, soldier's son has demonstrated his ability to confront such destructive forces. Being the hero that he is, Ivan, soldier's son not only copes with personal but also with collective shadows. But have we seen Ivan Tsarevich going through any such development?

For the civilized world, the question of the shadow is also closely

---

147   Jung, *Structure and Dynamics*, CW 8, §§ 778, 785.

connected to instinct. Here again, the relationship of Ivan, soldier's son to his horse gives ample proof of his ability to connect with this part of himself. He not only knows how to handle his horse, he trusts and relies upon it. However, Ivan Tsarevich's connection to instinct only appears in his going hunting, and even that he does for amusement.

We have interpreted the twins as representing two parts of the same personality. We have seen that they complement one another, and that they can therefore be considered shadow aspects of one another. We have, furthermore, realized that Ivan, soldier's son, despite all his mighty deeds, would have remained half a man had he not brought his brother back to life.

When Ivan, soldier's son first arrived in the kingdom to the left, he didn't have much time to think of his brother. His libido was engaged in fighting the serpents, saving the tsar's daughters and, last but not least, in marrying one of them. This was what was demanded of him in the first half of life. Ivan Tsarevich following the stag heralded the transition into the second half of life for both of them; their experiences at the white stone palace showed how very much connected the two brothers still were, despite their new relationships and responsibilities in life.

As already mentioned, the scene with the two ducks can be understood as an unconscious impulse alerting Ivan Tsarevich to possible trouble ahead, a form of compensation for his naive expectation of life. It emphasizes, yet again, the fragility of such threshold phenomena and the necessity of providing sufficient energy to enable their crossing over into consciousness. The tale offers no evidence of this happening; both brothers cook and eat their ducks, but this *integration* appears to remain limited to the conscious physical level, for shortly thereafter we witness Ivan Tsarevich succumbing to the lioness.

Were it not for Ivan, soldier's son, with his reliable instinct and his experience of confronting the shadow, Ivan Tsarevich would never have returned to life. We remember his first words upon being sprinkled with the water of life: "Ah, how long I have slept!" to which his brother answered: "You would have slept forever were it not for me."

But although Ivan Tsarevich has regained consciousness, he himself has done nothing to integrate the shadow. He is, so to speak, *pulled on board* by his brother. Even afterward, he continues to be passive; he is still in the same dependent relationship as at the crossroads scene. Here, it will be remembered, it was Ivan, soldier's son who decided which direction each of them would take, and Ivan Tsarevich just accepted the easier way.

We should not forget that the person who has just been revived is a tsarevich, a crown prince, one who will some day succeed to the throne and determine the values and rules of his people. We might have expected him to take more initiative; he might at least have supported his brother in passing judgement on the lovely maiden. But none of this happens. Ivan Tsarevich remains passive, and the tale only reports that Ivan, soldier's son takes pity on the lovely maiden and lets her go.

At this point, important information which is not known to the brothers is divulged to the reader, namely that this lovely maiden is actually the sister of the three serpents that Ivan, soldier's son had slain. It shows that the destructive powers in this tale are related, and alerts us to the perilousness of the situation.

This is the crisis, as well as the turning point, of the tale. Upon parting at the crossroads, the two brothers had each gone their own way and made their own experiences of life. Ivan Tsarevich's riding into the forest and catching sight of the fleet-footed stag heralded the transition into the second half of life. The shift in the flow of their psychic energy is at first hardly noticeable; for a while, both continue to live as they had before. Then suddenly Ivan Tsarevich is devoured by the lioness and, shortly thereafter, we realize that the *participation mystique* between them has become reactivated and they are forced together again.

This demonstrates the increased importance of the anima in the second half of life. Ivan Tsarevich's inability to fulfill the requirements of the first half of life now make it impossible for the brothers to take a united stand against the anima in her deceptive and destructive form. Sadly, we must also note that, upon reuniting with his brother, Ivan, soldier's son himself regresses; he lets the lovely maiden/lioness go unpunished. The renewed symbiosis of the twins' relationship appears to hinder any development beyond that of the lowest common denominator.

So far nothing has been said about the lioness. Let us first consider the life of this animal from a biological standpoint. Here we find that the responsibilities of the lion and lioness within the pride are quite different. The lion protects the pride's territory, but the tasks of procuring food, raising the young, teaching them to hunt, and introducing them into the social network of the pride all rest upon the lioness. In addition, as with most domestic cats, it is the lioness that chooses a mate when there are several males vying for her attention.

There is only one activity which both animals share in common and with an equal expense of energy, and that is copulation. The lioness comes into heat every six to ten weeks for a period of eight days. During this time, lions mate incessantly, forgetting everything, including hunting and eating. In the zoo of Dresden, a pair of lions was recorded copulating 360 times in one such eight-day period.[148] It should, therefore, not surprise us that the lion represents the hottest period of the year on the zodiac, the time between the twenty-first of July and the twenty-first of August. Since this is not only the hottest but also the lightest period, in alchemy the lion was considered a symbol of the sun and of *transformation through passion.*[149]

It is plain to see that the twins are both fascinated by the lovely maiden, but what is the source of this fascination? At the white stone palace, the twins are confronted by three manifestations of the feminine: the lovely maiden they first meet is the sister of the serpents who Ivan, soldier's son killed; she also transforms into the lioness and swallows Ivan Tsarevich. The cold-bloodedness of the serpent sister and the passionate nature of the lioness speak for the powerful energy which is constellated by this polarity. The twins are unable to see through to the triple nature of this being; they have no idea of what they are confronted with. Are they simply dazzled by the lovely maiden's beauty, or gripped by the numinosity of this triadic archetypal feminine? If the latter, might this be a challenge they need to face? Do they need to ask questions, to become conscious of what they have been exposed to?

---

148 Dolder, *Löwen*, 10-18.
149 Jung, *Children's Dreams*, 229.

Furthermore, we soon realize that it is not instinct in its polarity of serpent and lion that clouds their perception, for Ivan, soldier's son is ready to chop off the lioness's head after she regurgitates Ivan Tsarevich. It is only when she appears as a lovely maiden that the twins display a blindness that is difficult to comprehend. We originally interpreted their inability to see through her deception to their lack of experience with such women. We found Ivan Tsarevich's total amnesia of being swallowed by the lioness difficult to believe. Upon regaining consciousness, he sees the lioness and watches his brother raise his sword to chop off her head, but when she reappears in human form, he just splits off the negative experience. He asks no questions, he makes no deductions; he has gained no insight from having gone through this *night-sea-journey*. If a lovely maiden can turn into a ferocious lioness and then back again into a lovely maiden, it would seem reasonable to expect that she will make the switch again, most likely when he is off his guard and without the instinctive reaction of his magic steed.

What the twin heroes fail to realize is that this seductive woman is an inner problem; they only see her outer appearance, and ascribe the numinosity they experience via the unconscious to this outer image. The amplification of the lioness above, especially her sexual behavior, suggests seeing her as an instinctual image of the *coniunctio*. As any archetype, however, it can manifest both outwardly and inwardly; a man may experience it outwardly as a passionate sexual relationship with a physical woman, inwardly as an equally passionate union with the anima. This is not anything that either Ivan Tsarevich or Ivan, soldier's son can leave behind by simply pardoning the maiden and riding off into their kingdoms.

Sometimes we come upon a figure in a dream that we cannot recognize as mirroring a part of our personality. Even if we theoretically know that such a figure may be introducing us to an unconscious aspect of our psyche, we would be wrong to conclude that we can or need to incorporate it, *as is*, into our life. The reason for this is that the opposites exist together in unconscious material; only in consciousness can they be separated from one another and recognized by the ego.[150]

---

150 Jung, *Children's Dreams*, 140.

In considering the implications of such a figure, we would do well to first amplify and understand its nature in all its ramifications, and then try to imagine why we have been confronted with it. Such a procedure should help us decide what part of this image can legitimately be integrated into consciousness, and what cannot.

We had originally seen the twins as naive and overconfident. While we may be able to get away with such deficiencies in the first half of life, the demand for introspection which comes with the transition into the second half of life punishes such blindness severely. Because they do not ask themselves what the lioness represents and what this means for them, that part of the anima which is represented by the lovely maiden/lioness/serpent, slips away into darkness of their psyche and becomes invisible, that is, unconscious. In the second half of life where the goal is wholeness, it would have been of vital importance for the twins to gain insight into this part of their psyche, but because she got away with her deception the brothers were now in her power. Herein lies the tragedy of this tale; it marks the point at which all the positive libido that had been put into the development of the twins, as well as all they had themselves accomplished, loses its momentum. The fragility of the twin phenomenon was mentioned on several occasions, as well as the importance of the support they received from their family and from those they encountered on their way. Ivan, soldier's son's pardoning the maiden/lioness/serpent marks the turn in the road which seals their fate. The inability of the twins to acknowledge and accept the demands of the second half of life causes their individuation to take a negative form.

As von Franz writes in *Puer Aeternus* "If the growth is not accepted then it grows against you, at your expense, and then there is what might be called a negative individuation. The process of individuation, of inner maturing and growth, goes on unconsciously and ruins the personality instead of healing it."[151]

With this in mind, let us look at the final events of this tale and the lysis to which it leads. It will be remembered that upon leaving the

---

151   von Franz, *Puer Aeternus*, 55.

white stone palace the brothers spend three days celebrating in Ivan Tsarevich's kingdom. One might ask what they were celebrating. Was it their reunion; were they glad to be together again as they had been at the start of the tale? Was it Ivan Tsarevich's rebirth; was it relief at having solved the problem of the lioness, even magnanimously pardoning the lovely maiden? All these reasons are perfectly understandable on an outer level, but they are totally devoid of any introspection.

Some time after the twins return to their kingdoms, they both have a similar experience. Ivan, soldier's son meets a young boy while walking in an open field; several days later, Ivan Tsarevich comes upon an old man as he walks in his garden. Both strangers ask for alms and both brothers give them a gold coin. At this, the boy and old man begin to swell up; they turn into lions and devour the heroes. The tale makes it quite clear that their death was the lioness's revenge for her serpent brothers. This confirms, yet again, that the twins were two parts of the same personality, for Ivan Tsarevich had not been involved in the killing of the serpents.

It is a bit surprising to read that the twins were eaten up by lions; one might have expected the young boy and old man to turn into lionesses. This may perhaps indicate that the heroic defeat of the three male serpents, which took place in the first half of life, was invalidated by the inability to successfully confront the anima, and thereby achieve wholeness in the second. This would support the fact that different criteria are operative in the two stages. In addition, we note that the image of the masculine in the first case is an archaic, cold blooded spirit; in the second, it appears as its very opposite in the image of the lion. As mentioned above, in alchemy the lion was considered a symbol of the sun and, thereby, of consciousness, but also of passion. It is this unfulfilled condition which ultimately defeats the twin heroes.

The boy and the old man often appear as symbols of the Self in their polarity of *puer* and *senex*. In the case at hand they may well represent the whole span of a man's life, a life which is about to be extinguished. The gold coin given to them by the twins is reminiscent of the final goal of the alchemical opus. Here it alludes to the negative individuation which is now reaching its fulfillment.

But what went wrong? Surely it is worthy to give alms to the poor, just as it is to pardon a person asking for mercy. Why are the twins now being punished for such a humane gesture?

In his description of the transition to the second half of life, Jung mentions the stiffening of old convictions and principles, especially those concerning moral values. He explains this as an inability to accept the changes taking place within the psyche.[152] The twins' mother had brought them up to respect others and not to misuse their heroic strength. Having pity on a pleading person and giving alms to the poor mirrors this upbringing, but these are collective principles. The transition into the second half of life is now demanding a more differentiated and individual response, one in harmony with the changes taking place within the psyche.

This brings us to the sad end of the tale, and places the blame for the negative lysis on the twins' inability to make the shift into the second half of life. The unconscious had initiated this transformation in the forest scene when Ivan Tsarevich came upon the stag; it continued to provide opportunities for the ego to join in this development till the very end but, as we have seen, the brothers were unable to read these signs; they were incapable of more than one perspective on life.

The three serpents and their sister in this tale link these two stages. The battles with the three male serpents belong to the first half of life. As mentioned earlier, the hero usually fights a female serpent; the purpose of this battle is to separate the ego from the mother or from the world of the mother; from an inner perspective, this refers to the unconscious from which all consciousness emerges. However, this same unconscious has not only the power to bring forth but also to take back; therefore, in order to lessen the chances of being devoured, the ego must sever these symbiotic ties and anchor itself in the outer world.

Our tale differs from this scenario in that the serpents are male; therefore, one can say that, rather than confronting and conquering the negative aspect of the mother archetype, Ivan, soldier's son confronts and conquers the negative aspect of the father archetype.

---

152   Jung, *Structure and Dynamics*, CW 8, § 773.

The initial constellation in this tale was that of a missing father. It was not by design that this happened; moreover, the father left money for his children's future development into adult life. Nonetheless, he was not a part of the twins' experience of life. As we know, the absence of a father may lead to a lack of structure or an ignorance of the ways of the world. These deficiencies were tackled in exemplary fashion by the mother, supported by the tsar and the wise old man. This latter serves to illustrate another response to the missing father for, in the absence of a living experience, the archetypal expectation of the father is rechanneled into the spirit. As we have seen, these experiences were all positive. It should, therefore, not surprise us that, upon arriving in the kingdom to the left, Ivan, soldier's son is confronted with the *negative* aspect of the archetypal masculine, for this would be in keeping with the compensatory function of the unconscious.

After Ivan, soldier's son defeats all three serpents, there remains only one aspect of his psyche which he has never come to grips with, and that is the archetypal feminine in its negative manifestation. This blind spot results in both twins eventually succumbing to the serpent's sister, the lioness. This is indirectly confirmed by an alternative version of this tale where, after killing the three serpents, the hero fights a final battle with Baba Yaga, who turns out to be the mother of the three serpents. This leads to a positive lysis.

The twins' experience of the feminine in the first half of life was supportive and helpful; as we were to see all too vividly, however, this left them naive and vulnerable to the negative aspects of the feminine in the second half of life. Here the feminine, in the person of the lovely maiden, became a source of great danger and ultimately resulted in their death. The reason for this was that the demand for wholeness in the second half of life was not satisfied by the one-sidedly positive nature of the initial experience.

In attempting to find an explanation for the devastation caused by the serpents, we pointed to the subordination and inequality of the feminine in both kingdoms (p. 187). In the second half of life this would include the anima—the principle of Eros in a man's psyche. We noted that such a development had already begun during Ivan, soldier's son's confrontation with the third serpent. At that time, we not only saw a growing partnership between Ivan, soldier's son and the youngest tsarevna, but also an ability on the part of the tsarevna to stand up for herself, to reveal the true hero and denounce the water carrier; this was something her two elder sisters had not been able to do.

This was a development of vital importance, and had Ivan, soldier's son been a single hero it would probably have led to a different lysis. The negative feminine had not yet been confronted, but with the support of his wife—a more personal aspect of his anima—Ivan, soldier's son was better prepared to meet the challenge of the archetypal feminine in its negative manifestation. Thus, had his wife/anima witnessed the transformation of the lioness into the young maiden, there is no doubt that she would have seen through the deception and warned her husband of the danger ahead.

Let us now direct our attention to a seemingly insignificant detail in the text. Parting at the crossroads, the twin brothers had exchanged handkerchiefs, promising to wipe their faces with them each day and to hasten to the other's assistance should they find theirs stained with blood. After Ivan, soldier's son kills the third serpent, he returns to the old woman's house where he learns that the youngest tsarevna has been promised to the water carrier. He immediately makes his way to the palace where the wedding celebration is taking place. As he walks into the hall, the tsarevna recognizes him by "her precious kerchief on his sword." The similarity to the handkerchief connecting the twin brothers suggests that Ivan, soldier's son now has a double allegiance and that this may help him to differentiate his symbiotic relationship with Ivan Tsarevich.

Despite these positive developments in Ivan, soldier's son's life, the tale ends tragically. The bond between the brothers proves to be stronger than that of Ivan, soldier's son and his wife. When the twins are confronted by the transformations of the lovely maiden and the lioness, Ivan, soldier's son is pulled back into the original symbiosis with his brother and neither of them proves capable of standing up to this image of the archetypal feminine in its negative manifestation.

This underscores the fragility of the threshold phenomenon, and shows the inability of the twins to move beyond their symbiotic relationship. Both twins were now married and integrated into their respective kingdoms. They could very well have continued in these roles, and both would probably have succeeded to the throne. This was, in fact, prophesized for Ivan Tsarevich when he took the road to the right. Still, being only half personalities they would have continued to live their lives in a one-sided way. Many men do so without being devoured by a lioness.

But these are heroes, and as such they are born with a mission that goes beyond the mere biological requirements of life. Heroes are culture-bringers; they further humanity's development to a higher consciousness. And this higher consciousness is what Jung ascribed to the second half of life; it is not beyond the outer world, but connects that world with the unconscious roots of humanity. This is the wholeness we strive for in the process of individuation and the quest for the gold of the alchemical opus.

We cannot reach this goal without symbolic understanding. Calling it *symbolic* does not make it any less real, but assigns it to a different, psychic reality. "...real is what works," wrote Jung, though his original German text reveals his play on words: "*Wirklich...ist, was wirkt.*"[153]

In a man, this demand for wholeness is primarily directed toward the anima, toward a meaningful connection with the feminine principle of Eros, for Eros compensates the discriminating function of the Logos principle in him and mitigates its influence through relatedness. This appears to be the condition under which a man can access the unconscious part of his psyche. The goal is not only wholeness *per se*, but the ability to respond adequately to the unknown beyond the ego's reach. This explains why Jung understood the anima as a guide to the unconscious.

Such an understanding of the second half of life shows that a man cannot attain wholeness without having experienced both the positive as well as the negative aspects of the feminine. The anima holds the key to the inner world, but this is contingent upon a thorough awareness of her nature. If a man does not realize the ambivalence of this being, she may instinctively transform into any image of the feminine and wound him in his blind spot. But fairy tales also reveal that any such anima

---

153   Jung, *Two Essays*, CW 7, § 353; Jung, *Zwei Schriften* GW 7, § 353.

figure, be it Baba Yaga or the lovely maiden in our tale, will often test the hero before deciding how to react to him; what she tests is his knowledge of the duality of her nature, his respect for her power, and the strength of his ego in standing up to her.

This gives rise to the question about whether such a man would dare acquiesce to the dreadful sexual exploitation of women the world over; whether he would be capable of abusing women either inside or outside the home; whether he would even consider the possibility of paying women less than men for the same kind of work; whether such a man would even imagine not providing girls with an education; in short, whether he would not look upon women as equal partners sharing the same goal of attaining wholeness and being creative, and not only by bearing children.

Because the twin heroes could not consolidate the masculine part of their personality, they remained split, and because they never confronted the negative aspect of the feminine, they could not be whole. As a result, the contents they carried at birth did not make it over the threshold into consciousness. Psychologically, this shows a potential development within the unconscious which consciousness was unable to realize. The principle of Eros as well as the question of feminine equality—both for women as well as the anima—remained *in potentia*; this is a situation which is mostly true today. Most importantly, the reason the tale gives for this state of affairs lies in our inability to recognize the reality of the second half of life.

VI. The Seven Simeons

here once lived an old man, a rich peasant, who had neither son nor daughter. He began to pray that God send him at least one child to delight him in his lifetime and succeed him upon his death. Then it happened that seven sons were born to him in a single day, and they were all called Simeon. God did not grant them to grow up under the care of their parents; the Simeons were orphaned. Well known is the lot of an orphan; though young and ignorant, he will follow every trail, take up any task; so also did the Simeons. At harvest time, people got busy reaping, mowing, bringing grain to the threshing barn, plowing the earth and sowing the seeds. The Simeons thought for while and, although they had little strength, they went with the people to the wide fields and dug there like worms.

One day the tsar came riding by; he was surprised to see little children working beyond their strength. He summoned them and began asking them questions. Finding out that they had neither father nor mother, the tsar said, "I want to be your father; which trade do you wish to learn?" The eldest answered, "I, Your Majesty, will be a smith and will erect a pillar, the likes of which no tale has seen, nor pen described; it will almost reach the sky." "And I," answered the second, "will climb up on that pillar, look around in all directions and tell you what goes on in foreign kingdoms." The tsar praised him. The third answered, "I will be a carpenter and will build a ship." "Great!" the fourth said, "I will steer the ship and be its helmsman." "Good!" the fifth said, "and should this be necessary, I will take the ship by prow and hide it in the bottom of the sea." The sixth said, "And when necessary, I will bring it back from the bottom of the sea." "I can see that all of you want to be useful people! And you," said the tsar to the youngest, "what would you like to learn?" "I, Sire, will be a thief!" "Oh, that's not a very good idea! I don't need any thieves; I will have a thief executed." The tsar said good-bye to the children and rode away. The Simeons began to learn their trades. After a long time they grew up and completed their chosen apprenticeships. The tsar called them to himself to test their skills, to judge their achievements, and to examine their knowledge.

The smith forged such a high pillar that it hurt one's neck to look up at it; it almost reached the sky. The tsar praised him. The second brother ran up to the top, like a squirrel, and looked around in all directions; he saw all the kingdoms beneath him and began to describe what was going on in each of them. "And in such and such a land, in such and such a kingdom, lives Elena the Fair, a tsarevna of unimaginable beauty; red color spreads over her face, white down covers her breast, and one can see the marrow flowing from bone to bone." The tsar liked that best of all. Quickly, the third brother built a ship like a handsome house. The tsar was overjoyed. The fourth brother began to steer the ship; the ship swam on the sea like a live fish. The tsar was very pleased. The ship was sailing at full speed as the fifth brother grabbed it by the prow and brought it down to the bottom of the sea. The sixth brought it up again like little boat, and the ship stood there as if nothing had happened. The tsar liked this trick as well.

But for the youngest brother, the thief, gallows were erected and a noose was prepared. The tsar asked him, "And are you as skilled in your trade as your brothers?" "I am even more skilled than they!" They immediately wanted to hang him, but he cried out, "Wait, Your Majesty, maybe I too can be useful to you. Just order me to steal Elena the Fair for you; only let my brothers accompany me. I will sail with them on the newly built ship and Tsarevna Elena will be yours." The tsar could not get Elena the Fair out of his head; he had heard a lot about her, and his heart longed for her, but she lived far away, beyond thrice-nine lands, in the thrice-tenth kingdom. The tsar thought to himself, "This offer is attractive; to rely on a thief may be risky, but one could give it a try." He let the thief sail with his brothers and loaded the newly built ship with all sorts of riches.

Whether they sailed for a long time or not, they finally came to that kingdom where Elena the Fair lived. A thief doesn't need to be taught what to say or how to go about his business. He informed himself about everything. Learning that there were no cats in this kingdom, he dressed up as a merchant and got himself a cat; stroking and petting her, he led the cat on a golden cord past Elena Tsarevna's window. The tsarevna saw this; she liked the pretty little animal and ordered it to be bought. The thief answered that he was a wealthy merchant from a very rich kingdom, carrying many valuable rarities; he added that he wished to express his goodwill and asked her to accept the little cat as a present. He was invited into the palace, where the cat performed different tricks; the tsarevna admired them.

The thief spoke so much about his extraordinary goods; he spread before her such marvelous cloths, such magnificent finery, that she could not take her eyes off them. "But what else I still have!" he added. "These things I can show to everyone; whoever wants to buy them, can do so. But you, Tsarevna, would you like to see a priceless treasure, a treasure seen by no one? I keep it on my ship under heavy guard; to you alone would I show it. By night it replaces fire; during the day, the sun. It illuminates all darkness with a marvelous light; it is a stone of extraordinary beauty. To show it is impossible, to reveal this treasure is to put myself into great peril, because everyone would want to own it. I paid a dear price for it, but dearer still is the honor I would receive from my tsar for this wondrous gift." The tsarevna promised to come to his ship and to take a look at this treasure.

The next day, accompanied by nurses, governesses and maids-in-waiting, she left the palace and made her way to the ship. Her whole retinue remained on the shore, for only Elena was allowed to view the marvelous light of the incomparable stone. Everything was prepared for her arrival. All seven Simeons were in attendance, and no sooner had as she set foot on the ship, than the fifth brother grabbed the ship's prow and the ship fell to the bottom of the sea. There was a splash, the water swirled, and then the waves rolled on, as if nothing had happened; only on land the nurses and governesses were shouting and crying. The tsar, Elena's father, ordered his men in pursuit of the tsarevna, but they all returned empty-handed. Elena the Fair was already far away on the blue ocean. The sixth brother brought the ship up from the bottom of the sea; the ship sailed like a swan, rolling on the waves, and soon docked at the shore of their native land. The tsar was overjoyed; he had never dreamt of welcoming Elena the Fair in his kingdom. He generously rewarded the Simeons and exempted them from land and head taxes. He married Elena the Fair and a great feast it was for one and all!

I walked a thousand versts (kilometers) to be there. I drank beer and mead; it ran down my mustache and never got into my mouth! They gave me a horse of ice, a saddle of turnips, a bridle of peas; they put a blue caftan on my shoulders, an embroidered cap on my head. I went away from there in all this attire and stopped to rest; I took off the saddle and bridle, tied the horse to a tree, and lay down on the grass. Pigs came running from somewhere and ate the turnip saddle; chickens came and pecked the bridle of peas; the sun rose and melted the horse of ice. Grieved, I continued on foot; a magpie was jumping on the road and calling: "Blue caftan! Blue caftan!" I heard: "Throw the robe!" I took off my caftan and threw it on the road. And do I need the embroidered cap? I grabbed it and threw it on the ground and, as you can see, was left with nothing.

Alexander Afanas'yev, *Russian Folk Tales*, #147, trans. NB.

Interpretation

A childless couple, longing for a child ... this is a widespread motif in fairy tales, signaling the readiness or need to welcome something new into one's life. It is not just anything new, but something that is the product of this particular couple; symbolically, of a man with his anima or a woman with her animus.

In our tale, it is an old peasant who expresses such a wish—surprisingly, a wealthy one. At this time of serfdom in Russia, a wealthy peasant was highly unusual. Even more unusual are the peasant's reasons for wanting a child. Before the days of retirement privileges and old-age pensions, peasants were dependent upon their offspring to help with the hard work on the land and to ease their last days. This is not mentioned as the reason for our peasant's prayer; he expressly asks for a child "to delight him in his lifetime, and to succeed him upon his death."

And then we learn that his wish has been fulfilled many times over and that seven sons are born to him. The birth of seven sons to an elderly couple is again extremely unusual. They are all given the same name of Simeon. St. Simeon, the Stylite, was well known among the common people, where his name was converted to Semën (p. 85). This saint was a peasant's son, born in northern Syria in the fourth century. He left home to become a monk at eighteen and lived a severe, ascetic life, the last forty years of which he spent in a small cell on top of a pillar sixteen meters high. He became well known for his piety, and many sought his prayers and his counsel.

In the Eastern Church, St. Simeon's feast is commemorated on September first; this coincided with the Church New Year until 1699, when Peter the Great moved the New Year's celebration to the beginning of January. Because of this, in folk tradition St. Simeon became a Janus figure (p. 86 FN 65), and received the epithet of "the year's escort" (*Semën letoprovodets*). Even after Peter the Great's calendar reform, the celebration of St. Simeon's day retained many apotropaic rituals that it had in common with the celebration of the New Year. These were directed toward purging the land of evil and safeguarding against the devil, and took the form of plowing around fields and villages, reading of prayers, magic charms, and so on.[154]

These traditions were in large part connected with the gathering of the last harvest and with the beginning of the Indian Summer. In the yearly cycle, this marked the end of the period of growth and a preparation for winter.[155]

The amplifications above shed light upon the tale of "The Seven Simeons." The stage is set for the beginning of autumn, when vegetative growth is grinding to a halt and preparations are being made for the more introverted phase of life. The pillar to which St. Simeon retreats, devoting himself to the spirit, is interesting, for it mirrors the first Simeon's project as a smith.

We note that the peasant's wife, the mother of the seven Simeons, is hardly mentioned in this tale. We can imagine, however, that the birth of seven sons at this late stage in life is biologically highly improbable; it is a sort of biblical miracle comparable to Sarah giving birth to Isaac in Genesis 21. Something happens as the peasant turns to God that enables his wife to conceive, whereas she had not been able to do so earlier. In Jungian terminology, one would say that something quite unusual has become constellated, and that this marks the beginning of our tale. Note the epithet by which this saint was known in folk tradition: "the year's escort" (*Semën letoprovodets*).

If we consider this initial scenario objectively, we see a man approaching the end of his life. He has been successful in fulfilling his role in society, and has even amassed a considerable amount of wealth which he now wants to invest in a new beginning—one that will bring him satisfaction and joy while he lives, and continue to grow and develop upon his death.

As the tale shows, however, it is not the man's material wealth that enables him to fulfill his wish. Symbolically, money can be interpreted as energy; moreover, it is a reality principle. In addition to its outward

---

154   Shangina, *Russkiye traditsionnyye prazdniki*, 196.
155   Shaparova, *Kratkaya Entsyklopediya Slavyanskoy Mifologii*, 492 f.

value, money can be understood as psychic energy, as libido in its original meaning, which is not restricted to sexuality. Money as the reality principle can be understood as the reality of the psyche. "...everything that acts upon me" writes Jung," is real and actual."[156] As noted in Chapter V, in German this is a play on words: *"wirklich ist, was wirkt."* By this Jung meant that the psyche is no less real even though it is not tangible. The peasant's directing his prayer to God is an appeal to the non-rational, to the transcendent, to that which is beyond the power of the ego. The birth of seven Simeons would hence imply that something has become constellated that allows the irrational into life.

The above considerations suggest that this tale is concerned with the second half of life. The requirements of the first half of life have been satisfied and the birth of children which, for some reason, had not taken place earlier is now appearing in the context of the second half of life. This mirrors a very real situation where people who have been deprived of children, or who have consciously decided against having any, experience the need to be creative in an inner way.

Fairy tales present real-life constellations of archetypal content, meaning that such experiences have always been a part of human life and will continue to be so. Most importantly, fairy tales speak from the standpoint of the unconscious; in this way they are similar to dreams. They provide a window through which we can see how this other, unknown part of our psyche views our life. In order to do so, however, we need to change our perspective, for the language of the unconscious is, in large part, symbolic.

The unusual circumstances under which the seven Simeons were born bespeak their special nature. The birth of such children is often miraculous. In some cases they are abandoned or exposed to great danger yet, despite their fragility, are able to overcome obstacles that no normal child could cope with. Such a child can only be understood symbolically. It heralds the emergence of some creative impulse that can survive against all odds. When we are first confronted with such contents, we may be overwhelmed; we are not able to appreciate them because they are new to our experience. Our conscious impulse is to try to explain

---

156   Jung, *Structure and Dynamics*, CW 8, §§ 742, 747 f.

them, to connect them with what is familiar to us; psychologically, this means to bring them into the sphere of the ego's influence.

In "*The Psychology of the Child Archetype*," Jung shows that the core of such an unconscious content is an urge for independence. This is the divine child's distinguishing characteristic, which implies that such a child is not dependent upon any circumstances preceding it, or indeed that nothing *does* precede it. In fairy tales this is often expressed by its being an orphan, for an orphan has no parents and can, metaphorically speaking, be seen as being detached from its origin.[157] The divine child comes from the very depths of nature and, like every living creature, is driven by an irresistible urge to realize itself. In Jungian terminology, it represents the instinct of individuation.[158]

The striving for independence is part of every normal child's development. The way it does this is at times questionable and demands the guidance of an adult, but typically a child will be true to its instinct rather than influenced by expediency, and will not be afraid of making mistakes. In an adult, such spontaneity is often curtailed by the requirements of adaptation to life, or by social demands and the ethical values of the collective. We are indeed often afraid of making a mistake or of doing something that will not be acceptable in the eyes of the world. If, however, we understand the origin of our impulses, we are better prepared to allow them the independence they so badly need, even at the risk of failure. The appearance of the special or divine child in so many tales suggests that this is what the unconscious finds to be sorely lacking in our lives.

Jung saw this mirrored in alchemy. Here, the original substance or *prima materia* with which the alchemist begins his opus, is often referred to as an orphan or the son of a widow. Through endless, painstaking experiments, working very much in the dark and often accompanied by doubt and despair, the alchemist tried to bring his stone to perfection, indeed to turn it into gold.

Returning to the tale, we need to ask why there are seven sons born to the elderly couple when the peasant only asked for one? The hero most

---

157   Jung, *Archetypes*, CW 9i, § 285.
158   Jung, *Archetypes*, CW 9i, § 289.

often appears as a single person, and the twin hero motif symbolizes the approach of an unconscious content and its breaking up into opposites on the threshold of consciousness. In other tales, the hero may be accompanied by brothers, or a heroine by sisters, which refers to unrealized shadow aspects which need to be made conscious and dealt with. In such cases, the goal is to bring all parts of the personality together into a unified whole.

The same holds true for multiple heroes. In *Gegensatz und Erneuerung im Märchen* we find a vivid image for such a situation: the Self, breaking through into consciousness, is likened to a beam of light passing through a prism and becoming a spectrum of colors.[159]

Translated into psychological terms, this means that when the Self—represented here by the divine child—constellates in the psyche, its different aspects may begin to function as independent complexes. If these complexes pool their energies and work harmoniously, they are able to achieve the same effect as a single hero; if they don't, they could be considered as split-off parts of the personality, comparable to the dissociation in schizophrenia. Jung spoke of such fragmentation in normal people as an "...incomplete synthesis of the personality."[160] Here the therapeutic goal would be the same as in the case of the twin phenomenon or of shadow components of the hero, namely to bring together the different parts of the personality under the jurisdiction of the ego.

This is confirmed in the tale at hand, for none of the seven brothers is capable of finding Elena the Fair and bringing her to the tsar's court by his own efforts. In a parallel version, the tsar rejects Simeon, the thief, and gives him three days to leave his kingdom, but his nobles and generals, being more pragmatic and knowing of the tsar's wish to marry Elena the Fair, convince him to keep the thief around "for a while."[161] As it turns out, this brother plays a crucial role in procuring the princess; nevertheless, it is clear that even he would not have succeeded without the others. At the end of the tale, after the brothers have returned with

---

159   von Beit, *Gegensatz und Erneuerung*, 432. This book is presently in translation and will be published under Marie-Louise von Franz's name, probably as *Polarity and Renewal in Fairy Tales*.

160   Jung, *Archetypes*, CW 9i, § 279.

161   Afanas'yev, § 146.

Elena the Fair, the tsar appears to realize this, for he shows no intention of expelling the thief from the kingdom. Nor, however, does he raise the seven Simeons to royal status and designate the thief as his heir. Other versions of the tale have the princess reject the king and choose Simeon, the thief for her husband, but psychologically this is not as convincing as the present version.

But we have still not answered the question of why this tale speaks of seven Simeons and not some other number. What is so special about this number, and what does it add to the interpretation of the tale? Seven was the original measure of time, one that is connected with the moon's cycle. The four phases of the moon break this cycle up into seven-day periods, our weeks. This is a progression easily calculable and more helpful for longer periods of time than the daily rising and setting of the sun. The moon's cycle of twenty-eight days affects both animal and plant life. The human menstrual cycle is of the same length, and the mood swings to which some people are prone during a full moon have given rise to the word *lunatic*.

We remember the myth of the Sumerian goddess, Inanna, who undertakes the descent into the Underworld to visit her sister, Ereshkigal. On her way, she passes through seven gates where she is stripped of all her jewels and clothing, and hence of all her power. She arrives before her sister completely naked and is killed by the glimpse of death in Ereshkigal's eye. Her corpse is nailed to the wall. She is later revived and, as she starts to make her way back to life she is confronted by the seven judges of the Queen, the Anunnaki, who warn her that she cannot leave the Underworld without finding a substitute for herself.[162]

We find the number seven in the biblical account of the creation in which the last day, the day of rest, was—and still is—called the Sabbath by the Jewish people. In memory of the creation, they devote this day to God. Sabbatical breaks retain this connotation of rest from work in many, especially academic, professions. Such breaks, which are often for a year, are usually devoted to *soul work*, such as travel, painting, or fulfilling a dream for which one has never had enough time. The number seven occurs elsewhere in the Bible as well as in other religions

---

162   Eliade, *History of Religious Ideas*, v.1, 65.

and initiatory techniques, where it is always connected with *evolution* or *transition*.

For a long time, until science provided proof to the contrary, there were believed to be seven planets in the sky, seven colors (of the rainbow), and seven metals in the earth. All of these were thought to be related to one another. In classical astrology, the seven planets formed the basic elements of the horoscope, which charts the archetypal components of every personality, helping to foresee one's fate and destiny. The alchemists saw the seven metals as corresponding to the heavenly bodies; these provided the materials they worked with in their attempt to make gold. In the Bible, the seven colors of the rainbow appeared in the sky at the end of the flood and were described as a sign of reconciliation between God and Noah, and as a re-activation of God's covenant with his people.[163] We also have the seven notes of the scale whose eighth note begins another octave on the next level. This is particularly interesting from the point of view of individuation, where the psychic development can be seen as a spiral progression.

The alchemical opus was often described in seven steps. Thanks to Jung's fascination with alchemy, we can now relate this difficult and obscure science to the processes taking place within the human psyche. Jung realized that much of what the alchemists did not understand about matter was filled in by the projection of their own unconscious material. Since the unconscious usually speaks in images, which are symbolic in nature, there is no way of truly appreciating the contribution of alchemy without symbolic thinking. This was the key that opened up alchemy to psychology.

A seminal account of such an alchemical process may be found in *Aurora Consurgens*, the "Rising Dawn," interpreted by Marie-Louise von Franz. The authorship of this text has long been disputed; von Franz attributes it to the notes of a seminar given by St. Thomas Aquinas on the day of his death in the second half of the thirteenth century.[164]

The first five parts of *Aurora Consurgens* are devoted to the image of the *Sapientia Dei*, the Wisdom of God. This feminine aspect of God is de-

---

163   Genesis, 9.8-17.
164   von Franz, *Aurora Consurgens*, 24.

scribed as being contaminated with the impurities of the dark earth, here referring to worldy reality. The alchemist's goal was to liberate her from such impurities and return her to her proper place at the side of God.[165]

The problem with which alchemists in the Middle Ages were concerned is no less relevant in our world today, for it involves not only the position of women in society, but also the anima—man's inner feminine, his soul. In a more general sense, it refers to the Eros principle, to the principle of relatedness. This principle contends that nothing exists by itself, and that everything we say or do is related to, and affects, everything else.

But what is the image of the feminine in *our* tale? The only woman we meet in this kingdom is a mother. We know little about her except that she gives birth to the seven Simeons; shortly thereafter she dies together with her husband. And yet, the seven sons born of this couple provide the impetus for the tale ahead.

When we meet the tsar, we learn that he is not married; he has no tsaritsa, no queen, to reign with. On a physical level, this implies that he will have no children, no heirs to the throne, and no successors to continue his royal blood line. Because he is the dominant of collective consciousness, however, what happens to him affects all his subjects; if he is not fruitful, there will be no fertility in his land. Here we are moving from the objective to the symbolic. The tsar was considered to be a mediator between his people and God; he was responsible to both. Psychologically, he represents an image of the Self and, as such, he must be whole. His unmarried state alerts us to an important flaw in his nature, for the tsaritsa symbolizes his anima.

Such a view of the situation shifts the interpretation of the tale onto a level where both the rational and the irrational play a role. This is the reality of the second half of life. Whereas the peasant couple had done their part in satisfying the biological requirements of life, the further development of the personality is checked because there is no possibility for an inner *coniunctio*.

This is the problem constellated in the tale and the reason for the appearance of the seven Simeons as an incarnation of the Self; these

---

165   von Franz, *Aurora Consurgens*, 242.

seven little children, digging in the fields like worms will rectify the deficiency in the nature of the tsar; in a more general way, they will reintroduce the Eros principle into the collective. By adopting the seven orphans, the tsar raises them to the highest social class; this indicates that the problem concerns all mankind. The problem is universal and, as this tale shows, its solution comes from the common man; on a social level this refers to the lowest class, and on a symbolic level to the archetypal foundation common to all humans.

Before continuing with the tale, let us return for a moment to the text of *Aurora Consurgens*. As mentioned earlier, the first five parts of this manuscript are devoted to the *Sapientia Dei*, the Wisdom of God. After this figure has been introduced in the most glorious terms, the text continues with a description of an alchemical process which is aimed at freeing her from the shackles of the material world, thereby enabling her reunion with the Godhead.[166] This process is presented in the form of seven parables. Contrary to our expectations, the number seven does not refer to the seven steps of the alchemical opus; rather, each parable begins with the initial stage of the *nigredo* and culminates with a vision of the final goal.[167] The emphasis here is on the repetitive nature of the process, the constant working through of the problem from different angles. And yet, we cannot ignore the fact that the number designated for reaching the goal is seven. From a psychological perspective, this stresses that one cannot hope to solve any important problem quickly, but rather that some sort of evolution must take place, allowing one to outgrow the problem even if it proves to be insoluble. This is in keeping with the transformative symbolism of the number seven.[168]

Of particular interest for the tale at hand is the title of the first parable: "...of the Black Earth, wherein the Seven Planets took root."[169] This is an image of the *prima materia*, the substance with which the alchemist begins his work; it is likewise an image of the *nigredo*, the initial trans-

---

166   von Franz, *Aurora Consurgens*, 242.
167   von Franz, *Aurora Consurgens*, 242.
168   von Franz, *Alchemy*, 235; See also Jung, *Structure and Dynamics*, CW 8, § 771.
169   von Franz, *Aurora Consurgens*, 217.

formation of the raw, base, undifferentiated material from which the alchemist hopes to derive gold, a substance of the highest value.

Our tale provides a remarkable parallel to this first parable. We read that, upon losing their parents, the seven Simeons "...went with the people to the wide fields and dug there like worms." Without the care and direction of their parents, the seven orphans have no one to guide them and so, in order to survive, they turn to whatever comes their way.

In neurological terms, a worm is a very simple creature. Psychologically, this refers to life in compartments, with no possibility of synthesis, a preconscious state found in early development or, pathologically, in dissociation.[170] Jung uses the example of termites to illustrate such a psychic state which is completely collective and devoid of any individuality. This applies to all insects but also to those processes in our psyche that are not regulated by consciousness but activated and deactivated by the balancing of the sympathetic and parasympathetic nervous systems (p. 192 FN 130): "... digestion, inner secretions, the functioning of the liver and kidneys..." Jung adds that "...a serious deviation means upsetting the functioning of those nervous systems and we eventually risk a grave disturbance in our glandular organs or in our blood circulation."[171]

Particularly interesting is Jung's association of the sympathetic nervous system with participation mystique, for both are manifestations of the unconscious that can exert their influence without entering consciousness.

Before continuing with the narrative, we must return for a moment to the worm for it is undeniable that despite its biological simplicity the worm performs a very important function: with its excrement, it fertilizes the earth, the *prima materia*. Moreover, by its constant digging, it aerates the earth; symbolically, it introduces spirit into matter.

It just so happens that while this is going on, the tsar passes by. Had the tsar not witnessed this scene, there would have been no tale to tell. But the tsar not only sees the children digging in the earth, he takes a personal interest in the seven Simeons and, finding out that

---

170   Jung, *Dream Analysis*, 234.
171   Jung, *Zarathustra 1*, 749.

they have neither mother nor father, he decides there and then to adopt them. If the tsar had merely felt compassion for the children, he could very easily have provided them with some sort of financial support; but he does more than that—he gives them an opportunity to develop their potential, and the freedom to choose what they want to do in life. He doesn't impose his will upon them but gives them the independence to unfold in the way of their choice. His only requirement is that they make a decision; in doing so, he channels their energy and provides them with the structure and order necessary for any undertaking. These are truly the marks of a good father.

In Russia, the peasantry referred endearingly to the tsar as "father tsar" (*tsar batyushka*). This may be explained by their admiration of the monarch, and by their hope of being protected and taken care of by such a powerful figure. In this tale we witness a significant similarity between the father and the tsar. Both are interested in children without any material advantage to themselves. The father wants a child to delight in and to succeed him after death; the tsar acts out of compassion for the seven brothers. We can say that both are motivated by Eros, and that both make a significant contribution to the development of the story. Had the father not wished for a child, the seven Simeons might not have been born; had the tsar not decided to adopt them, he would not have married Elena the Fair at the end of the tale. Each of these two fathers played a part in this process. As we know from such mythical figures as Cronos and Uranus, or such fairy tales as Grimm's "The Devil and the Three Golden Hairs," this is not always the case. The positive attitude of both fathers suggests that some new spiritual development is being ushered in by the Self, and that there is a readiness to accept it at both the lowest as well as the highest level of society and, psychologically, of the personality.

The orphaned children are now connected to a new parent, and not just any parent, but the tsar himself. They have been raised to a higher social level and are now in a position to contribute to the collective development of the land. This is similar to giving children godparents. The essence of baptism is initiation, the only one remaining in our culture today. It is important to note that Jung considered the process of individuation, the confrontation with the unconscious, as modern man's version of initiation.[172]

In answer to the tsar's stipulation, the seven brothers now have to decide upon a trade. The first Simeon chooses to become a smith. This is a civilizing profession; it raises man out of the purely biological existence which he shares with all animals. Through his superior intelligence, man is able to exert his will over matter. It is for this reason that the smith was traditionally connected with medicine men and shamans, but also with sorcerers and even the devil. The ambivalence of this image speaks for its archetypal nature.

In this case, power refers to the potential effects of fire, for this is how the smith can change the shape of metal and transform it either into useful tools or destructive weapons. According to Greek mythology, the gods themselves were ambivalent about allowing mortals the use of fire, and we know that Prometheus had to suffer eternal agony for making this possible.

Fire in the symbolic sense refers to emotion or passion, and this is likewise necessary for shaping and transforming the personality. As Jung writes, "...emotion is the chief source of consciousness. There is no change from darkness to light or from inertia to movement without emotion."[173]

In Russian folklore and elsewhere, the smith was considered the patron of marriages; he was believed to weld two people and two fates together as he welds together two pieces of metal. This image often appears in wedding songs.

In alchemy, the *prima materia*, the original substance, is subjected to fire for the purpose of burning off all impurities. The same is true in the figurative sense, for the fire of passion enables us, or even forces us, to change our ways as we would never have done of our own accord. Fire not only produces heat but also light, and it is this light which brings consciousness into the experience we have suffered through.

Among all the inhabitants of the earth, humankind alone has always tried to rise above the purely instinctual demands of life. Science attempts to broaden our knowledge of the universe, while all initiation rites and

---

172   von Beit, *Symbolik des Märchens*, 454.
173   Jung, *Archetypes*, CW 9i, § 179.

religions strive toward a higher level of consciousness. Jung introduced the term *individuation* to denote this instinctual urge for inner development.

The alchemists applied all the knowledge at their command to extract the essence of each substance they worked with, to find the gold, so to speak, even in a heap of manure. This made a strong impression upon Jung, for he saw this in analogy to his work on the psyche.

The sky, the domain chosen by the first two brothers, has always been associated with spirit. The smith promises the tsar to forge a pillar reaching the sky. These two symbols—fire and sky—speak for a fiery spirit. We connect it with charismatic persons, with the wonder of Whitsun. It is highly energetic; it sets things into motion and exerts tremendous influence upon others. In alchemy this is referred to as the *rubedo*. Such energy is as vital for the beginning of the alchemical opus as it is for analysis. It provides the impetus for burning off superfluous material, or psychologically for confronting one's shadow; it results in a different orientation in life, which includes both the physical and the spiritual.

A few words about the pillar which the first Simeon intends to build. A pillar, especially one which will reach the sky, symbolizes the world axis in shamanism. It enables an initiated shaman to access all three cosmic regions; psychologically, this includes the unconscious.[174] The shaman's main purpose in undertaking such a voyage is that of finding, capturing, and bringing back a lost soul.[175] This is of particular interest for the tale at hand.

The first Simeon learns the trade of the smith and will make the pillar for climbing up to the sky, whereas the second Simeon learns how to make practical use of this construction. His task will consist of climbing it, looking around in all directions and informing the tsar of what is going on in foreign lands and kingdoms. These first two trades will serve to broaden the tsar's perspective; they will provide the overview and orientation for the work ahead.

This is exactly what happens in our tale. As the second Simeon climbs the pillar and surveys the surrounding lands, he spots the kingdom of Elena the Fair. Reporting back to the tsar, he says "... in such and

---

174   Eliade, *Shamanism*, 259-266.
175   Eliade, *Shamanism*, 215.

such a land, in such and such a kingdom..." In a later episode, we read that Elena "...lived far away, beyond the thrice ninth land, in the thrice tenth kingdom." Both of these expressions stand for the distant beyond, or psychologically for the unconscious.

There, in this land, the second Simeon espies a woman of such beauty as has never before been seen. His description of this lady's beauty is not necessarily what we may expect, but it convinces us of her extraordinary nature: "...red color spreads on her face, white down covers her breast, and one can see the marrow flowing from bone to bone."

Because these attributes are somewhat unusual, let us consider them more closely. Red is the color of blood, and is hence often seen as the essence of life and of the soul. For example, the latter is the reason for bleeding an animal before eating it, as in the preparation of kosher or halal meat. Red is also the color of fire, with all of its positive and negative implications: heat, passion, aggression, and so on.

In Old Russian, the word for *red* meant *beautiful*. Thus, for example, the expression *a red maiden* referred to a beautiful maiden, the corner of a house where the family's icons were placed was called the *red corner*, and the *red* in *Red Square* emphasizes its importance but, above that, its beauty. In these examples, which could be further elaborated, we find the essence of red in its connection to life, to the soul, and hence to the divine, to creativity and love in all its manifestations, but also to destruction.

The description of Elena the Fair continues with the following words: "white down covers her breast." This places her in the realm of birds and reveals her spiritual nature. But why is the white color emphasized? Why is this down not some other color or, for that matter, no specific color?

White light contains the full spectrum of visible light, which can be separated into different colors. For this reason it is commonly held to contain all colors and to be whole; it is therefore often ascribed to the deity, to virginity and purity, to transfiguration and enlightenment. Psychologically, it refers to the Self in its totality. It is connected with initiation because this has to do with transformation and development onto a higher level. White also carries apotropaic symbolism. The white dress of a bride includes three of these amplifications; it stands for purity, for initiation into another phase of life, and as protection against evil

Black, red and white are the basic colors of the alchemical *opus*, the equivalent of which Jung saw in the process of individuation. Our journey had begun with the seven Simeons digging in the fertile earth—a suitable image for the black *nigredo* stage. We then encounter red in the symbolism of the smith's fire as the *rubedo*, and now in the beautiful red color of Elena's face. Finally, we are told of the white down of her breast, which discloses her spiritual nature.

The final description of Elena is the most unusual one. Here, the second Simeon recounts that he can see the marrow flowing from bone to bone. This image describes her body as being translucent and leaves no doubt as to her spiritual nature.[176] It is reminiscent of Peter Birkhäuser's painting of "The Flame Dancer," an anima figure, holding the divine fire in her hand.

The emphasis on bones is particularly interesting. As Mircea Eliade writes in his book *Shamanism*, bones were considered "the final source of life" because the soul was believed to reside in them. This view stems from the fact that bones are the longest surviving parts of both animals and humans after death. It explains the shamanic practice of collecting the bones of all animals killed, taking care not to break any of them, and burying them in the prescribed manner so that the animals can be reborn from them.[177]

In the Bible, we have an impressive image of such resurrection. The Lord instructs the Prophet, Ezekiel, to preach to the bones of all the dead of the house of Israel:

> *Prophesy to these bones, and say to them, O dry bones, hear the word of the Lord. Thus says the Lord God to these bones: Behold...I will lay sinews upon you, and will cause flesh to come upon you, and cover you with skin, and put breath into you, and you shall live; And you shall know that I am the Lord.*[178]

Because of the Russian origin of this tale, it is interesting to note that the full text of this passage is always read at the Good Friday service in the Orthodox Church.

---

176   von Beit, *Symbolik des Märchens*, 432.
177   von Beit, *Symbolik des Märchens*, 159 f.
178   Ezekiel: 37, 4-6.

The three attributes ascribed to Elena the Fair make it clear that the second Simeon is describing no flesh and blood woman, but an anima figure. At first the images appear somewhat strange, but this is because we are seeing them in a literal sense. As soon as we consider them symbolically, we cannot help but experience their numinosity; our story has now made a shift onto another plane. This is the first time the tsar hears of Elena the Fair, but he is instantly fascinated by her. Such an experience of the anima often heralds a fateful turn in a man's life.[179]

The anticipation of the anima signals a shift in the psychic constellation of the tale, for she is the one who inspires and animates a man and builds a bridge to the unconscious.[180] At this point she is still *on the other side* but, upon hearing of her, the tsar is motivated and filled with longing. Hence he supports the Simeons' plan to find Elena the Fair and bring her back; against his better judgement he allows the thief to participate in this endeavor.

The tale now has a goal, and all the trades chosen by the remaining brothers will serve the purpose of securing Elena the Fair for the tsar. No tsaritsa was mentioned at the start of the tale, and we took this to mean that the tsar was not married. Nonetheless, it could very well be that a tsaritsa existed, but was of no importance to the story. What is becoming constellated in the tsar's psyche is the inner feminine, and this is what will now be spearheading the story.

We note that the next four Simeons are all applying their expertise in a new dimension, in that of water. Water is another important symbol of the unconscious; in contrast to the sky which symbolizes spirit, the primary significance if water lies in its being the source of all life, and hence connected with the mother archetype. Like every archetype it is ambivalent, and its positive motherly quality is balanced by a death aspect, for a human being cannot survive too long in its depths. The very first concern before venturing into water must therefore be to provide for one's safety, and to guarantee one's return.

The third Simeon's choice of profession is exactly what is needed at this juncture; he becomes a ship builder. A ship is a vessel and, as such,

---

179   von Beit, *Symbolik des Märchens*, 272.
180   Jung, *Alchemical Studies*, CW 13, § 62.

a feminine symbol. In contrast to the feminine nature of the sea, however, a ship is a human construction, a creation of the human spirit. It allows people to cover large distances over water and keeps them from drowning or, psychologically, from being overwhelmed by the unconscious. Symbolically, a ship can stand for any teaching, any tradition, any myth that provides structure in life and prevents us from losing our foothold in reality when confronted with unconscious contents.[181]

However, it is one thing to build a ship but quite another to steer it and bring it to its destination. This requires knowledge of the sea and its dangers, good orientation, focus on the goal at all times, and the ability to navigate the ship toward it. As in the case of the second Simeon who climbed the pillar built by the first brother, the fourth Simeon's task will be a practical application of the foregoing one. If we see the ship as a teaching or tradition which gives structure, then sailing the ship would imply the ability to apply this theoretical knowledge to practical life. This can be compared with the double approach in the alchemical *opus*: *orare*—prayer as a form of meditation, and *laborare*—physical work which moved the experiment forward.

The professions of the next two Simeons bring differentiation into movement over water. As shown earlier, the whole purpose of the ship is to allow people to travel over water without drowning. At times, however, it may become necessary to descend into the depths of the sea. The implication in such a descent is that it is not drowning, but a deliberate, conscious descent into the depths. In our tale this takes place when the seven Simeons are on their return trip, carrying Elena the Fair with them and escaping from her father. Had the king caught up with them, they would have been no match for his superior forces.

This can be likened to being in a difficult and dangerous situation with no way out. In such a case one would be wise to listen to the unconscious, for example, to watch one's dreams, consult the I Ching, or do active imagination. All such means of acquiring information from the unconscious would include the ego; moreover, any decision made on the basis of such information would be the ego's responsibility; instead of *drowning*, this would be better illustrated by *diving*.

---

181   von Franz, *The Cat*, 134.

But diving would necessitate a return to the surface. The motif is well illustrated in fairy tales where the hero goes in search of his beloved and finds himself in a glorious kingdom at the bottom of the sea. Sometimes he is invited to stay there for a certain length of time; at other times he is obliged to do so. If he leaves at the right moment, he may be able to bring the wisdom he acquired in the sea realm into life, whereas staying too long would result in his losing all contact with outer reality and living his life in fantasy.

Through the efforts and expertise of these six brothers, the ship has successfully reached its destination. And now the youngest of the brothers, the one who had learned the trade of the thief, is taking the stage.

It often happens that the hero in fairy tales is unappreciated or even scorned. In "The Speedy Messenger," both the hero's father and the tsar tell him that he is too young and foolish to be entering the tsar's service, but he manages to stand up for himself, and in the end do what no other can. In our tale, it is the seventh Simeon's wish to become a thief that makes him so undesirable in the tsar's eyes. Usually such a negative judgement of a hero is due to the incompatibility of collective expectations with new impulses arising from the unconscious. Because the hero represents that part of the ego which is in tune with the Self, he instinctively lives out such compensation.

The hero in this tale is condemned most vehemently by the tsar; the gallows are already up to hang him. Then, at the very last moment, the thief comes up with a proposition which causes the tsar to reconsider: Simeon offers to steal Elena the Fair for him.

We may interpret this as a shadow reaction; whereas before the tsar was concerned with upholding collective values, now, when it touches upon his own personal interests, he is willing to look the other way and take a chance on the thief proving useful to him.

If, however, we accept that a shift into the second half of life has taken place within the tsar's psyche, then we must revise our judgement, for in this phase it is perfectly legitimate for the tsar's libido to flow toward the anima. As a matter of fact, such a shift of values is not only legitimate but imperative.

We now follow the seventh Simeon, and see how he will go about securing Elena the Fair. We read that he informed himself about everything in this kingdom and discovered, among other things, that cats were unknown there.

The cat is a most independent creature, very sensual, and expert at expressing its needs. It comes when it wills, allows itself to be petted when it wills, and showers its attention onto the humans with whom it shares *its* house, but again, only when *it* wills. Since the cat, as any other animal, symbolizes instinct, we might ask what instinctive reactions it is compensating in Elena the Fair.

The amplification of Elena's attributes presented a one-sidedly positive, predominantly spiritual, image. When the anima appears in such a light, we can be sure that another, less positive and less spiritual, side of her is lurking somewhere close by. In many tales it is the demonic father who holds the anima in his power and prevents her from interacting with the outer world.[182] We will have the opportunity of meeting such a demonic father image in the tale of "Mar'ya Morevna" which follows. In the present tale, the image of Elena's father is a much more *civilized* version of this archetype, but nonetheless he is the one who tries to prevent his daughter from leaving his kingdom; she must be stolen and carried away by trickery, and it takes the unconventional ways of a thief to accomplish this.

Earlier we spoke of the alchemists' focus on liberating the feminine aspect of God from the impurities of the earth and restoring her to the side of the masculine. In our tale, the very opposite appears to be called for; here she must be freed from the distant world of her father and brought closer to everyday reality so that the tsar can unite with her as his anima.

The tale at hand does justice to both images. That part of the feminine which is contaminated with the impurities of the earth is the fertile peasant mother who bears the seven Semëns. This is, moreover, not restricted to a female being, for we recognize her in the peasant's wish for a child to rejoice in without the expectation of any personal advantage. We also see her in the tsar's concern for the seven little children as they toil in the fields, and even more so in his adopting them as his own and furthering their development. Both are examples of the maternal

---

182   von Beit, *Symbolik des Märchens*, 455 f.

structural form in a man's psyche.[183] Coming from the lowest and highest level of society, this demonstrates the widespread significance of the mother archetype in the collective over which the tsar reigns.

With the transition into the second half of life, the nature of a man's relationship to the feminine shifts from the woman who gave birth to him to the one with whom he, psychologically speaking, can give birth, that is, be fruitful, creative. What was long true in an outer sense now gains importance as an inner phenomenon.

The second half of life ushers in a flow of psychic energy toward this inner world. A man's relationship to his mother now shifts to his anima. This does not imply that the former relationship can no longer be meaningful, but his psychological development must now include the reality of both worlds.

As already noted, we saw the tsar in this tale as being unmarried, but he may very well have been married to a woman who satisfied the preferred feminine model of the collective. However, this no longer resonated with the inner image of the feminine in his psyche. From his emotional reaction to Elena the Fair, we can say that it is she who now pulls at his heart strings.

Not every man follows the call of the anima. In a world where so much is measured by outer standards, it is difficult to believe in anything that is not tangible. And yet such intangible experiences are part of every initiation, of every human development which goes beyond the instinctual. This is perhaps the reason why Elena the Fair appears in such strong contrast to the peasant mother. We might even speak of a split in the tsar's anima because there is no possibility for a direct transition from one experience of the feminine to the other.

This is the split which the seven Simeons set out to heal. They come from the world of the mother and have now successfully reached the kingdom of Elena the Fair. There is one small but intriguing detail that now comes to light. In this tale, the ruler of the original kingdom is always referred to as the tsar, whereas Elena the Fair's father is called the king. What might this imply? From the perspective of a Russian tale,

---

183   This illustrates one of the four structural forms of the psyche developed by Toni Wolff.

the tsar belongs to the collective since *tsar* would be the appropriate designation for the ruler of the land. Everything outside this collective is then the *other* and is designated by another name. Here king would imply not only another nationality, but also the other part of the psyche, the unconscious.

We return to our story as the seventh Simeon disembarks from his ship and gets his bearings in this new land. We note that he avoids contact with the king, but goes directly to where Elena lives. He parades the small kitten past Elena's window on a golden cord. Gold has always stood for the highest value and was a mark of royalty and of the well-to-do.

But a cord also connects. Initially, it connects the kitten with Simeon, but because Elena finds such pleasure in the kitten, Simeon is soon invited into Elena's chambers and a connection is made between them. Simeon impresses Elena with the kitten's stunts and finally presents it to her as a gift. This is very much a cat-and-mouse trick, one which any cat would understand, but since there are no cats in this kingdom, it falls right into Elena's shadow. Simeon acts instinctively; his actions are not based on collective principles of right or wrong, but on what is possible and, indeed, necessary, for the achievement of his goal.

The thief introduces himself as a wealthy merchant, and further captures Elena's interest by showing her some of his extraordinary goods. He "...spread before her such marvelous cloths, such magnificent finery, that she could not take her eyes away from them." Indeed, the thief is playing his cards most skillfully.

Finally, he tells her of the stone in his possession; a "priceless treasure," he calls it, one which "replaces fire by night and the sun by day, and illuminates every dark spot with a marvelous light." He tells her that she is the only person to whom he will show this treasure, that he dare not publically display it, for everyone would want to possess it.

We, too, are becoming fascinated by this "priceless treasure," for we recognize it as an image of the famous alchemical stone, also known as the philosopher's stone, the *lapis philosophorum*. It represents the goal of the alchemical opus, the result of the transformation of the *prima materia* through fire and water.

In psychological language, this stone represents the Self, a symbol for the bringing together of the extreme opposites. Its inherent structure permeates the whole universe; it is the very essence of life, one which cannot be shaken or undermined; it represents the eternal in us.[184] After exalting this priceless treasure, the wealthy merchant invites Elena to visit his ship and view it with her own eyes. Elena arrives with all her "nurses, governesses, and maidens-in-waiting," but they must stay on land; only Elena is allowed on board. All seven Simeons are there to receive her. No sooner has she boarded than the fifth Simeon takes the ship by the prow and brings it down to the bottom of the sea.

Let us now consider the psychological implications of this development. The motif of tempting the anima with precious objects is a frequent one in fairy tales, for example, in the Grimm tale of "Faithful John" and in "The Enchanted Ring" of Chapter IV here.

Outwardly judged, the hero's pragmatic deception is unworthy of the anima. If, however, we shift the emphasis from conscious trickery to a sign of his appreciation for the anima's extraordinary status, a different aspect of this motif reveals itself. By presenting the anima with such magnificent gifts, the hero is acknowledging her significance. Her admiration for what he lays before her confirms that he has chosen correctly and recognized her *taste*. In this sense, he is not merely tricking her but also letting her know that he understands what sort of being she is, for we must not forget that, as an archetype, the anima is a goddess.

Interpreting "Faithful John" in *Individuation in Fairy Tales*, von Franz suggests seeing such a tempting of the anima as a way of constellating the unconscious in active imagination.[185] By offering the anima such alluring fantasy images, one hopes to attract her attention and motivate her to enter into dialogue with the ego.

The seventh Simeon appears to have succeeded in winning Elena's trust, for she agrees to board his ship without her attendants. Later, after the ship has set sail, we hear of no displeasure or resistance at being abducted from her father's kingdom. Can we attribute this to the little

---

184   von Franz, *Archetypal Dimensions*, 335 f.
185   von Franz, *Archetypal Dimensions*, 172.

kitten on the golden cord? Has the anima been liberated from the con-
trolling spirit of the demon father? Is she now free to decide what *she*
wants? And could she be interested in getting to know this far-off tsar
for whom the wealthy merchant has procured this very special stone?

Judging from her reaction, or lack thereof, she appears to have
accepted her new role as a bride on her way to the bridegroom. After
the sixth Simeon brings the ship back to the surface, we read that it
sails like a swan, rolling on the waves. We remember the white down on
Elena's breast, which now receives an additional amplification, for it is
known of swans that they mate for life. Psychologically, we can say that
the anima has taken her proper place as a bridge between the conscious
and unconscious realm.

All this has been accomplished singlehandedly by the seventh Simeon.
Without awakening Elena's suspicions, he has won her trust and goodwill through the gift of the kitten and by allowing her to feast her
eyes on his extraordinary goods. By introducing himself as a wealthy
merchant from the wealthiest of kingdoms, he impresses her with his
credentials and further narrows the gap between them. He takes her
into his confidence by sharing his secret of the extraordinary stone,
and adds that he wouldn't show it to anyone but her. How can she
resist, especially since he asks nothing in return?

It is, of course, a ruse, but one which is carried out with amazing
skill, fine diplomacy and psychological instinct. He achieves his goal
without confrontation, and apparently to the mutual advantage of both
parties. Such were the typical characteristics of the Greek Hermes and
the Roman Mercury. Homer brilliantly captures the nature of this god
in his description of Hermes' first day of life in "Hymnus in Mercurium,"
an excellent shortened version of which can be found in Kerényi's book,
The Gods of the Greeks.[186]

For the alchemists, Mercury was the alpha and omega of the *opus*;
he was the *prima materia* as well as the final product, the *lapis*, the philosophers' stone, the gold.[187] At the beginning of our tale, we pointed
to the image of the seven Simeons digging in the earth like worms, and

---

186   Kerényi, *The Gods of the Greeks*, 162-170.
187   Jung, *Alchemical Studies*, CW 13, § 282 f.

equated it with the *prima materia* or *nigredo*; at the end, it was the promise to see that very special stone that persuaded the tsarevna to come aboard their ship.

Another important characteristic of Mercury was his extreme ambivalence. As a planet, Mercury is closest to the sun, and hence, in the alchemist's mind, connected to gold; as a metal, however, it was equated to the moon because of its silver color. But more than just the polarity of sun and moon, Mercury's ambivalence as quicksilver was seen in its capacity to dissolve that very same gold which represented the alchemists' aspired goal.

Mercury was called a hermaphrodite because he contained all possible polarities. He was the alchemists' friend and adviser and a helpful spirit in their work, but he was also a trickster, often deceptive and insidious. Evasive, like quicksilver, he could never be caught or pinned down. For this reason the alchemists also spoke of him as *cervus fugitivus*, the fleeting stag.[188]

In mythology, Mercury / Hermes was the messenger of the gods, and therefore free to cross all borders, even those between the living and the dead; psychologically, this means between the conscious and unconscious parts of the psyche. Note that it was only the seventh Simeon who set foot in Elena's kingdom; the other six brothers remained on board. It will be remembered that shamans were also capable of accessing cosmic regions, and that the main purpose for doing so was to find, capture and bring back lost souls.

As far as ethics are concerned, Jung saw Mercury as amoral. He further explained that Mercury could best be understood as a process beginning with evil and ending with the good.[189]

On the first day of his life: Mercury stole Apollo's sacred cows, but when confronted he blatantly denied doing this before both Apollo and Zeus; he also tried to cover up his footprints by putting his sandals on backward. Subsequently we learn, however, that he did this in order to ingratiate himself before the Olympians; he burned the cows and their scent rose up to the gods as a sacrificial offering. This resulted in Mercury and his mother being accepted into their midst.

---

188   Jung, *Psychology and Alchemy*, CW 12, § 84.
189   Jung, *Alchemical Studies*, CW 13, § 276.

Similarly, in his role as wealthy merchant, the hero lured Elena onto his ship to view the miraculous stone, and later kidnapped her. Without this deception, Elena would never have married the tsar and the royal *coniunctio* would never have taken place. In order to accomplish this, the thief in our tale needed to free Elena from the backward pull of the unconscious, personified by the *demonic* father. There appears to have been some sort of *participation mystique* between father and daughter, and this could not have been broken with rational arguments.

This exemplifies a morality which at times deviates from that of collective Christianity. Our tale speaks of a tsar who is reigning without a feminine counterpart, or psychologically, without his soul. Because the tsar represents the dominant of collective consciousness, this deficiency affects his whole land. An old peasant, a common man but in this case a wealthy one, who has a wife, that is, who is still connected to the feminine, prays to God for a child. Together with his wife, the two produce the seven Simeons who provide the solution to the problem constellated in this kingdom. From the amplification, we see that this takes on the form of an alchemical opus and that the hero, the seventh Simeon, turns out to be Mercury—a pagan god and a master thief.

Jung's intense preoccupation with alchemy made him realize that this *science* had retained everything that had, over time, been eliminated from the Christian teaching to make Christianity lighter, clearer, more comprehensible. Alchemy, with its chaos and complexity, was mostly misunderstood and unappreciated, even though it provided a more complete image of the psyche.[190]

This led Jung to understand the alchemical Mercury as an archetypal image of the collective unconscious, and the alchemical opus as a projection of the process of individuation.[191] As our tale shows, when collective consciousness proves incapable of providing an adequate solution to any given problem, the collective unconscious breaks through, bringing up contents foreign to our values and understanding of reality. This explains why so much of what the seventh Simeon does or says seems wrong, strange, incomprehensible, immoral.

---

190   Jung, *Alchemical Studies*, CW 13, § 289.
191   Jung, *Alchemical Studies*, CW 13, § 277.

In closing, I would like to refer to one small detail, which may have gone unnoticed by the reader, namely, that after the ship sets out on its return voyage, the stone is never mentioned again. We remember Simeon saying to Elena, "I paid a dear price for it, but dearer still is the honor I will receive from my tsar for this wondrous gift." Judging from the importance that Simeon ascribes to it, we could have expected the stone to be presented to the tsar with great ceremony, but this does not happen.

The Self, in the form of the stone, enters this tale at a critical moment. Had it not been for the stone, Elena would never have come aboard the ship. But why does it disappear from the story after the ship sets sail? May it be that its purpose has been fulfilled? If that is the case, we must assume that the return of the anima to the conscious world, bringing about wholeness in the reigning principle of the land, was willed by the Self.

Another possibility for explaining Elena's shift in allegiance from her father to the seventh Simeon lies in her realizing the true nature of the wealthy merchant as soon as he begins to speak of the precious stone. This allows her to escape the bond with the demon father and to put herself willingly into the service of the Self.

"I walked a thousand versts (kilometers) only to be there. I drank beer and mead; it ran down my mustache but did not get into my mouth..." is a typical ending to a Russian fairy tale. It is comic relief, meant to bring the listener back to everyday reality, and therefore requires no interpretation. Here it is pure gibberish, partly a play on words which becomes even less understandable in translation. One small example of this is the speaker's using the feminine form throughout and relating how the beer and mead flowed down her [sic] mustache.

VII. Mar'ya Morevna

In a certain kingdom in a certain land lived Ivan Tsarevich (Prince Ivan); he had three sisters—Mar'ya Tsarevna (Princess Maria), Ol'ga Tsarevna (Princess Olga), and Anna Tsarevna (Princess Anna). Their father and mother died, leaving these parting words to their son: "Give your sisters to the first who woos them; do not keep them long with you." The tsarevich buried his parents, and in his sorrow went to walk with his sisters in the green garden. Suddenly a black cloud covered the sky and a terrible storm gathered. "Let us go home, sisters," said Ivan Tsarevich. No sooner had they entered the castle than they heard thunder, the ceiling was cut in twain, and a bright falcon flew into the room; he struck the floor, turned into a brave youth, and said, "Hail, Ivan Tsarevich! Formerly I came as a guest, now I come as a suitor; I want to woo your sister, Mar'ya Tsarevna." "If my sister finds you to her liking, I will not stand in her way; let her go with God." Mar'ya Tsarevna consented, and the falcon married her and carried her off to his kingdom.

Days followed days, hours followed hours; a whole year went by unnoticed. Ivan Tsarevich went walking in the green garden with his two sisters. Again, a great cloud darkened the sky, bringing a storm, wind and lightning. "Let us go home, sisters," said the tsarevich. No sooner had they entered the castle than they heard thunder, the ceiling was cut in twain, and an eagle flew in; he struck the floor and turned into a brave youth. "Hail, Ivan Tsarevich! Formerly I came as a guest, now I come as a suitor." And he wooed Princess Ol'ga. Ivan Tsarevich said: "If Ol'ga finds you to her liking, let her marry you; I do not oppose her will." Olga Tsarevna consented and married the eagle; he lifted her up and carried her off to his kingdom.

Another year went by. Ivan Tsarevich said to his youngest sister, "Let us go walking in the green garden." They walked a while; again a cloud darkened the sky, bringing thunder and lightning. "Let us return home, sister." They returned home and, before they had time to sit down, they heard thunder, the ceiling was cut in twain, and a raven flew in; he struck the floor and turned into a brave youth. The other two were handsome, but he was handsomer. "Well, Ivan Tsarevich, formerly I came as a guest, now I come as a suitor; give me Anna Tsarevna in marriage." "I will not oppose her will; if she finds you to her liking, let her marry you." Anna Tsarevna married the raven, and he carried her off to his kingdom.

Ivan Tsarevich was left alone. For a whole year he lived without his sisters, and he became lonely. "I will go and look for my sisters," he said. He made ready; he walked and walked, and he came upon a mighty army lying slain on the field. Ivan Tsarevich asked, "If any man is alive here, let him speak; who slew this great army?" One man answered him, "This whole great army was defeated by Mar'ya Morevna, the beautiful princess." Ivan Tsarevich continued on his way; he came upon white tents, and Mar'ya Morevna, the beautiful princess, came out to meet him. "Hail, tsarevich, whither is God taking you, and is it of your own will or by compulsion?" Ivan Tsarevich answered her, "Brave youths do not travel by compulsion." "Well, if you are not in a hurry, rest for a while in my tent." This pleased Ivan Tsarevich and he spent two nights in her tent. Mar'ya Morevna found Ivan Tsarevich to her liking, and he married her.

Mar'ya Morevna, the beautiful princess, brought Ivan Tsarevich to her kingdom; they lived together for some time, then the princess decided to make ready for war. She left Ivan Tsarevich in charge. "Go everywhere and oversee everything, but never look into this closet." Ivan Tsarevich could not restrain himself; as soon as Maria Morevna had gone, he rushed to the closet, opened the door and looked inside. There he saw Koshchey the Deathless hanging, held fast by twelve chains. Koshchey implored Ivan Tsarevich, "Take pity on me, give me to drink! For ten years I have suffered without food or drink; my throat is all parched." The tsarevich gave him a whole pail of water; he drank it and asked for more. "One pail will not quench my thirst, give me another!" The tsarevich gave him another pail; Koshchey drank it and asked for a third. After he had drunk his third pail he recovered his former strength, shook his chains, and broke all twelve of them at once. "Thanks, Ivan Tsarevich! Never again will you see Mar'ya Morevna, as you will never see your own ears." He flew out of the window in a terrible whirlwind, caught up with Mar'ya Morevna, the beautiful princess, seized her, and carried her off. Ivan Tsarevich wept bitterly, then he made ready and set out on his way. "Whatever happens," he said, "I must find Mar'ya Morevna."

He walked one day, then another and, as the third day dawned, he saw a marvelous castle; near the castle stood an oak, and on the oak sat the bright falcon. The falcon flew down from the oak, struck the ground, turned into a brave youth, and exclaimed, "Oh, my dear brother-in-law! How does the Lord favor you?" Mar'ya Tsarevna ran out, greeted Ivan Tsarevich with joy, inquired about his health, and told him about her life. The tsarevich stayed with them for three days and said, "I cannot stay longer with you for I am searching for my wife, Mar'ya Morevna, the beautiful princess." "It will be hard for you to find her," said the falcon. "In any case, leave us your silver spoon; we shall look at it and think of you." Ivan Tsarevich left his silver spoon with the falcon and went on his way.

He walked one day, then another, and as the third day dawned he saw a castle more magnificent than the first; near the castle stood an oak, and on the oak sat an eagle. The eagle flew down from the tree, struck the ground, turned into a brave youth, and called out, "Arise, Ol'ga Tsarevna, our dear brother is coming!" Ol'ga Tsarevna immediately ran out to greet Ivan Tsarevich; she embraced and kissed him, inquired about his health, and told him about her life. Ivan Tsarevich stayed with them for three days, and said, "I can no longer stay with you for I am searching for my wife, Mar'ya Morevna, the beautiful princess." The eagle said, "It will be hard for you to find her. In any case, leave us your silver fork; we shall look at it and remember you." Ivan Tsarevich left his silver fork and went on his way.

He walked one day, then another, and as the third day dawned he saw a castle more magnificent than the first two; near the castle stood an oak, and on the oak sat a raven. The raven flew down from the oak, struck the ground, turned into a brave youth, and called out, "Anna Tsarevna, come out quickly, our brother is coming!" Anna Tsarevna ran out, greeted him with joy, embraced and kissed him, inquired about his health, and told him about her life. Ivan Tsarevich stayed with them for three days and said, "Farewell! I must go now to search for my wife, Mar'ya Morevna, the beautiful princess." The raven said, "It will be hard for you to find her. In any case, leave us your silver snuffbox; we shall look at it and think of you." The tsarevich gave them his silver snuffbox, said farewell, and went on his way.

He walked one day, he walked another, and on the third day he came to Mar'ya Morevna. When she saw her beloved, she threw her arms around him, cried bitterly, and said, "Ach, Ivan Tsarevich! Why did you disobey me, why did you look into the closet and release Koshchey the Deathless?" "Forgive me, Mar'ya Morevna! Do not recall the past. Instead, come with me while Koshchey the Deathless is away; perhaps he will not catch up with us." They made ready and left. Koshchey had been out hunting; at nightfall as he was returning home his good steed stumbled under him. "Why do you stumble, hungry jade, or do you sense some mishap?" The steed answered, "Ivan Tsarevich was here and has carried off Mar'ya Morevna." "Can we overtake them?" "We could sow wheat, wait till it grows, reap it, thresh it, grind it into flour, bake five ovenfuls of bread, and eat that bread; after that we could set out in pursuit, and even then we would overtake them." Koshchey galloped off and overtook Ivan Tsarevich. "Well," he said, "the first time I forgive you, because of your kindness in having given me water to drink; the second time I will also forgive you; but the third time, beware, I will chop you up into pieces." He took Mar'ya Morevna away from him and carried her off, and Prince Ivan sat on a stone and wept.

He wept for a while and then went back again for Mar'ya Morevna. Koshchey the Deathless happened to be away. "Let us go, Mar'ya Morevna," he said. "Ach, Ivan Tsarevich! He will catch up with us." "Let him catch us; we shall at least have spent an hour or two together." They made ready and left. As Koshchey the Deathless was returning home, his good steed stumbled under him. "Why do you stumble, hungry jade or do you sense a mishap?" "Ivan Tsarevich was here and carried off Mar'ya Morevna." "And can we catch up with them?" "We could sow barley, wait till it grows, reap and thresh it, brew beer, drink ourselves drunk, sleep our fill; after all that we could set out in pursuit, and still overtake them." Koshchey galloped off and overtook Prince Ivan. "Did I not tell you that you would not see Mar'ya Morevna any more that your own ears!" He took her and carried her off.

Once again, Ivan Tsarevich was alone. He wept for a while and went back again for Mar'ya Morevna. At that time Koshchey happened to be away. "Let us go, Maria Morevna!" "Ach, Ivan Tsarevich, he will catch up with us and chop you into pieces!" "Let him chop me up! I cannot live without you." They made ready and left. As Koshchey the Deathless was returning home, his good steed stumbled under him. "Why do you stumble, or do you sense some mishap?" "Ivan Tsarevich was here; he carried off Mar'ya Morevna." Koshchey galloped off, overtook Ivan Tsarevich, chopped him into small pieces, and put the pieces into a tarred barrel; he took this barrel, reinforced it with iron hoops, and threw it into the blue sea. Then he carried Mar'ya Morevna off.

At that very moment the silver that Ivan Tsarevich had left with his brothers-in-law darkened. "Ach," they said, "it appears that our brother-in-law has met with misfortune." The eagle rushed to the blue sea, seized the barrel and pulled it ashore; the falcon flew for the water of life and the raven for the water of death. They all got together, broke the barrel, took out the pieces of Ivan Tsarevich's body, washed them, and put them together in the right order. The raven sprinkled them with the water of death, and the pieces grew together and joined; the falcon sprinkled the body with the water of life, and Ivan Tsarevich shuddered, rose up, and said: "Ach, how long I have slept!" "You would have slept even longer had it not been for us," answered the brothers-in-law. "Now, come and visit us." "No, brothers, I shall go in search of Mar'ya Morevna."

He came to his princess and said, "Find out from Koshchey the Deathless where he got himself such a good steed." Mar'ya Morevna found an opportune moment and began to question Koshchey. Koshchey answered, "Beyond thrice nine lands, in the thrice tenth kingdom, beyond a river of fire, lives Baba Yaga. She has a mare on which she flies around the world every day. She also has many other splendid mares. I herded her mares for three days without losing a single one, and for this she rewarded me with a colt." "But how did you get across the river of fire?" "I have a special handkerchief; if I wave it three times to the right, a very high bridge appears which the fire cannot reach!" Maria Morevna listened carefully to him, repeated everything to Ivan Tsarevich, stole the handkerchief, and gave it to him.

Ivan Tsarevich crossed the river of fire and made his way to Baba Yaga. He walked for a long time without eating or drinking. Then he came upon an exotic bird with her young. "I shall eat one of the chicks," said Ivan Tsarevich. "Do not eat him, Ivan Tsarevich!" pleaded the exotic bird. "Some day I shall be useful to you." He went on and saw a beehive in the forest. "I shall take some honey," he said. "Do not touch my honey, Ivan Tsarevich! Some day I shall be useful to you," said the queen bee. He did not touch the honey and went on. He met a lioness and her cub. "Let me at least eat this lion cub, I am so hungry that I feel wretched." "Do not touch him, Ivan Tsarevich!" the lioness pleaded, "Some day I shall be useful to you." "Very well," said Ivan Tsarevich.

He continued on his way; still hungry, he walked and walked until he came to the house of Baba Yaga; around the house were twelve stakes, and on eleven of these were human heads; only one stake was without a head. "Good day, grandmother," said the tsarevich. "Good day, Ivan Tsarevich! Have you come of your own free will or out of need?" "I have come to earn a mighty steed from you." "You are welcome to try, tsarevich! You need not serve a year with me, but only three days. If you can tend my mares, I will give you a mighty steed; if you cannot – do not hold it against me – your head will go on the last stake." Ivan Tsarevich consented; Baba Yaga gave him food and drink and bid him to set to work. No sooner had he driven the mares into the field than they raised their tails and scattered over the meadows; before the tsarevich could even look around, they vanished from sight. He was saddened and wept, then he sat on a stone and fell asleep. The sun was already setting when the exotic bird appeared and roused him from sleep. "Arise, Ivan Tsarevich! The mares are already at home." The tsarevich stood up and returned to the house. Baba Yaga got angry and shouted at the mares, "Why did you come home?" "How could we help coming home? Birds flew in from every corner of the world and almost pecked our eyes out!" "Well, tomorrow don't run in the meadows, but scatter though the deep forests."

Ivan Tsarevich went to sleep. In the morning Baba Yaga said to him, "Mind you, tsarevich, if you do not tend the mares, if you lose even one of them, your bold head will go on the stake." He drove the mares into the field; they immediately raised their tails and scattered in the dark forests. Once again Ivan Tsarevich sat on a stone, wept and wept, and then fell asleep. The sun was setting over the forest when the lioness ran up to him. "Arise, Ivan Tsarevich! The mares are all gathered together." Ivan Tsarevich rose and returned to the house; Baba Yaga got angry and shouted at her mares even more than before, "Why did you return home?" "How could we help going home? Wild beasts from every corner of the world attached us and almost tore us to pieces!" "Well, tomorrow run into the blue sea."

Ivan Tsarevich went to sleep. In the morning Baba Yaga sent him to herd the mares. "If you lose any of them, your bold head will be on the stake." He drove the mares into the field; straightway they raised their tails, disappeared from sight and ran into the blue sea; they stood in the water up to their necks. Ivan Tsarevich sat on a stone, wept and fell asleep. The sun was setting over the forest when the bee flew up to him and said, "Arise, tsarevich! All the mares are gathered together; when you return home do not show yourself to Baba Yaga, but go to the stable and hide behind the manger. There you will find a mangy colt wallowing in a dung heap. Steal him and leave the house in the darkness of midnight."

Ivan Tsarevich arose, made his way to the stable and lay down behind the manger. Baba Yaga got angry and shouted at her mares: "Why did you return?" "How could we not return? Bees from all over the world swarmed around us and fell to stinging us so that we bled."

Baba Yaga fell asleep. At the stroke of midnight Ivan Tsarevich stole her mangy colt; he saddled him, then mounted and galloped off to the river of fire. When he came to the river, he waved his handkerchief to the right three times, and suddenly, as though from nowhere, a high, marvelous bridge hung over the river. The tsarevich rode over the bridge and waved the handkerchief to the left only twice, and there remained a very thin bridge above the river. Next morning Baba Yaga awoke and found the mangy colt gone. She rushed off in pursuit, galloping as fast as she could in an iron mortar, spurring it on with a pestle, and covering her tracks with a broom. She galloped up to the river of fire, looked and thought, "The bridge is fine." As she reached the middle of the bridge it broke, and Baba Yaga fell into the river, where she died a cruel death. Ivan Tsarevich let his colt graze in the green meadows and it turned into a marvelous steed.

The tsarevich rode on to Mar'ya Morevna. She ran out and threw her arms around him. "How has God brought you back to life?" "In such and such a way," he said. "Come with me." "I am afraid, Ivan Tsarevich. If Koshchey catches us, he will once again chop you to pieces." "No, he will not catch us! I now have a magnificent, mighty steed that flies like a bird." They mounted the steed and rode off.

Koshchey the Deathless was returning home; his steed stumbled under him. "Why do you stumble, you hungry jade, or do you sense a mishap?" "Ivan Tsarevich was here; he has carried off Mar'ya Morevna." "Can we overtake them?" "God knows! Now Ivan Tsarevich has a mighty steed, better than me." "No, I can't accept this!" said Koshchey the Deathless. "I will go after him!" After a long time or a short time, he caught up with Ivan Tsarevich, jumped to the ground and was about to cut him down with his sharp saber. At that moment Ivan Tsarevich's steed struck Koshchey the Deathless with all his might and smashed his head with his hoof, then Ivan Tsarevich finished him off with his mace. Thereupon the tsarevich gathered together a pile of wood, made a fire, burned Koshchey the Deathless, and scattered his ashes to the wind.

Mar'ya Morevna sat on Koshchey's steed, and Ivan Tsarevich on his own, and they went to see the raven, then the eagle, and lastly the falcon. Wherever they went, they were received with joy. "Ach, Ivan Tsarevich, we had given up hope of ever seeing you again. Indeed, you have not taken all this upon you without reason; such a beauty as Mar'ya Morevna could not be found in the whole world." They stayed a while and feasted together, and then Mar'ya Morevna and Ivan Tsarevich rode back to their kingdom to live and prosper and drink mead.

Alexander Afanas'yev, *Russian Folk Tales*, #159, trans. NB.

INTERPRETATION

The tale of Mar'ya Morevna is one of the longer tales in the Afanas'yev collection. In interpreting such a tale it is especially helpful to consider the symbolism of the numbers, for they mirror the unconscious order which underlies the narrative.[192] Knowing the symbolism of the numbers which appear in the tale enables us to better understand what is constellated at any time below the surface of consciousness.

The text is not quite clear about the disappearance of the tsar and tsaritsa; nonetheless, their death is very much a part of the initial situation, and emphasizes the transition from one rule to the next. It is, therefore, worthwhile to consider the symbolism of the number six as constellated by the older couple and their four offspring.

We find this number in many natural forms, for example, in snowflakes and flowers like the lily. It also appears in the extraordinary life of bees, in the way they build their cells; three bees each make two walls and one-third of the floor, and then they fit the parts together to form a hexagonal cell. Geometrically, a perfect hexagon can be constructed within a circle by joining points around the circumference with straight lines the length of the radius. By connecting alternative points on the circumference this figure also produces a six-pointed star or two triangles pointing in opposite directions. All these examples display a natural order.

The beginning of this tale is very much in harmony with the above symbolism. We see the tsar and tsaritsa preparing to hand over the kingdom to their son; this is in sharp contrast to many tales where the tsar tries to hold on to his power. In our tale there is no quarrel, no conflict. Surprisingly, the tsar and tsaritsa die together, apparently of natural causes; it is as if they step down when the time comes for them to do so.

Peaceful as this may seem, such transitions always bode potential danger because they usher in the new and unexpected. The old is known,

---

192   Jung, *Structure and Dynamics*, CW 8, § 870.

and therefore familiar; the development of the new world order has not yet been established. For this reason, critical moments such as these are often accompanied by disorientation and confusion.

This may explain why Ivan Tsarevich, the heir to throne, doesn't jump at the opportunity to take his father's place. We read that he "... buried his parents, and in his sorrow went to walk with his sisters in the green garden." This garden represents a piece of nature which has been tamed and cultivated for leisure and contemplation. While other tsareviches go hunting in the forest, Ivan Tsarevich accompanies his sisters in this idyllic setting. What are we to think of this?

At this point the numerical constellation has shifted from six to four. Usually, we attribute totality and completion to this number. Like any even number, four is archetypally feminine and passive. Totality and completion implies that something has been fulfilled, but also that some experience of life has come to an end. This suggests that one has to start anew, that one must redirect one's energy toward a new goal. The demand for change may come from within or without. But how does one decide where to go, what to do? If the change is inwardly motivated, how will the collective respond to it? Will this be the right decision? Such uncertainty throws one back upon oneself; it is unsettling because it disrupts the *status quo*. The alchemists referred to this condition as chaos or *nigredo*.[193] Psychologically, it represents a regression into the unconscious.

Jung discovered that such situations are often compensated by images of the circle or a quaternion; both are principles of order, both provide orientation and stability. The emotional impact of chaos and *nigredo* can be attributed to the conflict which now arises between the conscious (the known) and the unconscious (the unknown).[194] In our tale, this would represent the void left behind by the death of the tsar and tsaritsa, regardless of how benevolently and justly the transition was carried through. It is this situation that Ivan Tsarevich and his three sisters are now facing. The passive or feminine aspects of the number four call for a time of reorientation and of getting in touch with one's

---

193 Jung, *Aion*, CW 9ii, § 304.
194 Jung, *Aion*, CW 9ii, § 304.

psychic roots. To take the time to do this instead of rushing into action would be a feminine way of responding to the situation. Psychologically, it therefore makes perfect sense that Ivan Tsarevich is "walking in the green garden with his sisters," for, on an inner level, the sisters represent his anima and can best connect him with this part of his psyche.

The fact that there are three sisters, and not some other number, can easily be explained by the necessity for the constellation of the number four at this critical moment of transition. It also gives us information about the role of the feminine in the tale. As an uneven number, three is archetypally masculine and active; it brings dynamism into a situation. It can represent a child that furthers the development of the opposites in whom they have been united; moreover, as something born of the opposites, it can also stand for consciousness. In nature, such dynamism may appear as a wind; in this connection it also symbolizes spirit, for, like the wind, it is invisible and can only be perceived indirectly through its effect on what it comes into contact with. The number three also symbolizes time in its movement from the past to the present and on to the future.

The archetypal significance of numbers in general can be seen in the way they have been projected onto the divine; an example for the case at hand is the triadic goddesses of fate in ancient Greece. These goddesses determined the fate of human beings, and their decisions could not be challenged even by Zeus himself. In Christianity, we have the Holy Ghost or Spirit as the third member of the Trinity. Its masculine attribution should not be misunderstood as pertaining exclusively to males as opposed to females, but rather to the active and dynamic in both sexes.

If we interpret the three sisters as aspects of the hero's anima, we must conclude that the feminine is strongly constellated in his psyche. Till now the sisters have contributed to the stabilizing effect of the number four; they have made it possible for him to express his grief and to reconnect with his soul. This was important in the emotional turmoil after the parents' death. We might, therefore, understand the dynamism represented by the three sisters as channeling Ivan Tsarevich's libido away from the conscious world and establishing a connection with the unconscious part of his psyche. The further development of the tale shows just how important this connection will become.

And yet, the parents' parting injunction calls for Ivan Tsarevich to sever these close ties with his sisters; he is explicitly ordered not to keep them long with him, and told to marry them off to the first suitor. Psychologically, this is very wise council, for the sisters' presence would tie him to the past, to the parents' worldview, and this would keep him from following his own destiny. With his sisters, he would remain forever a brother, and he would never be able to unite with a woman and be fruitful with her; psychologically, to become whole.

The motif of the passive hero is widespread in Russian fairy tales. Psychologically, it points to the constellation of the mother archetype, to that unconscious force which, independent of the real mother's influence, pulls a man away from life and makes him passive. Such an experience is common among creative people, for what looks like passivity to the outside world may be the result of an immersion in the unconscious. The true hero can survive this immersion and bring back the treasures acquired in the unconscious realm, but something usually has to happen to make this possible. In the "Speedy Messenger," it is the appearance of two old men who promise to fulfill the hero's wish. In the tale at hand, it is the wise instruction of the parents that nudges the hero out of his comfortable nest.

The nature of the suitors, who—one by one—woo the tsarevnas and carry them off to their kingdoms, supports this development. All three of them are birds, who appear in a storm of almost cosmic proportions. Each time, a black cloud suddenly covers the sky, causing the tsarevich and his sisters to seek shelter in the castle. Only recently this symbol of the Self belonged to the old tsar and tsaritsa. The destruction brought about by the storm makes it clear that this castle can no longer provide the necessary protection against the new spirit now breaking into Ivan Tsarevich's life. In fulfillment of his parents' wishes, he dutifully accepts the suitors' proposals and parts with his sisters.

Psychologically, the image of the storm can be seen as a powerful affect compensating the regression into the idyllic brother-sister-relationship. How long would they have continued to wander about in their garden had the storm not shocked them out of their complacency?

It is worthy of note that the three sisters are courted and married not by suitors from other kingdoms, but by birds. Birds symbolize thoughts, intuitions, fantasies; more generally, they represent spirit. By marrying birds, the sisters testify to the spiritual nature of the anima.

One of the anima's functions is to inspire a man. Because she is part of the collective unconscious, the anima has access to human patterns of experience not always available to consciousness; this we can observe in what now follows. One after the other, each of the three sisters marries and starts a new life with her avian husband; they leave their brother but, by so doing, they show him the way out of the incestuous stasis.

And yet, even after they have gone, Ivan Tsarevich continues to live alone. Finally, after a whole year goes by, he gets lonely and decides to go to look for his sisters. He doesn't seem to have any other interest in life, and he certainly does not seek adventure as so many other heroes do. This shows that his libido is still directed toward the sisters and to his former life. The pull of the mother archetype has not diminished, and he continues to choose the old and familiar over the new and unknown. This regressive attitude could easily have led to the proverbial Oblomovian lethargy (p. 185) had fate not prepared a different scenario for him.

Before continuing with the story, let us consider the symbolism of the numbers constellated thus far. We last spoke of the number three, as exemplified by the three sisters. This number introduces dynamism into the situation, propelling the action out of the static nature of the four; it also draws our attention to the uneven distribution of the masculine and feminine within the hero's psyche. This would represent a man whose energy is largely determined by unconscious feminine values; it pulls him back and hinders him in fulfilling his masculine role in life.

The arrival of the first suitor strengthens the masculine component of the hero's psyche by altering the ratio between the masculine and feminine. Whereas before, the masculine represented a quarter, now it is two fifths. Without going through each step of this process, we can say that each suitor increases the proportion of the masculine and, upon flying away with one of the sisters, decreases the proportion of the feminine. This leads to a gradual transformation within Ivan Tsarevich's psyche. With the departure of all three sisters the hero's psychic energy is entirely masculine. This is a rather significant development in the psyche of a man with a mother complex for it provides him with a much-needed spurt of masculine energy to counteract the backward pull of the unconscious.

We saw a similar development at the beginning of "The Speedy Messenger," where the process of combatting the laming effect of the swamp could not even be conceived until the father had three sons to help him. The masculine element had reached wholeness in the total absence of any human feminine being. It was only the swamp, with its life-devouring and stagnating influence, which represented the feminine principle.

The number seven, which in this tale represents the sum of the sisters, their suitors and Ivan Tsarevich was discussed in considerable detail in connection with the tale of "The Seven Semëns" (p. 228). Its relation to the four phases of the moon made it the original measure of time. The fact that these phases also represent a progression in time is an example of the active nature of the number seven. As also mentioned there, the number seven appears in the Biblical story of the creation where, as the Sabbath, it represents the culmination of the creative process. This day is not meant as a day of idleness, but of contemplation or consciousness of God's role in creation. Psychologically, this touches upon the question of hubris or inflation, of attributing that which is within the competence of the Self to the ego. More generally, it indicates the need for humility in working with psychic contents.

It is for this reason that the number seven appears in many rites of initiation. Both the practices of the shamans and the experiments of the alchemists strove for a higher, more spiritual understanding of the human condition. Their goal never implied a rejection of the material, but invoked the inclusion of the divine to create a product of both matter and spirit, leading to wholeness.

The number seven can, therefore, stand for transformation and evolution. The constellation of this number at the present moment in the tale may be expressed by the image of an airplane waiting in line for takeoff. It is an exciting, but also frightening, time; it carries the possibility of a new beginning, of realizing one's own individual fate, but it is filled with anxiety because of the unknown challenges ahead. At such moments one is thrown back upon oneself. This is the meaning of the number one which has now become constellated in Ivan Tsarevich's psyche. Will he rush into life and face its challenges, or return to his still warm, albeit empty, nest?

Before continuing with the story, let us take a closer look at his three brothers-in-law, who appear in the shape of a falcon, an eagle, and a raven.

The falcon has already been discussed in detail in "The Tale of Finist, the Bright Falcon" (p. 104). Because of its fast flight and aggressive mode of attack, it was often seen as a bird of warriors, and because of its devotion to its mate and offspring, it became a term of endearment for a young man in Old Russian.

The eagle has earned itself the title of *king of birds* by its grandiose appearance and majestic flight; it appears on many coats of arms. Like the falcon, the eagle is a solar bird. Many indigenous peoples use its feathers in their headdress, symbolizing the sun. Hence, in many mythologies the eagle represents the chief god of the pantheon, and is thereby connected with power and victory. In Russian folklore, warriors were often called eagles. In a Russian song, a maiden speaks with longing of her love as *a dashing Cossack, an eagle of the steppes.*

Psychologically, the eagle, as any bird, symbolizes intuitive thoughts and fantasies; in this case these attributes are raised to the highest degree, to intense enthusiasm and high-flying thoughts which are capable of sustaining man in the most perilous situations.[195] Seen as aspects of the hero's shadow, the falcon and eagle would speak for the tremendous spiritual potential within the hero's psyche, for strength and prowess, for courage and clarity of vision. So far in the tale, we have not witnessed any such traits in Ivan Tsarevich. The advent of the falcon and eagle would therefore suggest that these unlived parts of his personality have now come closer to consciousness.

But what about the raven? What does it herald for Ivan Tsarevich's future? We read that each of the suitors flies into the castle through the roof ripped open by a thunderbolt; each bird strikes the floor and transforms into a brave youth. As the third one appears, he is introduced

---

195   von Franz, *The Golden Ass*, 125.

with the following words: "...the other two were handsome, but he was handsomer." It is surprising that the raven should be singled out in this way. Seen outwardly, it would appear to be the least "handsome" of the three, and yet this description suggests that the raven is of special significance for the hero.

From a purely biological perspective, the raven is a most impressive creature. It is highly intelligent, capable of learning and adapting to changed circumstances. It has a complex social structure and a capacity for teamwork; moreover, it is capable of play and of imitating others, and it is very curious and inventive.[196] One can easily see how these highly developed traits might have influenced many of the beliefs connected with the raven.

In Nordic mythology, ravens sit on Wotan's shoulders, informing him of all that goes on in the universe. Von Franz sees the ravens as Wotan's extra-sensory perception or absolute knowledge, a knowledge characteristic of synchronistic phenomena.[197] The raven was Wotan's messenger, and was thought to disclose the god's intentions to those who could read the signs through divination.

Similarly, in Russian mythology, the raven was held to be a wise bird with secret knowledge of life and death. Moreover, it was believed to have connections to the world of the dead and to all dark forces; it forebodes, or even brings, death. Edgar Allen Poe's famous poem, "The Raven" is a suitable example of the melancholy and dark thoughts which this brings. In alchemy, the raven symbolizes the *nigredo*, the darkness and suffering which accompanies the beginning of the *opus*. This stage calls for continuous washing and burning off of impurities, something we usually experience through the long and painful work on the shadow, especially in the initial stages of analysis.

In addition, the raven was believed to possess immeasurable wealth. Of special significance to the tale at hand is the water of life and death, which could only be obtained from the other world, and to which the raven had access. It was this water which saved the hero's life after he was killed and dismembered by the villain, Koshchey the Deathless.[198]

---

196   Zürchertierschutz, "Krähenvolk"; Grzimek, vol. 7, 339; vol. 9, 520 f.
197   von Franz, *Shadow and Evil*, 211; Jung, *Structure and Dynamics*, CW 8, § 948.
198   Shaparova, *Kratkaya Entsyklopediya*, 192-194.

Much in the above echoes the shamanic experience and, thereby, introduces the idea of initiation into this new stage of Ivan Tsarevich's journey. The first two birds compensate the hero's passivity and lack of manliness; without the warrior attributes of the falcon and eagle, the night-sea journey which lies ahead would have proved insurmountable;[199] but still there would have been no psychic development without the raven. Another way of expressing this is that the falcon and eagle inspire Ivan Tsarevich to courageous and mighty outer acts, while the raven prepares him for the difficult inner journey of individuation. This begins with the *nigredo*, confronting him with the collective as well as the personal shadow, for as a hero it is his lot to confront both. Such is the significance of this "most handsome" suitor.

We return now to the point in time where Ivan Tsarevich has given away all three sisters in marriage and is now left to decide what to do with his life. This was the implication we drew from the symbolism of the number one. The example set by his sisters might have motivated Ivan Tsarevich to go out into the world, and his parents' parting injunction about marrying his sisters off at the first opportunity had, in all probability, the same intention. This, however, was not what Ivan Tsarevich decided to do; rather he chose to remain living alone in his castle.

After a whole year went by, Ivan Tsarevich began to miss his sisters and set out to look for them. His attitude toward life doesn't seem to have changed, for he is still clinging to his sisters as part of his past. And yet, what looks like a digression leads to an unforeseeable and fateful change in his life. He seems to be doing something right for the wrong reasons; by deciding to follow his sisters, he gets out of the old environment, exposes himself to the outside world and allows the world to impact him. This is a beautiful example of the unconscious maneuvering us into fulfilling its intentions.

Ivan Tsarevich's first encounter with the outside world is a battlefield full of corpses. Subjectively, this may symbolize the huge crisis within his soul, for in leaving his former way of life he is entering uncharted territory and distancing himself from the comfort and safety he had previously known under the influence of the mother complex. It is difficult

---

199   Jung, *Letters* 1, 86 n. 2; Jung, *Symbols of Transformation*, CW 5, § 308 f.

to imagine anything more different than this battlefield from the idyllic setting of his former life. Short as the reference to this crisis may be, psychologically it carries wide-ranging implications, for if the hero continues upon this new path, he will be making room for another image of the feminine within his psyche. This is indeed what now happens.

Inquiring of a survivor, Ivan Tsarevich discovers that it is Mar'ya Morevna, the beautiful princess, who is responsible for this carnage. Undaunted, he goes to seek her out and soon arrives at her camp. Mar'ya Morevna greets him with a question we most often hear from Baba Yaga. She asks if he is coming of his own will or by compulsion. "Brave youths," answers Ivan Tsarevich, "do not travel by compulsion." One begins to feel the impact that his brothers-in-law made upon his psyche. So far, so good; he has impressed Mar'ya Morevna and she invites him into her tent. After two nights Mar'ya Morevna decides she likes him and they get married.

In another version of this tale, the hero Ivan finds Mar'ya Morevna sleeping when he reaches her campsite. He lies down next to her. When she awakens, she asks him if they should fight or make love. Ivan suggests they go out and see how their horses are doing. They find the two horses grazing peacefully next to one another. Then Mar'ya Morevna and Ivan Tsarevich decide to marry. So easy, so quick!

We sense a completely new energy in this relationship. As an anima figure, Mar'ya Morevna is quite different from Ivan Tsarevich's sisters. The hero himself has changed upon leaving the old setting, and his brother-in-law shadows have now come closer to consciousness; their strong masculine energy is, in fact, beginning to free him from the inhibiting influence of the mother complex.

The infatuation he experiences is often a necessary first step in fairy tales, as it is in real life. For example, in Grimm's "Faithful Johannes," just seeing a portrait of a beautiful princess fills the young king with such longing that he is willing to overcome great obstacles to find her and make her his own. Such intense love, often mostly sexual, holds couples together through the necessary adjustment and adaptation period in which they learn to live with one another. This is even clearer in the parallel version given above, where Mar'ya Morevna and Ivan Tsarevich take their cues from their horses. Seen psychologically, the fascination is the magic experienced through the constellation of the archetype of the *coniunctio*. The number one has transformed into a two, and now supports their union.

What happens next may be seen as their first *marital crisis*. After they have lived together for a while in her kingdom [*sic*], Mar'ya Morevna informs Ivan Tsarevich that she is, once again, going off to war. She leaves everything in his care, but warns him against entering a certain closet. In fairy tales this is a warning most often given by a man to a woman, but we have already noted the reversed roles in this relationship.

We may wonder why Mar'ya Morevna suddenly decides to make war. Does such harmonious living threaten to bring stagnation? Has the hero once more regressed into his "green garden"? Has the archetypal mother begun to pull him back into his former passivity? In marital situations, we often see a woman becoming active and aggressive when the man is passive.

Likewise noteworthy is the speed with which Ivan Tsarevich seeks out the forbidden closet. The woman in fairy tales usually tries to resist the temptation, to curb her curiosity. Not so with Ivan Tsarevich: "...as soon as Mar'ya Morevna had gone, he rushed to the closet, opened the door, looked in." Curiosity is usually considered a feminine trait; that Ivan Tsarevich acts in such an exaggeratedly feminine way is no wonder when we remember that three-quarters of his psyche was originally feminine.

Let us consider the motif of the forbidden door. Most often something terrible is hidden behind this door; psychologically, this is something repressed and incompatible with consciousness.[200] It takes a hero or heroine to bring such contents to light without succumbing to their power. In the Grimm tale of "Fitcher's Bird," the first two sisters are not up to the challenge and are cut into pieces. It is only the third sister who knows how to deal with the situation and who, subsequently, saves the others.

Because the anima, like every figure in the unconscious, is contaminated with the whole of the unconscious, union with her often exposes a man to deeper layers of the psyche. Such contents may pose an existential

---

200   von Franz, *The Interpretation of Fairy Tales*, 124.

threat to consciousness.[201] The prohibition against entering a certain room may, therefore, be seen as psyche's attempt to protect the human ego against this danger.[202] And yet the fascination of going against a prohibition also appears to be universal. Here the unconscious, once again, discloses its ambivalent nature; it warns and challenges at the same time.

Genesis 2-3 is an example of such a situation. After God creates the world, He fashions a beautiful garden and instructs man, the highest of His creations, to be its guardian. Man is free to eat of every fruit in this garden except that of the tree of life, which imparts the knowledge of good and evil. This tree, standing in the very center of the Garden of Eden, is a test of man's response to such an ambivalent prohibition by the Creator; here too, it presents a warning and a challenge. It is, furthermore, interesting that Eve, and not Adam, disobeys this ruling. Whether we see Eve as woman or as anima, here psychic development is attributed to the feminine.

The question now is how this relates to the tale at hand. Upon opening the forbidden door, Ivan Tsarevich is confronted with Koshchey the Deathless, a most dangerous demon, hanging by twelve chains. Koshchey begs Ivan Tsarevich to have pity on him, saying that he has been without food and drink for ten years. In his kindheartedness, Ivan Tsarevich brings him—one after another—three pails of water to soothe his thirst; Koshchey recovers his strength and breaks all twelve chains. He then storms off in pursuit of Mar'ya Morevna, telling Ivan Tsarevich that he will never see her again.

Our hero was a bit naive in showing so much goodwill toward Koshchey; he doesn't seem to realize that, in the face of such evil, pity can be a dangerous weakness. His gullibility may be attributed to his experience with life, and in particular with women. Till now all the women in Ivan Tsarevich's life have been positive. Even such a dangerous warrior as Mar'ya Morevna falls in love with him and agrees to become his wife. Ivan Tsarevich has trust in the feminine and, as we have seen, he is connected to his emotions and able to express them; in short, he has a positive attitude toward life. How else could he have

201   Jung, *Structure and Dynamics*, CW 8, § 430.
202   von Beit, *Gegensatz und Erneuerung*, 570.

approached Mar'ya Morevna's tents after learning of the carnage she had wrought? However, this positive experience of the feminine has also made him naive and passive. He is like a child who expects to be taken care of, protected, understood, and supported. When he sees Koshchey hanging in Mar'ya Morevna's closet, he never suspects that this could be someone dangerous, someone he should not let loose.

We might compare this to Psyche's refusal to save a drowning man as she crosses the river Styx. In that episode, Psyche restrains her impulse to come to the man's assistance. Later we learn that this would have jeopardized her chances of reuniting with Eros and of being included into the assembly of the gods.[203]

The actions of both Eve and Psyche ultimately lead to a broadening of consciousness. Psyche's union with Eros represents a *coniunctio* with the animus, and enables her acceptance into Olympus; it attributes divinity to the soul. Eve's transgression marks the end of the couple's life in paradise, and confronts them with the realities of human existence.

The same is true in the tale at hand, for had Ivan Tsarevich not freed Koshchey there would have been no story to tell, nor any further development for the hero. Let us, therefore, return to this critical moment when Ivan Tsarevich defies Mar'ya Morevna's prohibition and opens the forbidden closet. As noted above, the psychological significance of this act is the confrontation with some dreadful, unconscious content which no human response can mitigate. Moreover, if we consider Koshchey subjectively as a part of Ivan Tsarevich's psyche, we realize that it is through union with the anima that this deeply repressed aspect comes to light.

The response of the ego to confrontation with unconscious contents is, to a large degree, determined by the strength of the ego. This is, of course, the reason why so much emphasis is placed on strengthening the personality in the first half of life. Clinically speaking, the possible effects of such an invasion of the unconscious may lead to neurotic dissociation, fragmentation, or even full-blown psychosis.

If the ego is strong enough, it may try to assimilate these contents; because of their intensity, however, the ego will inevitably become a passive

---

203   von Franz, *Golden Ass of Apuleius*, 126.

observer, unable to exercise its will. Another possibility is that the ego may become so impressed by their numinosity that it will identify itself with them; this could trigger a power complex as a compensation for the vulnerability of the ego.

Should the ego be unable to hold its own against the unconscious, it would itself become overwhelmed and assimilated; in that case, its experience of the world would be from the perspective of the unconscious. Such a person would live in a mythological world with no possibility of translating its images into concrete reality. Jung refers to this as a state of preconscious wholeness.[204] It is as if the ego was swallowed up by the unconscious, or symbolically, the hero by the devouring mother.[205] This is particularly significant in the present context, for here we are concerned with a mother complex. By going out into the world and distancing himself from his sisters, Ivan Tsarevich may have managed to free himself from the personal implications of this complex, but now he is challenged by its more archetypal aspects.

The above is a clinical image of the possible reactions to the intrusion of heavily repressed unconscious contents into consciousness. This is now the challenge that awaits Ivan Tsarevich in the forbidden closet. How can we explain the fact that the fairy tale hero manages to survive such a destructive onslaught? The answers appear to lie in the definition of the hero, for he represents that part of the ego which keeps a door open to the Self and respects its might without losing himself in the process. It also confirms Jung's belief that both the ego and the Self are transformed in such a confrontation.[206]

But who is Koshchey and what is his relationship to Mar'ya Morevna? We know that he is held prisoner in her palace but the present tale provides no explanation of how this came to be. N.V. Novikov, a Russian folklorist, mentions a parallel version in which the heroine vehemently rejects Koshchey's advances, destroys his mighty army and takes him prisoner.[207]

---

204   Jung, *Structure and Dynamics*, CW 8, § 430.
205   von Beit, *Gegensatz und Erneuerung*, 558.
206   Jung, *Structure and Dynamics*, CW 8, § 430.
207   Novikov, *Obrazy*, 74.

Koshchey is one of the three most important demonic figures in the fairy tales of the Eastern Slavs; the other two are the serpent and Baba Yaga. The motifs which circle around Koshchey all have to do with women. Sometimes they are his daughters;[208] at other times they are taken captive by Koshchey and forced to live with him.

The motif of this villain follows two basic scenarios, both connected to the cause of his death. According to the first of these, Koshchey has no heart and therefore cannot die, but this is only partially true. Koshchey has no heart *in his body* because he has hidden it in an egg in a faraway place known to him alone. It is only the hero who can find the egg and kill the demon by destroying it. This version is probably the older one; it portrays him as the mighty king of the World of the Dead; the word *koshchuna* refers to myths of this world. The contemporary word *koshchunstvovat'* means to blaspheme, and vividly expresses the attempt of the Church to eradicate pagan beliefs and practices in the land.[209]

The second cause of Koshchey's death is attributed to a magic horse. This is the case in our tale, and we will have more to say about it in what follows.[210] I have described the first cause in some detail because, although this is not the scenario in our tale, it reveals the basic nature of this villain.

Common to both versions is Koshchey's desire to possess a woman and to keep her for himself. He appears to have tremendous power over her, and opposes anyone who tries to take her away from him. This is vividly portrayed in the tale at hand; Mar'ya Morevna is a warrior princess who is capable of subduing a whole army, and yet she is powerless against Koshchey. If she did capture him in battle, as a parallel version describes, why didn't she kill him outright, and why did she leave him hanging in her closet for ten years? Why, moreover, did she have to resort to trickery to get at his secrets later on in the tale?

How alarmingly similar this is to the sexual abuse and overt incest which is increasingly coming to light in our day! How unjust of those with power to exert their will over others, and to hold them in bondage! How great is the victims' suffering, both physical and psychic!

208 Novikov, *Obrazy*, 70.
209 Rybakov, *Yazychestvo drevney Rusi*, 326 ff.
210 Novikov, *Obrazy*, 193.

How difficult, at times almost impossible, it is for the victim to free herself or himself from the guilt of involvement! How long does it take to restore one's sense of integrity?

That Koshchey can get away with such evil by hiding his heart on a faraway island is an apt illustration for the splitting off of a complex; it is the opposite of individuation which strives for wholeness. Koshchey is stronger without his heart because this allows him to function through power alone, with no concern for the other or for morality. But individuation is an archetypal principle which governs all of life and, as the example of Adam and Eve shows, the consciousness it brings comes with a price.

From a subjective standpoint, Koshchey is a part of Ivan Tsarevich's psyche; he would represent a negative aspect of the father archetype in both its personal and collective manifestations. In his hitherto peaceful and harmonious life, Ivan Tsarevich had never been confronted with such an evil spirit; he would, consequently, never have had the opportunity of becoming conscious of it, still less of coming to terms with it. Because of the ambivalent nature of all archetypes, the father archetype would, of necessity, include both the positive and the negative aspect. Mar'ya Morevna, as a new and more archetypal aspect of Ivan Tsarevich's anima, has opened his heart, thereby exposing him to deeper layers of his psyche to which he previously had no access.

This triangle is an image of what is now constellated in the hero's psyche. The appearance of Koshchey sheds light upon the existence of a hitherto unconscious aspect of Ivan Tsarevich's psyche; one which has power over the anima and, moreover, whose aim it is to prevent a union between her and the ego. As we see from the outcome of the tale, it is only the hero who can win this battle because of his relationship to the Self; as fairy tales show more generally, however, this can never happen unless the hero has the anima on his side. Outwardly, this shows that a solution to the problem of sexual abuse cannot be found without a man's proper relationship to the inner feminine, without the experience of the inner *coniunctio*.

Let us for a moment consider the twelve chains that hold Koshchey imprisoned in the forbidden closet. A chain is put together from little pieces, from links. The expression *chain of events* shows clearly that many different parts are connected in a sequential way. Another expression, *the chains that bind us*, places the emphasis on holding together. But a chain can also restrict movement; it can connect in a forcible way. If we assume that Mar'ya Morevna captured and imprisoned Koshchey, then all the above amplifications apply: There must have been a long story behind his being held captive in her closet, and the fact that he has been there for ten years suggests some sort of relationship between them. He is the skeleton in her closet, the dangerous secret which had been repressed and kept well hidden. If we were responding to such a woman, we might say that this cannot go on indefinitely, that some more permanent solution must be found to this problem. Perhaps that's why Ivan Tsarevich is now opening the door to the forbidden closet; perhaps this is a call to the ego to bring consciousness into the situation.

Likewise significant is the fact that Koshchey is not held by one chain, but twelve. Twelve is another number connected with time: the twelve hours of the day and night, as well as the twelve months of the year. The twelve signs of the zodiac introduce the element of fate into this symbolism. As the product of three and four, twelve symbolizes the interaction of these two numbers, and hence of matter and spirit, of the active and passive. Like the number seven, twelve often appears in the initiations of mystery cults. We can, therefore, say that twelve stands for completion or wholeness in time, and that this is connected with destiny and individuation. Such an understanding of the number twelve allows us to postulate that the time for Koshchey's imprisonment has reached completion, and that it is a necessary that the chains are now broken and Koshchey freed from his captivity; the time is ripe for further growth, and a new development has been set into motion. It should not surprise us that this change is brought about by three figures: Mar'ya Morevna, Koshchey, and Ivan Tsarevich. We are, once again, witnessing the constellation of the number three, bringing dynamism and movement into the tale.

Let us turn now to Mar'ya Morevna, the beautiful princess. As the reader will have noticed, Ivan Tsarevich's eldest sister is also called Mar'ya. This draws our attention to nuances in the names of the two women. In the Russian tradition, apart from the family name, each person carries two other names. The first of these is freely decided upon at birth; the second name is a special form of the father's name, called the patronymic. In the original text, the sister is called Mar'ya Tsarevna, which means Mar'ya, daughter of the tsar. The father's name is replaced by his title, because the tsar is not a private individual. The same is true of the hero who is called Ivan Tsarevich.

The name Mar'ya Morevna, the beautiful princess, offers additional insights. The suffix in *Morevna* is the typical grammatical form of the feminine patronymic. The root of this word is *mor* and refers either to the sea, *more*, or to death, *mor*. In the first case the name would be translated as *Mar'ya, daughter of the sea*, which is symbolically very fitting for an anima figure. The older meaning of the word *mor* has been traced by ethnologists to the pagan rites of spring, in which a straw figure representing winter would be burned in a fire, thereby heralding a new cycle of fertility; this figure was called *Morena*. It is, therefore, very probable that the name of this pagan figure became transformed into the patronymic in the present tale.[211] In contrast to Ivan Tsarevich's sister, Mar'ya Morevna carries the epithet of "beautiful princess." This small nuance shows that she is not regarded as daughter of the tsar, but "korolevna," which means daughter of a king.

Summarizing, we can say that this tale speaks of two Mar'yas, both related to Ivan Tsarevich; one is designated as daughter of the tsar, the other as the daughter of a king. Taking into account that this is a Russian fairy tale where the ruler is a tsar, we can make the assumption that the daughter of a king would belong to the non-Russian world. Psychologically, that other, non-Russian world could be seen as the unconscious. This distinction is often made by Baba Yaga who, in her blindness, sniffs the air and recognizes the smell of the hero as coming from the *Russian world*. Her reaction clearly shows that she is juxtaposing this world to her own world of the unconscious. Mar'ya Morevna's coming from this other, unconscious, world testifies to her being a deeper, more archetypal, aspect of Ivan Tsarevich's anima.

In his book, *Paganism of Ancient Russia*, the ethnologist Boris Rybakov gives valuable information about the religious practices of the

---

211 Rybakov, *Yazychestvo drevney Rusi*, 392.

early Slavs.[212] Many of these practices disclose remnants of a matriarchal society, which became incorporated into fairy tale imagery. Such examples are mostly connected with Baba Yaga, but some also refer to Morena. The information Rybakov provides suggests a contamination between these two feminine figures. In our tale, Mar'ya Morevna first appears as a fierce warrior who destroys a whole army of men, and Baba Yaga is sometimes also described as leading a whole army of women—her daughters. Sometimes her daughters appear as mares, as in the present tale. As we had already noted, upon first meeting Ivan Tsarevich, Mar'ya Morevna asks him whether he is coming of his own will or by compulsion. This is a question most often put to the hero by Baba Yaga. We will return to the similarities between these two women in the further development of this tale.

Let us now go back to the moment where Ivan Tsarevich inadvertently frees Koshchey, and where the latter flies off to capture Mar'ya Morevna and to carry her off to his house. The power of this demon has been unleashed through the hero's naiveté, and this now leads to a reversal of roles between Koshchey and Mar'ya Morevna; whereas Koshchey was her prisoner for ten years, she has now become his. Psychologically, this shows that the anima has once again fallen under the influence of the father archetype in its negative manifestation.

Our hero is once again alone, as he had been before setting off to visit his sisters. This time, however, he is facing the consequences of his own actions; he himself has opened a door to a side of his psyche of which he has, till now, been unaware. It is a dark, demonic aspect which now confronts him. The beginning of Ivan Tsarevich's life was harmonious and stable; he had the love of his parents and sisters and all his needs were satisfied. After his parents died and his sisters were married off, Ivan Tsarevich meets an amazing woman, loves and is loved by her, until, quite suddenly, he finds himself faced with a demon of Koshchey's proportions.

Ivan Tsarevich weeps bitterly. This is his usual response to misfortune, which is surprising because in patriarchal society weeping is for women, not men, and especially not for heroes. We have repeatedly seen

---

212 Rybakov, *Yazychestvo drevney Rusi*, 230 ff.

that Ivan Tsarevich has a very pronounced feminine side, and this includes the ability, indeed the need, to express his feelings. Here he shows himself to be related, to suffer, and to grieve. We see, however, that this suffering now spurs him to action. He immediately makes ready and sets out on his way. "Whatever happens, I must find Mar'ya Morevna," he says. When he left his own kingdom at the start of the tale, it was out of loneliness; now he is focused and has a conscious goal.

The first steps on this way, however, look suspiciously like a regression, for his intended goal is to visit his sisters and brothers-in-law. Despite his resolute intention to seek out Mar'ya Morevna, could Ivan Tsarevich be seeking solace in the familial and reliable after his painful experience with Koshchey and his subsequent loss? This situation warrants looking into.

One after another, Ivan Tsarevich comes upon the three castles. Before each castle stands an oak tree, and on each of these oak trees sits one of his brothers-in-law in his bird manifestation. Seeing Ivan Tsarevich, they fly down, hit the earth and take on human form. This was just like their initial appearance when they flew in through the torn roof of Ivan Tsarevich's castle. The image is important because it shows that these spiritual aspects of his sister-animas are able to become human by making contact with the earth; they do not remain mere thoughts, fantasies or intuitions when applied to waking reality.

A castle is a stronghold, a place of safety, of nourishment, and of culture. In the castles he now visits, Ivan Tsarevich becomes reconnected to his family and experiences their support. This strengthens and centers him, and prepares him for the difficult journey ahead. We must not forget the clinical implications of his opening the forbidden door described above. The visits to his family must, therefore, be seen as a reconnection with his roots, rather than as a regression.

A further connection can be seen in Ivan Tsarevich's leaving three of his possessions with his sisters and brothers-in-law: a silver spoon, fork, and snuff box. Silver is related to the moon, and hence symbolizes the feminine principle of Eros, of relatedness. The spoon and fork are used in eating, and the snuffbox for smoking, that is, the first two for bodily, and the third for spiritual, nourishment. As we see from the further development in the tale, they provide a link between Ivan Tsarevich and his brothers-in-law. When he is dismembered by Koshchey, their darkening alerts them to the danger he is in. This is another example of *participation mystique*, expressed in other tales by the bloody or rusty knife, or by the handkerchief which turns red when the hero is faced with danger. Because a castle is also an image of order and a locus of energy, it is an important symbol of the Self. The increase in the size and splendor of the castles indicates a growth and strengthening of this inner stronghold.

In front of each of the castles stands an oak tree. In many cultures, including Russian, the oak is an attribute of the chief pagan god; it is often connected with thunder and lightning (Zeus, Thor, Jupiter, Perun). As the eagle is *king of birds*, and the lion *king of animals*, so the oak is *king of trees*. It has great longevity, durability and strength. Just as the castle is a man-made image of stability, the oak is a natural one. Its mighty roots anchor it in the earth; its branches reach up into the sky.

Coming to the castles and oak trees brings the attributes connected to these symbols closer to consciousness. They give Ivan Tsarevich the self-confidence he needs to continue on his way. The dynamism of the number three is also indicative of the focus which now propels the hero to the next stage of his journey. As a fourth step, Ivan Tsarevich now arrives at Koshchey's home. The number four, which symbolizes completion, now also indicates the beginning of the next series of repetitive events. Three times Ivan Tsarevich tries to flee with Mar'ya Morevna, and three times Koshchey catches up with them and recaptures her.

When Ivan Tsarevich arrives at Koshchey's house, the latter is out hunting. Koshchey's steed warns his master of Ivan Tsarevich's flight with Mar'ya Morevna. In answer to Koshchey's question about whether he will be successful in catching up with them, the steed says: "We could sow wheat, wait till it grows, reap it, thresh it, grind it into flour, bake five ovenfuls of bread, eat that bread, and after all that set out in pursuit—and even then we would overtake them." The second time the horse says: "We could sow barley, wait till it grows, reap and thresh it, brew beer, drink ourselves drunk, sleep our fill, and after all that set out in pursuit—and even then we could overtake them." Boris Rybakov sees these poetic descriptions as remnants of an early measurement of time in agrarian society. They are pre-Christian because no reference is made to the Church calendar, but only to natural events.[213] This supports tracing Mar'ya Morevna's name to the old pagan ritual of the Morena which heralded spring. Such amplifications attest to the deep roots of Russian folklore in fairy tales.

Having caught up with Ivan Tsarevich and Mar'ya Morevna, Koshchey tells the tsarevich that, out of gratitude for his freeing him from the closet, he will pardon him for running off with Mar'ya Morevna two times; he warns him, however, that he will chop him up into pieces the third time. This doesn't appear to intimidate the hero, for he now realizes that giving up his claim to Mar'ya Morevna is not an option, regardless of the consequences. The first time he merely expresses the hope that they will escape Koshchey; the second time, he responds to Mar'ya Morevna's concern with: "Let him catch us; we shall at least have spent an hour or two together." The third time, when Mar'ya Morevna reminds him that Koshchey means to chop him up into pieces, he answers: "Let him chop me to pieces. I cannot live without you." We must understand Ivan Tsarevich's responses on two levels, expressing his love and devotion not only to Mar'ya Morevna as a partner, but also as an anima figure.

Mar'ya Morevna is also beginning to show her feelings for Ivan Tsarevich. When he first arrives at Koshchey's home, she throws her arms around him and, after scolding him for his disobedience, she accompanies her reprimands with bitter tears. She too is changing. Does she realize that she almost lost him? Or does she sense that his visits to his sisters and brothers-in-law have centered and strengthened him and made him even more worthy of her love? Despite the fact that Mar'ya Morevna must know from experience what a grave danger Koshchey presents, she agrees to flee with Ivan Tsarevich. This mighty princess who brought death to a whole army of men is also powerless against Koshchey, but she entrusts herself to Ivan Tsarevich out of an equal inner need to be together with him whatever may be.

The two are now closer than ever. If we see Koshchey as that evil spirit that strives to keep the anima from uniting with the ego, that is, of becoming conscious, then we must realize just how much is at stake

---

213 Rybakov, *Yazychestvo drevney Rusi*, 334.

at this particular moment in the tale. The archetypal nature of this experience becomes even clearer if we place it into our own times, for it emphasizes the importance of not losing contact with the soul, of not abandoning it regardless of circumstances.

The tale is moving toward that very critical moment when Koshchey comes upon them the third time, and carries out his promise to chop Ivan Tsarevich into pieces. Clinically, this would represent the total fragmentation of the personality mentioned earlier. The unity of the ego would be destroyed and the personality, as such, cease to exist. The text reads, "Koshchey ... overtook Ivan Tsarevich, chopped him into tiny pieces, and put the pieces in a tarred barrel; he took the barrel, reinforced it with iron hoops, threw it into the blue sea..."

Of interest here is the mention of the tarred barrel into which Koshchey puts the pieces of Ivan Tsarevich's body, reinforcing it with iron hoops. He does not just throw the dismembered hero into the sea, to be scattered and eaten by fish; that would clinically amount to psychosis and the total dissociation of the personality. Difficult as it is to believe, he instead leaves the possibility of salvation and transformation open. From this we can infer that even Koshchey is in the service of the Self.

The motif of dismemberment is a central motif in alchemy, as well as in the shamanic initiation rites of many cultures. It symbolizes a fundamental disruption of the prevailing conscious attitude, marking a point in the individuation process where nothing but a completely new orientation is called for. It is an intervention by the Self with radical consequences for the personality, and it is experienced by the ego as total destruction.

This is now constellated in the tale. We saw earlier that Ivan Tsarevich's visits to his sisters and brothers-in-law had strengthened and centered him. The three silver objects which he left behind created a bond between them which now manifests in the darkening of the silver. This calls the brothers-in-law to the scene, and they work together to revive Ivan Tsarevich.

The way they go about it can be compared with the therapeutic process. First the barrel with Ivan Tsarevich's dismembered body is raised up out of the sea; this symbolizes bringing consciousness into an unconscious situation. Breaking the barrel, taking the different pieces out, and washing them represents the continual work on the shadow which accompanies this process. Finally, putting the parts together "in the right order" speaks of reintegrating the personality, correcting things which may perhaps have been "out of order"; this also belongs to work on the shadow.

But despite all the work, nothing happens. Now the raven flies off and returns with the water of death. It should not surprise us to learn that the raven is connected with the water of death, for it often represents the *nigredo* in alchemy. This refers once again to the shadow or the *massa confusa*, the unformed mass representing a return to primordial chaos; it is the original substance which must be re-created, that is, transformed. According to the text, it is only after the raven sprinkles Ivan Tsarevich with the water of death that the pieces grow together.

Still Ivan Tsarevich shows no sign of life. This can only imply that what now lies before them is the old ego, and that this ego must die before any meaningful transformation can take place. And surely enough, after the falcon sprinkles the dead body with the water of life, Ivan Tsarevich shudders, gets up and utters the usual words of heroes in such situations: "Ah, how long I have slept!"

After this happy ending, the brothers-in-law invite him to return home with them. These positive shadows, which are intimately connected to his sisters, have been instrumental in bringing him back to life. They do not appear to understand, however, that this ordeal has but opened a new chapter in Ivan Tsarevich's journey. Whereas his visits to his sisters and brothers-in-law had previously strengthened and supported him, at this stage they would have sidetracked him from his new task. Ivan Tsarevich's answer is clear and firm: "No, brothers! I shall go look for Mar'ya Morevna."

What happens next reveals Ivan Tsarevich's new attitude toward Koshchey. His recent experience has made him realize that there is no escape from this demon, that Koshchey must be destroyed; this is substantially different from his compassion at their first meeting in the forbidden closet. We recognize a similar change in his response to Mar'ya Morevna. His very first words to her are: "Find out from Koshchey the Deathless where he got himself such a good steed." No welcoming words, no embraces, no tears of joy. The tale has shifted onto another level.

With the help of Mar'ya Morevna, Ivan Tsarevich now acquires important information about Koshchey. He learns that there is a greater power behind this demon, and realizes that he cannot hope to win against him without first confronting Baba Yaga. Psychologically, this is very significant, for it shows that he has to face the negative aspect of the mother archetype before he can confront the demonic father.

What Ivan Tsarevich has just gone through is an initiation into the second half of life, in which a man's interest and responsibility shift toward the inner world, more specifically, toward the world of the anima. In this initiation, his original relationship with the feminine as son is now broadened to include the role of partner. Similarly, the confrontation with his personal shadow is extended to that of the collective shadow, and his relationship with his parents will now encompass the archetypal father and mother. In a more general way, this can be expressed as a shift in emphasis from the personal to the collective unconscious, whereby the former is not rejected but expanded and deepened.

Such are the implications of Ivan Tsarevich's initiation. He cannot accept the invitation of his brothers-in-law before finding a solution to the threat which Koshchey poses to his relationship with Mar'ya Morevna. This is not a mighty warrior who sweeps his lady away from the enemy's grasp as she sits passively, despairing over her approaching doom. Rather, this is a hero who has realized that he is no match for this villain, and that he needs to work together with his anima to solve their mutual problem. As we recall, Mar'ya Morevna herself was not able to permanently get rid of Koshchey; she could only temporarily incapacitate him and keep him hidden in the secret closet of her home.

Ivan Tsarevich's contribution to this joint effort is his realization that the key to Koshchey's power lies in his steed. He arrives at this conclusion either through deduction or intuition, for he has never witnessed the steed's mantic capabilities; he never overheard the advice it gave its master. We can, therefore, attribute his knowledge either to the enhanced Logos of his more masculine ego or to the increased access to the unconscious which he has obtained through his initiation. Because the relationship between the two men is so hostile, Ivan Tsarevich is wise to stay out of Koshchey's way, and so he relies on Mar'ya Morevna to obtain the necessary information.

After killing and dismembering Ivan Tsarevich, Koshchey is probably confident of having secured Mar'ya Morevna for himself. Why shouldn't he brag about his steed and his connection with Baba Yaga? Obviously Mar'ya Morevna goes along with this deception, and manages to extract all the necessary information from Koshchey. She takes advantage of his interest in her, and uses a semblance of Eros to achieve her ends.

Till now, neither Mar'ya Morevna nor Ivan Tsarevich could match or overcome Koshchey's power. His is a power with no Eros, for it doesn't take the other into account. Even if Koshchey's principal interest is in women, this is always for his satisfaction and for the fulfillment of his own needs. As mentioned earlier, this mirrors all too well the sexual abuse of our day!

Seeing Koshchey as an archetypal figure provides additional insight, for it implies that the potential for such a manipulative aspect of the masculine exists in every psyche. The message of this tale is, therefore, that a *coniunctio* with the soul is the only means of preventing such abuse in its outer manifestation. This does not only pertain to men; the same holds true for a woman who allows the animus to rule her life, for then it is not a *coniunctio* but a possession by this Koshchey spirit.

Mar'ya Morevna now informs Ivan Tsarevich of what she learned from Koshchey. Not having suspected her motives, Koshchey disclosed that he received a colt from Baba Yaga as reward for herding her mares for three days. He also told Mar'ya Morevna where Baba Yaga lives, and described the way to her kingdom: "Beyond the thrice nine lands, in the thrice tenth kingdom, beyond a river of fire, lives Baba Yaga." In Russian tales, this is one of the typical descriptions symbolizing the deeper layers of the unconscious. Mar'ya Morevna also reports that Baba Yaga has many splendid mares, one of which she uses to fly around the world each day. This information, together with the fact that Koshchey had to work for his colt, divulges her superior power. The importance of the horse for Baba Yaga testifies to the tremendous libido of this cosmic goddess. Last but not least, Koshchey reveals the secret of the handkerchief, without which it is impossible to cross the river of fire. Mar'ya Morevna listens carefully, steals the handkerchief, and reports all to Ivan Tsarevich.

Learning that this handkerchief provides the only means of crossing the river of fire, Ivan Tsarevich wastes no time in overcoming that hurdle and seeking out Baba Yaga. This raises an interesting question for, by doing so, Ivan Tsarevich is now using Koshchey's weapons. This suggests that there are situations where collective morality does not apply, where one must do the wrong thing for the right reasons. As we have seen in the case of the mercurial thief in "The Seven Simeons," such are the amoral ways of the unconscious. Had the hero followed collective values, he could never have freed Mar'ya Morevna from Koshchey's regressive pull; he would never have made it into the realm of Baba Yaga.

The fire which bars Ivan Tsarevich's way to the realm of Baba Yaga represents the powerful emotions triggered by his intrusion into the archetypal world of the unconscious. This river of fire, separating the known world from that of Baba Yaga, is a paradoxical image. As a river, it is something that flows; without it there would be a static gorge. Fire does not flow, it spreads, but even then, it does not confine itself to a riverbed. Neither do we have any indication of it being lava. It appears to be water *and* fire, a juxtaposition of opposites that is inconceivable to the conscious mind. This supports our assumption that Ivan Tsarevich is now standing at the threshold of the unconscious. For the normal ego, this could spell psychosis; only the hero has the means of averting this danger because of his connection to the Self.

In the case at hand, it is the handkerchief which Mar'ya Morevna steals from Koshchey that offers a solution, and provides access to the realm of Baba Yaga. This handkerchief, waved three times to the right (the direction of consciousness), causes a high bridge to appear, upon which the river can be crossed; waved three times to the left (the direction of the unconscious), it causes this bridge to disappear. To the conscious mind this is magic, totally against the laws of nature. It is yet another example of what Jung said of magic, namely that it is an indication of unconscious influence.[214] We likewise recall the quote from his *Zarathustra Seminars*: "In habentibus symbolum facilior est transitus"; for those who have a symbol, that is, for those who are capable of thinking symbolically, the passing from one side to the other is easier.[215]

---

214   Jung, *Structure and Dynamics*, CW 8, § 725.
215   Jung, *Zarathustra 2*, 1248.

Koshchey's handkerchief is such an example; as a symbol, it connects the conscious with the unconscious part of the psyche. It is manmade, but of a natural material and, being square, it carries the numerical symbolism of totality and the geometrical symbolism of a quaternion or mandala, that is, the Self. Summarizing, we can say that what makes the transition from the conscious to the unconscious realm possible is the wholeness constellated by the physical effort of producing such an object (matter), coupled with the psychic quality of the number four (spirit).

Let us return for a moment to the river of fire. At first glance it appears that this is meant to keep humans from entering Baba Yaga's territory; however, as we later see, she too is dependent upon the bridge to get over to the other side, as when she pursues the hero out of her territory, riding in a mortar and pestle. And yet, we recall Koshchey's words to Mar'ya Morevna about Baba Yaga flying around the world each day on her mare. This raises the question of whether it is the horse which makes Baba Yaga into a cosmic goddess. Whatever the answer, this is the kind of energy that Ivan Tsarevich is out to get.

The symbolism of the horse has been discussed in detail in the tale of "Two Ivans, Soldier's Sons" (p. 169). Internalizing this horse aspect of the psyche allows us to appreciate the tremendous power which can result from balancing the instinctual, non-human part of the psyche with ego consciousness. This is another aspect of wholeness, one which can never be achieved by force, but only through mutual respect and appreciation. What holds for the relationship between a human and their horse is equally valid for the attitude toward one's psyche. As we shall see in Ivan Tsarevich's final battle with Koshchey, it is the reason for the hero's ultimate defeat of the villain.

Upon successfully crossing the river of fire, Ivan Tsarevich finds himself in the realm of Baba Yaga. Here he meets three sets of animals, three mothers with their offspring; despite his hunger, he accepts the mothers' pleas and spares their young, then continues on his way. Von Franz holds that in fairy tales there is but one rule without an exception: Whoever acquires the gratitude and help of an animal always wins. Psychologically, this would imply that success only comes to one who acts in accordance with their instincts; neither good nor evil can prevail if it goes against this animal soul in a human.[216] This echoes what has been said of the relationship to the horse.

The first animal our hungry hero meets is a bird. Calling it a bird "from beyond the sea" is a literal translation of the Russian adjective, which refers to something exotic or fantastic. As any bird, it belongs to the realm of the sky and symbolizes spirit. In a letter written in 1959, Jung speaks of the bird as a messenger of the gods, an *angelus*, a symbolic being which introduces a higher, transcendent quality.[217] Earlier in the tale, we had already met Ivan Tsarevich's brothers-in-law in bird form, but these were all masculine beings. Here the bird is clearly designated as a female of the species.

A bird can symbolize intuitions, thoughts or fantasies. Here too, it is important to see all these aspects as related to the nature of the feminine, as being governed by Eros. This exotic bird is reminiscent of the firebird in other Russian fairy tales, such as "The Maiden Tsar," "The Firebird and Princess Vasilisa," and "Prince Ivan, the Firebird, and the Gray Wolf." In all these tales the bird represents an anima figure in her spiritual form. The appearance of this mother bird with her young may be imagined as a signpost, announcing to the hero that he has now entered the world of the Great Mother.

Next, Ivan Tsarevich comes to a beehive. By now he is very hungry and wants to strengthen himself with some honey, but the queen bee asks him to refrain from doing so. Here it is a bit more difficult to understand why this is denied him, for it would not have harmed the bees or the beehive. Perhaps the emphasis is on ritual fasting; perhaps he will now be exposed to another form of initiation.

Bees live in a matriarchal society. They were sacred to the mother goddesses as they represented Eros and eroticism, the latter being depicted beautifully in the biblical "Song of Songs." Honey is used to make mead, the drink of the gods and inspiration of poets.

As insects, bees have no individuality, but function in a perfectly organized and disciplined way, and have been doing so for millions of years. In our psyche they would represent all those functions of our

---

216   von Franz, *Archetypal Dimensions*, 89.
217   Jung, *Letters 2*, 476 f.

body which do not need consciousness to carry out their work, but are governed by the sympathetic nervous system. We can, therefore, interpret them as symbolizing the unconscious functioning of the body.

After the bee, Ivan Tsarevich meets a lioness. Here, for the first time, we have a mammal and a predator. As the eagle is *king of birds*, so the lion is *king of animals*, and the lioness is his queen. This is, of course, a very patriarchal view of animal symbolism, indicative of our culture, but this was not so in matriarchal society where the lioness had a close connection to the Great Mother, and hence a significance independent of the lion.

Eric Neumann traces the lioness in the imagery of the Great Goddess throughout the ages, from the Mesopotamian Lilith to the Christian Maria.[218] Neumann's comparison of the male and female attitude toward animals in mythology and folklore is interesting: "Whereas the male god in myth, like the male hero, usually appears in opposition to the animal that he fights and defeats, the Great Goddess, as Lady of the Beasts, dominates them but seldom fights them..."[219]

In the wild, the duties of the lion and the lioness are quite different; the lioness is the main provider of food,[220] whereas the lion guards against invaders of his territory. She is the one who takes care of the cubs, teaches them to hunt, and introduces them into the pride.[221] What she does share with the lion, however, is a passionate sex life.[222]

What does this excursion into the nature of the lioness add to our understanding of the fairy tale? What part of Ivan Tsarevich's psyche is activated by this encounter? Surely this confronts him with a wild, instinctive aspect of the feminine with its ferociousness and its sensuality.

Let us now rejoin our hero as he makes his way to Baba Yaga. Upon crossing the river of fire, Ivan Tsarevich met up with three different aspects of the mother archetype: the exotic bird symbolizing the female spirit; the bee, the unconscious functioning of the body; and the lioness, instinctive femininity.

---

218   Neuman, *The Great Mother*, 272 f.
219   Neuman, *The Great Mother*, 272.
220   Dolder, *Löwen*, 31.
221   Dolder, *Löwen*, 22 f.
222   Dolder, *Löwen*, 15.

Approaching the house of Baba Yaga, Ivan Tsarevich finds it surrounded by twelve stakes, with a human head impaled on all but one. This sight leaves no doubt about her intentions, and yet Ivan Tsarevich is not daunted by such a welcome. He greets Baba Yaga, addressing her as "grandmother," and doesn't allow her to provoke him by asking whether he has come of his own free will or out of need. Ivan Tsarevich gets straight to the point, and tells Baba Yaga that he has come to earn a mighty steed from her.

Ivan Tsarevich's arrival at Baba Yaga's house marks another crucial moment in the tale. We spoke of the symbolism of the number twelve in connection with the twelve chains holding Koshchey in Mar'ya Morevna's closet. There the time had come to completion, and a new development was initiated by Ivan Tsarevich's freeing Koshchey; here, all but one of the twelve stakes have heads impaled upon them, and it is clear that if Baba Yaga has her way this last one will soon carry that of Ivan Tsarevich. This would also constellate wholeness in time, but with dire consequences for the hero, for then ego consciousness would be wiped out by the devouring mother; then fate would take a negative turn for Ivan Tsarevich.

Anyone but a hero would have been terrified by what was now taking place, so it is impressive that Ivan Tsarevich addresses Baba Yaga cordially as "grandmother." This minor detail is psychologically very meaningful. In *Dream Analysis* Jung writes that in dealing with the unconscious nothing is quite as dangerous as fear. "If you are afraid," writes Jung, "you are gone, the game is already lost."[223]

Panic is even more dangerous; in speaking of a patient confronting his wife, Jung says: "If my patient *keeps his head* (italics mine), he may be able to handle the situation...if [he] is in the least afraid he would most likely handle the situation awkwardly, he would infect her with panic and cause the powder to explode...he must be cautious..."[224]

As in Jung's example, Ivan Tsarevich must also exercise extreme caution in confronting Baba Yaga. The emphasis here is once again on the strength of ego consciousness. Ivan Tsarevich must "use his head";

---

223   Jung, *Dream Analysis*, 205.
224   Jung, *Dream Analysis*, 205.

he must curb his instinct to act emotionally. An animal faced with a comparable situation might try to attack, flee, cower, or play dead. We can be reasonably sure that none of these reactions would have been successful with Baba Yaga. Apart from any pragmatic considerations, what the hero displays in this instance includes respect and humility toward an archetypal content, independently of whether this is constellated in its positive or negative aspect. This is similar to the heroine's response to Baba Yaga in "Vasilisa the Beautiful."

Judging from Baba Yaga's reaction, this seems to have the right effect. She responds to Ivan Tsarevich in like manner—courteous, but firm and straightforward. Very possibly, she is impressed with the respect and good manners he shows her, as well as by his standing up for his needs. She then sets her own conditions, and makes it clear that non-compliance will cost him his head. This potentially dangerous episode is followed by her offering him food and drink.

The motif of eating in the other world is a frequent one in fairy tales. In some instances it appears to be right for the hero to do this, but in others it binds him to that world and prevents him from returning home. This ambivalence suggests that a deeper, psychological meaning underlies this situation. Jung discusses this issue in connection with incest. Both incest and hunger are characteristic of a regression to the mother. Jung argues that if such regressive libido is denied realization, it can be rechanneled into symbolic form and redirected toward the inner mother, the collective unconscious. Fasting is a means by which this libido can be redirected into such an inner experience; this is the reason why it is often a necessary preparation for initiatory rites.[225]

In the present tale, the libido which would have gone into eating the animals or the bees' honey falls into the unconscious and activates an aspect of the mother archetype which Ivan Tsarevich has not experienced before. For the sake of wholeness, which becomes ever more important in the second half of life, he now needs to confront the negative feminine in the person of Baba Yaga.

---

225   Jung, *Symbols of Transformation*, CW 5, § 519.

It is interesting to note that feeding the hero is one of Baba Yaga's typical actions.[226] At times, the hero himself refuses to answer her questions until she has fed him, given him to drink, heated up the bath for him and let him sleep. This illustrates the necessity of bringing such negative aspects of the unconscious closer to consciousness where they can be humanized and more easily dealt with. Indeed, after the hero has made the above demands of Baba Yaga, and after these demands have been met, she often rewards him with gifts and good counsel. Here again, it is the hero's ability to stand up for himself and even to set his own conditions that constellates such a conciliatory response. We may even postulate that she is testing him to find out if he is worthy of her trust.

Sometimes Baba Yaga makes unreasonable demands of the hero. Tales in which the hero is preceded by his elder brothers show them to be incapable of responding adequately, with the result that they are usually eaten by the Baba Yaga. If the elder brothers are seen as earlier attempts of the ego to solve a problem, their being eaten implies that they are rendered unconscious. Both the hero and his brothers enter the unconscious, but the hero does so actively or intentionally, whereas the brothers do so passively, against their will. This could be the reason for Baba Yaga's initial question to the hero about whether he is coming of his own free will or not.

As the condition for receiving a mighty steed from Baba Yaga, Ivan Tsarevich must tend her mares for three days, not losing a single one and bringing them all back by night. It is here that the helpful animals come to his aid, and accomplish a task which he could never have managed by himself. Psychologically, we would say that, faced with an unsolvable problem, Ivan Tsarevich relinquishes ego control and allows his instincts free reign, just as a lost rider entrusts their horse with getting them back home.

Throughout the tale we have seen Ivan Tsarevich freely expressing his emotions. Each time Mar'ya Morevna is taken away from him, he cries, but then he gets up and continues on his way. In the three episodes

---

226   This is paralleled in other cultures where eating is a prerequisite for entering the world of the dead, for example, Egypt, Babylon, ancient Greece (Lotus-eater motif of the Odyssey).

with the mares, when he loses all hope of bringing them back by night-fall, his response is the same; he sits on a stone and weeps, but then, strangely enough, he falls asleep. It is difficult to imagine how one can physically fall asleep sitting on a stone, but symbolically it is another example of relinquishing ego control and allowing the unconscious to provide the necessary solution. "The morning is wiser than the evening," says the Russian proverb. In English, one might express this by *sleeping on something*. During sleep, consciousness is submerged into the uncon-scious and better able to integrate unconscious contents. Apart from being an important symbol of the Self, the stone on which Ivan Tsarevich sits while weeping and sleeping is also a solid part of the earth, and shows that he is well grounded in trusting his emotions.

At the setting of the sun, Ivan Tsarevich is awakened by each of his helpers and informed that the day's task has been accomplished. Returning to Baba Yaga's house, he overhears her scolding her mares for coming home. If before he was not fully aware of her evil designs, now he can no longer doubt her intentions. The extreme measures taken by Baba Yaga to destroy the hero shows her reluctance to give up any of her instinctive energy to consciousness, even the sickly, mangy colt that she herself had rejected. Moreover, it reveals Baba Yaga's sen-sitivity to exposing her dark side. Examples of this motif can be found in "The Black Woman's Castle"[227] or in "Vasilisa, the Beautiful."[228] In such tales, the heroine succeeds only by showing extreme respect to this dark side of the archetype.

On the eve of the fourth day, after the bees had successfully dealt with the last trial, Ivan Tsarevich receives additional instructions to cope with Baba Yaga. The queen bee tells him to keep out of her sight; he is to hide in the manger and to make his escape "in the dark of midnight," stealing the mangy colt. The sympathetic nervous system symbolized by the bees is now responsible for this final *coup de force*, which we might also describe as a gut instinct. Baba Yaga's response to Ivan Tsarevich's success in meeting her demands makes it clear that she will not abide by her promise and willingly allow him to leave her kingdom with the "mighty steed" he asked for.

---

227   Von Franz, *Archetypal Dimensions*, 174.
228   Afanas'yev, § 104.

The number symbolism now alerts us to another critical moment in the tale. The dynamic energy of the number three is approaching its climax, but it demands extreme vigilance to arrive at the wholeness of the number four.

Ivan Tsarevich's experience in Baba Yaga's realm has taught him to curb his conscious will and submit to the guidance of the unconscious. We now see him following the queen bee's instructions explicitly, and thereby escaping Baba Yaga's wrath by the skin of his teeth. Interestingly enough, the reader is informed that, on that evening, Baba Yaga fell asleep and missed Ivan Tsarevich's escape. Did she not instinctively realize that she needed to remain watchful at such an important moment, or was she too sure of herself?

When Ivan Tsarevich first arrived at Baba Yaga's house, he used willpower to curb his fear. It was an *opus contra naturam* not to be ruled by his instinct. In pursuing him, Baba Yaga's anger gets the better of her, and she cannot realistically assess the strength of the bridge before her. She is tricked by Ivan Tsarevich, but only because she is blinded by her own affect. The river of fire, which cannot be crossed without the right kind of transition—the bridge—now spells her defeat. This confirms yet again that this is not Baba Yaga's river, but one that has been assigned by the Self as a boundary between the two realms. Whereas Ivan Tsarevich shows respect for the power of Baba Yaga and acts accordingly, she fails to acknowledge the superior power of the Self, and is destroyed by her own inflation.

This last episode with Baba Yaga brings up another important consideration, namely that a certain kind of evil cannot be transformed or done away with permanently. There are many fairy tales that show how the hero's attitude can influence Baba Yaga in a positive way. In the present tale, we have seen Ivan Tsarevich defuse her destructive power by being cautious and not provoking her, but later on he tricks her into falling into the river of fire. Nonetheless, it would be foolish to think that this has permanently solved the problem presented by her. The fact that she perishes in the river of fire cannot be seen as a final solution, any more than a happy end guarantees the permanent well-being of those who are said to "live happily ever after." Both of these endings mirror the outcome of this fairy tale; they represent the solution to the specific problem which has been constellated. From a psychological point of view, it would be highly optimistic, indeed unrealistic, to presume that any archetype can be permanently destroyed.

Let us now take a closer look at the mangy colt that Ivan Tsarevich steals from Baba Yaga. According to Webster, the word "mange" refers to "any of various skin diseases due to parasitic mites affecting animals and sometimes man and characterized by loss of hair and scabby eruptions." The mangy colt is sick and left to lie on a dung heap. With so many mares in the stable, one would think that some motherly animal would take pity on it, but this colt is rejected and not cared for. Is this because it is a male? Earlier we noticed that everything in Baba Yaga's realm is feminine: the exotic bird, the queen bee, the lioness. Is it possible that Baba Yaga destroyed all male beings in her territory?

Such reasoning is reminiscent of the Amazons in Greek mythology, who were believed to maim or kill any male children born to them, and only suffered the presence of men for procreation. This myth was probably inspired by the nomadic Sarmatians who occupied the northern shores of the Black Sea in the third to the second centuries B.C. Women played an important role in this society; they rode horses, hunted, and accompanied their men into battle. This area was the cradle of the Slavic peoples, and such accounts may well have left traces in Slavic folklore.[229]

Novikov places Baba Yaga's roots in matriarchal society. His study of Slavic folklore reveals that her primary connection has always been with women, predominantly with her daughters, whom she often transforms into mares; any men she deals with are suspect and scorned. A variant of our tale speaks of the mangy colt as her son; the present one shows just how *motherly* her treatment of him is. In his description of Baba Yaga, Novikov notes that she appears both positively and negatively inclined, and ascribes this ambivalence to the long and bitter struggle between matriarchy and patriarchy.[230]

Novikov's views are compatible with Jungian psychology, in which Baba Yaga would be seen as an image of the Great Mother, and her

---

229 Rybakov, *Yazychestvo drevnich slavyan*, 575, 616 ff.
230 Novikov, *Obrazy*, 180.

ambivalence directly attributable to her archetypal nature; her negative response is then a compensation to the one-sided attitude toward the feminine in patriarchal society.

But how can we explain such animosity toward women in patriarchy? Could it be attributable to fear? The feminine is, after all, an archetypal force no less powerful than the masculine. If a man is incapable of meeting the challenge of this active life force, he may experience it as destructive and aggressive; its positive aspects would then be acknowledged and welcomed, while all that threatens him would be viewed with suspicion and repressed. As we know, however, everything that is repressed falls into the unconscious and takes on an archaic, undifferentiated, autonomous, and negative form. This results in a vicious cycle which, if not broken, causes blindness and leads to projection on both sides.

This mirrors Ivan Tsarevich's experiences with Baba Yaga. Firstly, her territory is far removed from the rest of the story and cut off by a formidable barrier—a river of fire; this already suggests repression. Secondly, her antagonism and evil intent toward the hero reveal the negativity arising from the repression. The benevolent aspect of this archetype appears in the instinctual, non-human aspects of the feminine; the bird, the lioness and the bees all respond to the hero in a related way and subsequently save him from Baba Yaga's animosity.

It will be remembered that Ivan Tsarevich's motivation for seeking out Baba Yaga was his inability to cope with Koshchey, because after his dismemberment and rebirth he realizes that the demon's power lies in his horse. He has Mar'ya Morevna question Koshchey, and thereby finds out that the horse was received in payment for herding Baba Yaga's mares.

The psychological importance of this scenario lies in the fact that the ego, the hero Ivan Tsarevich, works together with his anima. In effect then, we can say that Koshchey caused his own demise by not realizing the importance of ego consciousness. This episode also shows that the solution to Ivan Tsarevich's problems with Koshchey required him to confront the negative aspect of the mother archetype; this too, would have been impossible without his anima.

The original weakness of the hero's consciousness was gradually overcome by the strengthening of his ego. Jung saw this as the major task of the first half of life. As we learn from archaic initiation rites, this could not be accomplished without repression and without the rechanneling of energy into other, more acceptable, forms. At that earlier stage, repression was legitimate because of the ego's vulnerability to the power of the unconscious; as the ego became stronger, such repression could be turned increasingly into a use of force against the unconscious.

Every hero has the task of harmonizing the relationship between the two parts of the psyche. Tales with archaic material show the male hero killing the female dragon, symbolically asserting himself against the devouring unconscious. With further development, the hero is called upon to differentiate between what can be incorporated into consciousness and what must be rejected. As Ivan Tsarevich demonstrates, however, this needs to be done with relatedness and humility, not with arrogance. Often, when confronted with an insurmountable challenge, the hero can only be saved through the intervention of a helpful animal. This shows that no success is possible without a connection to one's instinctual roots. In our tale such an admission of powerlessness is exemplified by the stone, the ground of hard reality, on which Ivan Tsarevich sits, weeps, and sleeps.

As we have seen in the tale of "The Seven Simeons," a hero's actions do not always conform to collective norms (p. 247). Here too, Ivan Tsarevich doesn't ask whether using Koshchey's handkerchief to get across the river of fire is right or wrong. He has no scruples about stealing the mangy colt, nor does he refrain from tricking Baba Yaga into crossing the weakened bridge and falling into the flames. But what he does manage to do is avoid inflation, something that neither Baba Yaga, nor later Koshchey, is capable of doing. Inflation reflects an inability to realize that stronger forces are at work.

After crossing the river of fire, Ivan Tsarevich stops to put his mangy colt out to pasture in green meadows. It is understandable that he had no time to do so while escaping from Baba Yaga, but this existential source of energy, symbolized by the horse, now needs to be strengthened; its vitality needs to be restored. In life-threatening circumstances, we are sometimes able to force our energy far beyond normal limits, but we cannot hope to continue in this way for long without replenishing our resources. Doing that requires a conscious decision, and it is therefore appropriate that Ivan Tsarevich feeds the colt after crossing to the other, conscious side of the river of fire.

The tale now moves swiftly to its end. Ivan Tsarevich rides his magnificent steed to Koshchey's house and carries Mar'ya Morevna off for the fourth time. As Koshchey returns home, his horse stumbles; when questioned, it informs its master that Ivan Tsarevich has, once again, run off with Mar'ya Morevna; it also discloses that this time Ivan Tsarevich has a superior steed, and that success is not guaranteed. Koshchey is furious; he refuses to accept the possibility of defeat. Blinded by rage, he does not heed the words of his steed, words that had been proven true on previous occasions. Here, hubris leads to Koshchey's defeat, just as it did to Baba Yaga's.

Koshchey pursues Ivan Tsarevich and, upon catching up with him, engages him in battle. Rather than remaining on his horse, however, Koshchey dismounts and attempts to cut Ivan Tsarevich down with his saber. This seemingly insignificant detail is quite meaningful from a symbolic perspective. By dismounting, Koshchey has separated himself from his horse, and thereby deprived himself of the tremendous power of his instincts. Actually, he had already sealed his fate by not heeding his horse's advice.

Koshchey now relies upon his saber. Like any weapon, a saber is used for killing, even though symbolically it can represent differentiation. In the hands of this villain, however, who does not allow his instincts to correct the intentions of his will, one cannot speak of differentiation. Here, his use of the saber shows Koshchey to be power-driven and completely unrelated. His warped reasoning works against him, for he doesn't realize that being on the ground while his adversary is mounted makes him vulnerable.

At this moment, Ivan Tsarevich's horse smashes Koshchey's head with a strike of its hoof. Although it is Ivan Tsarevich who subsequently finishes Koshchey off with his mace, it is the mighty steed which has made this possible—a perfect example of a joint effort. The goodwill which Ivan Tsarevich had previously shown the mangy colt now pays off, just as it had with the bird, the bee, and the lioness.

After Koshchey has been killed, Ivan Tsarevich gathers wood for a fire and burns the body; he then scatters Koshchey's ashes to the wind.

It was previously mentioned that tradition places Koshchey into one of two categories, based on the cause of his death. The second of these categories assigns his death to a mighty steed. Although this is the case in our tale, it is psychologically significant that here Koshchey's death cannot be attributed solely to the horse, but is the result of a joint effort by the hero and his horse. Psychologically, this is only possible if the instinctual part of the psyche works together with ego consciousness.

The fire, which was the key element in the death of both Baba Yaga and Koshchey, carries an important symbolic connotation, for it represents the inflation and fury which blinds them and leads to their demise.[231] Like any archetypal force, however, fire is ambivalent; it can destroy, but it also purifies and transforms. Both aspects play a role in the present situation, for even though Baba Yaga's and Koshchey's physical remains are dissolved in the river of fire or burned and scattered in the wind respectively, their instinctual energy continues to serve Ivan Tsarevich and Mar'ya Morevna as the latter's steeds. Psychologically, this would indicate that the tremendous energy of these negative aspects of the mother and father archetypes, which had formerly hindered the development of both Ivan Tsarevich as the ego and Mar'ya Morevna as his anima, are now free to enter life in their positive manifestations.

Having put an end to Koshchey, Ivan Tsarevich now visits his sisters and brothers-in-law with Mar'ya Morevna. They are greeted with great joy, and Ivan Tsarevich's efforts at winning Mar'ya Morevna back from Koshchey are unanimously applauded: "...such a beauty as Mar'ya Morevna could be sought throughout the world, but her equal could never be found." Such euphoric praise speaks more of the anima than of any mortal woman.

This final passage brings the archetypal experiences of the tale back to waking reality. It allows Ivan Tsarevich and Mar'ya Morevna to return to normal life and to incorporate the manifold transformations they have experienced: "... they began to live and prosper and drink mead." Here drinking mead would allow for a double interpretation—the enjoyment of the sweetness of life and the inspiration which the true union of ego and anima brings.

---

231   Jung, *Civilization in Transition*, CW 10, § 643

Because this is such a long and intricate tale, I will now summarize some of its most significant moments. The hero is presented as a kind, loyal, empathic man, who trusts in life, or rather, who trusts that life will provide him with what is necessary to continue in the way of his father. He embraces and furthers all the good things that come his way. At the start of the tale, however, he does not show much personal initiative; he displays little curiosity, and does not appear to have any particular goal in life.

The first experience that jars his placid temperament is a meeting with a powerful warrior princess, a woman unlike any he had experienced before; opposites attracting one another could have no better example. It is love at first sight, and the two decide to marry.

Then Mar'ya Morevna takes Ivan Tsarevich to live in her kingdom. This is a bit unexpected, for his castle stands empty and there would seem to be no reason why he wouldn't want to bring his bride back to his home. Viewed subjectively, however, his following her can be seen as a particularly fateful experience of the anima, one which pulls him into her sphere of influence, and reroutes his whole psychic development. It marks the beginning of a process which ultimately frees the hero from the grip of the archetypal mother and channels his libido toward the anima.

Shortly thereafter, Mar'ya Morevna decides to go to war. Marriage doesn't seem to have changed her very much. Before leaving, she puts the whole household into Ivan Tsarevich's care, and forbids him access to a certain closet. This is rather surprising because fairy tales usually attribute this role to a man. It is obvious that Mar'ya Morevna is still in charge; she is active and focused, and she is out to kill.

None of this appears to concern or upset Ivan Tsarevich, and after she leaves his first reaction is to run to the forbidden closet and open the door. There he discovers Koshchey, hanging suspended on twelve chains. This discloses the terrible secret in Mar'ya Morevna's home. Did she intend for this to come to light? Is this perhaps her reason for bringing Ivan Tsarevich to her house after they married?

In a parallel version, Mar'ya Morevna is said to have subdued Koshchey in battle and held him captive in a closet of her house. It is surprising that she didn't kill him but, as noted in connection with both

Baba Yaga and Koshchey, an archetype can never be destroyed. It is therefore all the more impressive that, in his final battle with Ivan Tsarevich, Koshchey inadvertently takes part in his own defeat by dismounting from his steed, thereby severing himself from the instinctual part of his being. What follows is Ivan Tsarevich's amazing victory over the villain which, psychologically, can only be attributed to the differentiating faculty of consciousness; this enables Ivan Tsarevich to channel off the instinctual energy of Koshchey's steed, subsequently making it available to his anima, while putting an end to the villain. This would have been impossible without Ivan Tsarevich's experiences in the realm of Baba Yaga. There, for the first time, he is confronted with the negative feminine. For a man with a mother complex, learning to cope with this aspect of the mother archetype is of existential importance, for only then he will have experienced the feminine in both its positive and negative aspects. From the standpoint of number symbolism, it makes perfect sense that Ivan Tsarevich can only free Mar'ya Morevna on the fourth try, for it is through the episode with Baba Yaga that he has gained a more complete experience of the feminine.

And yet none of this would have happened had Mar'ya Morevna not obtained the relevant information from Koshchey. This marked her first involvement in the conflict between Ivan Tsarevich and Koshchey. In general, we note that Mar'ya Morevna becomes more related and devoted to Ivan Tsarevich; she supports him, waits for him, and suffers from his misfortunes. There are changes in Ivan Tsarevich as well. The sorrow he experiences each time Koshchey snatches Mar'ya Morevna away now transforms into a more active and forceful attempt to free her from the villain's grip. The two are growing closer together.

When Ivan Tsarevich and Mar'ya Morevna first met, it was their extreme polarity that brought them so fatefully together. The experience with Koshchey appears to have constellated different aspects of their personalities; Mar'ya Morevna, the warrior princess, becomes more passive and, at the same time, more related to Ivan Tsarevich; and Ivan Tsarevich, who had gone through life in such a passive way, now becomes more active. In one very important respect, however, the new roles do not alter their basic relationship, for it remains compensatory and mutually dependent.

Let us, for a moment, consider Mar'ya Morevna's relationship to Koshchey. Fairy tales never depict him as a young rival, but always as an older man; in fact, he can best be seen as a negative father figure. We saw Mar'ya Morevna cowed by Koshchey, but at the same time we know that she fought against being forced into a subordinate relationship. By her actions, she shows that she is, and intends to remain, a "virgin" in Esther Harding's understanding of this term, that is, a woman who is "one with herself."[232] Perhaps this explains Ivan Tsarevich's lack of concern upon learning that his wife has decided to go to war; it is rather a sign of trust and respect for Mar'ya Morevna's decisions.

Because Eros and power are mutually exclusive,[233] Mar'ya Morevna can only respond to Koshchey's destructive spirit with the death-bringing aspect of the feminine; she fights, she kills, she imprisons. Here, it is helpful to recall that the etymology of her name has been traced to the word for sea—*more*, or death—*mor*, images which contain the polarity of life and death.

The significance of Koshchey's preference for women who are connected to the hero reveals the archetypal nature of this situation. Since the hero is that part of the psyche which acts in accordance with the Self, Koshchey's interference can be seen psychologically as an attempt to obstruct the union of the ego with the anima, which is a goal of the second half of life, the inner wholeness one strives for in the process of individuation.

Since the nature of the unconscious is ambivalent, one can expect that the wished-for union of the hero and the anima must meet with an opposing tendency to swallow up any such development. Such a counteroffensive forces the ego to confront the shadow, and to choose between what it wants and what it doesn't. This creates friction, but also energy; like the biblical Judas, it has its legitimacy and its purpose. In the end, it depends on the ego's response to the challenges it is faced with; there would be no story without Koshchey, nor would there have been any transformation.

---

232 Harding, *The Way of All Women*, 103 ff.
233 "Where love reigns, there is no will to power; and where the will to power is paramount, love is lacking." Jung, *Two Essays*, CW 7, § 78.

Throughout this chapter we have repeatedly pointed to similarities between Baba Yaga and Mar'ya Morevna. This raises the question of whether Mar'ya Morevna might be seen as an attempt on the part of the Self to introduce a more positive version of Baba Yaga. Both are strong, independent, and active women; both are capable of standing up for themselves. Baba Yaga is definitely older than Mar'ya Morevna, and one might wonder if she would have become less aggressive had she met a man like Ivan Tsarevich in her earlier days. In his contacts with Baba Yaga, Ivan Tsarevich appears to know instinctively how to approach her and how to respond to her without being eaten or otherwise annihilated. He treats her with respect, but nonetheless he sees through her to her evil designs; most importantly, he is capable of standing up to her. In a real-life situation, no man could survive a confrontation with such a *Baba Yaga* unless he was convinced of her qualities without being threatened by them.

This kind of woman is exemplified by the mythical Amazons. Although they never existed, the many accounts of them testify to their compensating role for the image of the feminine in Ancient Greece, which was a patriarchal society. Artemis, their patron goddess, was a huntress and closely connected with all animals. Toni Wolff describes the Amazon woman in her positive manifestation as an "independent and self-contained" companion to man. However, she turns vicious when not given her due and when her concerns are not honored.[234]

The very first thing we learn of Mar'ya Morevna in this tale is that she is responsible for the slaughter a whole army of men. After she marries Ivan Tsarevich they move into her home, but shortly thereafter she decides to go to war again. This is a familiar scenario in fairy tales, but it is almost always the man who leaves the home. Here, however, Ivan Tsarevich responds to Mar'ya Morevna's decision in the same way that a wife would do in other tales; he accepts her will and gives her the freedom to do what she thinks is right. As the story unfolds, we realize that there would have been no tale to tell if she hadn't taken this step. It transforms both of them, and ultimately brings them together in a

---

234 Wolff, *Structural Forms*. Toni Wolff follows the pattern of Jung's typology in describing four different aspects of the feminine.

more meaningful way. Most importantly, Ivan Tsarevich does not succumb to the will of Mar'ya Morevna, nor does she to his. The relationship between them is one of respect and trust, and if either of them needs to go their own way, it is always in keeping with their common fate, for if this were endangered, they would both be radically affected.

Such may be the desired culmination of a human relationship, or psychologically the union of a man with his anima and a woman with her animus. Ultimately, neither can be achieved without the other, for if there is no harmony between these inner and outer manifestations of the psyche there will be no lasting effect leading to wholeness.

Conclusion

The tales in this volume all portray different psychic situations that illustrate familiar life experiences.

The initial image in "The Water of Life" is the loss of energy, a disturbing realization that one is not what one was yesterday.

"The Speedy Messenger" starts with stagnation, with an inability to develop, to broaden one's horizons.

"The Feather of Finist the Bright Falcon" illustrates a maiden's transition into womanhood.

"The Enchanted Ring" and "Two Ivans, Soldier's Sons" are both introduced by the motif of the missing father but their stories are very different, and the lysis of each diametrically opposed.

"Seven Simeons" is a burst of creative energy studded with alchemical imagery.

And finally, "Mar'ya Morevna," where we witness a remarkable transformation of a passive man and an active woman.

Seeing fairy tales as illustrations of life experiences explains why they are so important in Jungian analysis and psychotherapy, but the same can be said for other psychological schools. Since this book is concerned specifically with the Jungian understanding of fairy tales, I will now summarize two of Jung's basic principles, relevant in this regard.

The first of these principles concerns Jung's general view of the psyche, namely that it contains conscious and unconscious parts, that the two are related and dependent upon each other, and that, moreover, psychological wellbeing can only prevail if they are in harmony (whereas neurosis results when they are discordant).

Fairy tales depict these two parts as separate worlds. In this book we encounter different examples of this motif. In both "The Water of Life" and "Two Ivans, Soldier's Sons," crossroads mark the boundary between the two worlds. In the first of these tales, a second border is designated by a wide ditch over which the hero spurs his horse as he rides into the realm of the Tsar Maiden; in the second tale, a river of fire separates the world of the hero from that of the Baba Yaga. The seashore constitutes the boundary in "The Speedy Messenger," and the increasing austerity of nature in "The Feather of Finist, the Bright Falcon." Often this other world is introduced by phrases such as "beyond thrice nine lands, in the thrice tenth kingdom."

The hero or heroine experiences the two worlds as real; going from one to another, he interacts with different figures, he confronts unfamiliar situations, and then he carries his experience back into the world from which he came. Often, it is the information he receives from this other world that provides him with a solution to an insolvable problem in his own world.

Such a fairy tale view of life is very much in keeping with Jung's concept of the *reality of the psyche*.[235] Jung considered the two aspects real because they both influence human life. The ego has to consider not only its own position but that of the unconscious; moreover, where possible, it needs to seek consensus between the two and be ready to incorporate the latter. It is clear that such an attitude is highly problematic for someone who only acknowledges the world of conscious reality, for it requires the ability to accept the irrational as a part of the psyche.

Jung's concept of the *reality of the psyche* lies at the core of his whole psychology. The ego learns to heed the compensatory function of the unconscious; at the same time, it must be aware of the latter's different and often opposing manifestations. The hero or heroine, who represents the model ego, must be able to stand up for themselves despite the overwhelming power of the unconscious. In "The Water of Life," we had an example of the hero's answer to Baba Yaga as she tries to intimidate him by questioning the seriousness of his intentions.

In fairy tales, the hero's/heroine's deeds are often described as superhuman and magical. This reveals their connection to the unconscious, for though they are part of the ego, that is, of the conscious psyche, they have the distinctive feature of being in tune with the Self. This holds true irrespective of their different manifestations, even for a "questionable" example of the hero such as the thief in "The Seven Simeons." Jung's

---

235   Jung, *Structure and Dynamics*, CW 8, §§ 742, 747 f.

description of the Self as "...unity of the personality..."[236] reverts to the *"reality of the psyche"* and to the necessary connection between consciousness and the unconsciousness.

The second concept which I would like to introduce into this discussion is that of objective and subjective interpretations. This directly relates to the two parts of the psyche, *objective* referring to images and experiences from the outer world, *subjective* to those of the inner world. Here the difference is a matter of perspective; the content of each is viewed as belonging to either the outer or the inner world. This further emphasizes the correspondence between the two parts of the psyche.

Thus, for example, the three tsareviches in "The Water of Life" may be seen as the tsar's sons (objective perspective) but they may also be his young shadows (subjective perspective). We recognize the youngest as the hero because he finds the solution to the problem. We cannot but marvel at the instinctive way in which he moves through the tale: at the crossroads he follows the middle road despite its leading to death; he knows how to reply to Baba Yaga when she threatens to eat him; he follows the advice of the three Baba Yagas explicitly, apart from the caution against being tempted by the Tsar Maiden's beauty, and so on. All of these decisions prove to be correct despite the fact that they are initially suspect to the conscious mind.

To what can we attribute the hero's actions? The lysis supports his decisions but what may the source of his wisdom be? We only see that he acts instinctively, and certainly for a young man to be overwhelmed by the beauty of the maiden is a plausible explanation for his sleeping with her. This would be a perfectly acceptable interpretation from the objective perspective, that is, from conscious deliberations. However, instinct is deeply rooted in the unconscious part of the psyche, and here we must consider the images of the archetypal world and their validity for all mankind. In this other part of the psyche, the union of man and woman symbolizes the wholeness which creates and heals; consequently, from a subjective perspective, the woman he unites with is the feminine within his own psyche, the anima.

---

236   Jung, *Psychological Types,* CW 6, § 789.

Let us consider the episode of hero's making the *mistake* of divulging his experiences to the brothers. The perfidious tsareviches cut him up into pieces and steal the phial with the water of life. What at first appears as the hero's demise ultimately results in his rebirth. From the objective perspective, his *mistake* would be judged as naive and foolish but, as the further development of the tale shows, his instinct leads him to a deeper and more meaningful lysis.

Let us now compare this scenario with "Two Ivans, Soldier's Sons." Here, twin heroes receive magic steeds from an old man. The tale never speaks of their riding any other horses but these. One of the brothers even combats three, twelve-headed serpents with the help of his steed. Toward the end of the tale however, this strong bond between man and animal appears to slacken, following the appearance of the lovely maiden at the white stone palace. As the hero invites her to join him for a meal, she expresses fear of his magic steed. Both brothers assure her that they have left their magic steeds behind, a statement which is later proven false. A subjective interpretation would attribute the magic steeds to an archetypal aspect of the heroes' instinct. Consequently, by denying the magic nature of their steeds, the heroes cut themselves off from a powerful source of intuition and instinct within their own psyches. At the end of the tale this results in their being torn apart by a lion. The reader is then told that the culprit was the disguised sister of the same three, twelve-headed serpents killed by one of the brothers.

The reason for the heroes' demise is their inability to differentiate between the outer and inner manifestations of the unconscious. The brothers do not suspect the lovely maiden of evil designs, even though they had just experienced her transformation into a lioness. Apparently, they are only capable of believing what is before their eyes; they are no longer open to the inner experience. They have forfeited the valuable potential they once possessed by cutting themselves off from their deeper instincts.

This is what Jung meant by *"reality of the psyche."* What brought the hero success in "The Water of Life" was his instinctive response to everything he experienced, regardless of which part of the psyche it came from, whereas in "Two Ivans, Soldier's Sons," it was the brothers' inability to integrate the subjective component that sealed their fate. Such a negative lysis in the latter clearly indicates that this is the *sine qua non* of individ-uation.

The interaction of the inner and outer parts of the psyche is im-pressively described in the tale of "The Speedy Messenger." The back-drop of this tale is provided by the unconscious; it is portrayed by a huge swamp, a regressive force exemplifying the archetypal mother complex. We also learn that the father has three sons and that he has decided to clear the swamp. Consciousness is now getting involved as it has become activated by the increase in masculine energy. On the symbolic level, this can be attributed to the wholeness constellated by the number four; the time is right for this new development and the necessary energy has now been liberated. Even more importantly, there is consensus between the two parts of the psyche, and this brings life into motion.

The four men set about making the swamp passable for "travelers by foot and for those on horseback." Afterward, the father directs his sons to find out what people think of their accomplishment. This extraverted impulse results in a new spurt of energy from the unconscious; this time it is the Self in the guise of two, wise old men. The old men praise the work and reward the sons' efforts. As noted in the interpretation (p. 59 f.), this is done in a way that furthers their development out of the mother complex.

Another example of the interconnection between the two perspec-tives is given in the interpretation of "The Enchanted Ring." Here, the subjective perspective enriches and deepens the understanding of the tale. The problematic relationship between the hero and his wife is raised to a different level, allowing for a solution which satisfies both the conscious and the unconscious parts of the psyche.

Before seeking help in analysis with some difficult problem, one usually tries to solve it by the means at one's disposal, but this rarely includes the potential of the irrational psyche. This is where dreams and fairy tales can be a valuable tool, for they contain images which open up windows into this other world. As model egos, their heroes and heroines reflect the unconscious view of any such solution. We note, for instance, that although the hero or heroine is usually aware of the final goal of their quest or the right solution to their problem, they rarely know how to get there. They just set out on their journey. In "The Feather of Finist, the Bright Falcon," the heroine's goal is to find her love. She knows that she must equip herself for a long journey but she has no plan for getting there. In "Mar'ya Morevna," Ivan Tserevich leaves his castle to find his sisters out of boredom, but he, too, has no idea where to go. In "The Enchanted Ring," the hero doesn't even have a final goal. He takes the money his father left him and takes to the road.

Sometimes the hero comes to a crossroad, but the directions are not the roadsigns we look for on our highways. At other times, advice is offered by an animal, but who would trust an animal to even understand what the hero is looking for?

In "Two Ivans, Soldier's Sons," we hear the mother say to her adult sons: "Listen to me, children! As you travel to town, bow to anyone whom you encounter." The heroes follow this advice and are rewarded for doing so. For the ego, this implies a readiness and humility to acknowledge the other and to heed the unknown and the unexpected. If we have already decided what one's problem is and how to solve it, one is not as open to what comes one's way. Moreover, if one knows the solution in advance, one is already prejudiced against anything new. But, given that the unconscious is ambivalent, it is understandable if one doesn't quite know what to believe. It is here that the hero's definition as a model ego as well as his being in tune with the Self is so helpful.

I close with "Mar'ya Morevna," a tale which describes a highly differentiated view of the relationship between man and woman. The two main actors form a strong bond from the moment they meet in Mar'ya Morevna's camp, and their relationship grows as the tale develops. At first glance, her name in the title suggests seeing the tale from the feminine perspective, that is, as referring to a feminine psyche. She outshines the good-natured hero by her brilliance and martial exploits. As the story develops, this appraisal of the two becomes more complicated. With time she loses her militant image, whereas he becomes increasingly more active and resolute. The polarity between them remains throughout the tale, but gradually and harmoniously it shifts to another complementary relationship.

This tale is a beautiful illustration of the interrelatedness of the objective and subjective interpretation: the woman outside and the anima for a man; the man outside and the animus for a woman. That this image is projected against the backdrop of so much belligerence and power only makes it more realistic, for such a positive relationship would not be whole without evil. We can perhaps see the lysis of this tale as a new image of the *coniunctio* to which consciousness makes an important contribution.

Among the most interesting and, at the same time, humbling experiences in revisiting a tale is finding that it has new insights to offer. It may be that we have now broadened our knowledge of the subject; more likely, however, it is our inner growth and experience of life that enables us to recognize these deeper aspects. We come to realize that each tale has a greater treasure chest than we are capable of opening at any given time. This may also explain why it can be more enriching to work on a tale together with others, and why so many people from different walks of life and stages of development can relate to the same tale. All of these factors provide strong evidence for the unconscious origin of fairy tales and their archetypal nature.

Bibliography

Afanas'yev, Alexander. *Narodnye Russkiye Skazki* [Russian Folk Tales]. 3 vols. Moscow: Nauka, 1984-5. All tales appearing in the current document have been translated by Nathalie Baratoff.

Baratoff, Nathalie. *Oblomov: A Jungian Approach; A Literary Image of the Mother Complex*. Bern: Peter Lang, 1990.

Becker, Udo. *The Continuum Encyclopedia of Symbols*. Lance W. Garmer, trans. New York: Continuum, 1994.

Birkhäuser-Oeri, Sibyle. *The Mother: Archetypal Image in Fairy Tales*. Toronto: Inner City, 1988.

Bolen, Jean Shinoda. *Goddesses in Everywoman: A New Psychology of Women*. New York: Harper, 1984.

Bulfinch, Thomas. *Bulfinch's Mythology*. New York: Crown Publishers, 1978.

Campbell, Joseph. *The Masks of God: Occidental Mythology*. New York: Penguin Books, 1964.

Chudyakov, I. D., comp. *Velikorusskiye Skazki* [Great Russian Fairy Tales]. Moscow: Nauka, 1964.

Dal', Vladimir. *Tœlkovyi Slovar'* [Explanatory Dictionary]. 4 vols. Moscow, 1955.

Dolder, Willi & Ursula. *Löwen*, Freiburg: Herder, 1988.

Deutsche Märchen seit Grimm, Zürich: Ex Libris, 1964.

Eliade, Mircea. *History of Religious Ideas*. 3 vols. Chicago: University of Chicago Press, 1978-1988.

------. *Rites and Symbols of Initiation*. New York: Harper & Row, 1958.

------. *The Sacred and the Profane*. New York: Harvest, 1959.

------. *Shamanism: Archaic Techniques of Ecstasy*, Princeton: Princeton University Press, 1974.

Federer, Yvonne. *The Animal Within*. Eglisau: Federer, Y., 2002.

Fierz, Heinrich Karl. Jungian Psychiatry. Einsiedeln: Daimon Verlag, 1991.

Gawriluk, T. R. et al., Comparative analysis of ear-hole closure identifies regeneration discrete trait in mammals. *Nature Communications*, 2016; 7: 11164 DOI: 10.1038/ncomms11164.

Grzimek, Bernhard. *Grzimek's Animal Life Encyclopedia*. 13 vols. New York: Van Nostrand, 1972-1975.

Gura, Aleksandr Viktorovich, *Simvolika Zhyvotnych v Slavyanskoy Narodnoy Traditsii* [Animal Symbolism in Slavic Folk Traditions], Moscow: «Индрик», 1997.

Hannah, Barbara. *The Cat, Dog and Horse Lectures*. Illinois: Chiron, 1992.

------. *Encounters with the Soul: Active Imagination as Developed by C.G. Jung*. Santa Monica: Sigo, 1981.

Harding, M. Esther. *The Way of All Women*. New York: Longmans, Green & Co., 1956.

Hillman, James. "Salt: A Chapter in Alchemical Psychology" in *Salt and the Alchemical Soul*. Wookstock: Spring, 1995.

Il'ya Muromets. Compiled with commentary by A.M. Astachova. Moscow: Academia Nauk, USSR, 1958.

Jung, Carl Gustav. *The Collected Works [CW]*, 2nd ed. Edited by H. Read, M. Fordham, and G. Adler and W. McGuire. Translated by R.F.C. Hull. 20 vols. Princeton, NJ: Princeton University Press, 1953-1979.

------. CW 5. *Symbols of Transformation*. 1967.

------. CW 6. *Psychological Types*. 1971.

------. CW 7. *Two Essays on Analytical Psychology*. 1966.

------. CW 8. *The Structure and Dynamics of the Psyche*. 1969.

------. CW 9i. *The Archetypes of the Collective Unconscious*. 1968.

------. CW 9ii. *Aion: Researches into the Phenomenology of the Self*. 1968.

------. CW 10. *Civilization in Transition*. 1970.

------. CW 12. *Psychology and Alchemy*. 1968.

------. CW 13. *Alchemical Studies*. 1968

------. CW 14. *Mysterium Coniunctionis*. 1970.

------. CW 16. *The Practice of Psychotherapy*. 1966.

------. *Letters. Vol. 1. 1906-1950*. Edited by G. Adler and A. Jaffe. Translated by R.F.C.Hull. N.J.: Princeton University Press, 1973.

------. *Letters. Vol. 2. 1951-1961*. Edited by G. Adler and A. Jaffe. Translated by R.F.C.Hull. N.J.: Princeton University Press, 1973.

------. *Children's Dreams: Notes from the Seminar given in 1936-1940 by C.G. Jung*. Edited by L. Jung & M. Meyer-Grass. Translated by E. Falzeder & T. Woolfson. N.J.: Princeton University Press, 2008.

------. *Dream Analysis: Notes of the Seminar given in 1928-1930 by C.G. Jung*. Edited by W. McGuire. N.J.: Princeton University Press, 1984.

------. *Nietzsche's Zarathustra: Notes of the Seminar given in 1934-1939*. Edited by J. Jarrett. 2 vols. N.J.: Princeton University Press, 1988.

------. *Visions: Notes of the Seminar given in 1930-1934 by C.G. Jung*. Edited by C. Douglas. 2 vols. N.J.: Princeton University Press, 1997.

Jung, Emma. *Animus und Anima*. Zurich: Spring, 1974.

Jung, Emma and Marie-Louise von Franz. *The Grail Legend*. N.J.: Princeton Univ. Press, 1998.

Kerényi, Carl. *The Gods of the Greeks*. New York: Thames & Hudson, 2002.

------. *The Heroes of the Greeks*. London: Thames & Hudson, 1997.

Novikov, N.V. *Obrazy vostochnoslavyanskoy volshebnoy Skazki* [The Imagery of East Slavic Magic Tales]. Leningrad: Nauka, 1974.

Propp, V.Ya. *Istoricheskiye Korni volshebnoy Skazki* [Historical Roots of the Fairy Tale], Leningrad: Izdatel'stvo leningradskogo gosudarstvennogo ordena Lenina Universiteta, 1946.

Roob, Alexander. *Alchemie & Mystik*. Cologne: Benedikt Taschen Verlag, 1996.

Russkoye dekorativnoye Iskusstvo [Russian Decorative Art]. 3 vol. Moscow: Izdatel'stvo Akademii Chudozhestv SSSR, 1962-1965.

Rutten, Ellen. "Koshchey the Immortal versus the People: Viktor Vasnetsov and the Political Interpretation of Folk Tales in Russian Culture" in *Russian Legends, Folk Tales and Fairy Tales*. Edited by Patty Wageman. Groninger Museum Exhibition; Rotterdam: Nai Publishers, 2007.

Rybakov, B. A. *Yazychesto drevney Rusi* [Paganism of ancient Russia]. 4th ed. Moscow: Akademicheskiy proyekt, 2016.

------. *Yazychestvo drevnich Slavyan* [Paganism of the ancient Slavs]. 4th ed. Moscow: Akademicheskiy proyekt, 2016.

Sager, Hans Walter. *Die Überwindung der Mutter* [Overcoming the Mother]. St. Gallen: Zollikofer, 1977.

Shandler, Robert, trans. *Russian Folk Tales*. New York: Random House, 1980.

Shangina, I. *Russkiye traditsionnyye prazdniki* [Russian traditional holidays]. St. Petersburg: Azbuka-klassika, 2008.

Shaparova, N.S. , Kratkaya Entsyklopediya Slavyanskoy Mifogolii [A Short Encyclopedia of Slavic Mythology]. Moscow: Astrel', 2001.

Slovap' Russkogo Yazyka [Dictionary of the Russian Language]. 4 vols. Moscow: Gosudarstvennoe Isdatel'stvo Inostrannych i Natsional'nych Slovarey, 1957-1961.

Topkov, V. A., comp. *Fol'klor Voronezhskoy oblacti* [Folklore of the Voronezh District]. Voronezh: Voronezhskoye Oblastnoye Knigoiszdatel'stv, 1949.

Tschitschetow, Wladimir. *Russische Volksdichtung* [*Russian Folk Literature*]. Berlin: Akademie Verlag, 1968.

Vasmer, Max. *Russisches Etymologisches Wörterbuch.* 3 Bände. Heidelberg, Carl Winter, 1953-55.

Voet, Donald and Judith G. *Biochemistry.* New York: John Wiley & Sons, 1995.

Vries, Ad de. *Dictionary of Symbols and Imagery.* 3rd rev. ed. Amsterdam: North-Holland Publishing Company, 1981.

Von Beit, Hedwig. *Symbolik des Märchens* [Symbolism in Fairy Tales]. Bern: A. Franke Verlag, 1952.

------. *Gegensatz und Erneuerung im Märchen* [Polarity and Rebirth in Fairy Tales]. Bern: A. Franke Verlag, 1957.

Von Franz, Marie-Louise. *Alchemy,* Toronto: Inner City Books, 1959.

------. *Archetypal Dimensions of the Psyche.* Boston: Shambhala, 1999.

------. *Creation Myths,* Zurich: Spring, 1975.

------. *The Golden Ass of Apuleius: The Liberation of the Feminine in Man.* Boston: Shambhala, 1992.

------. *Individuation in Fairy Tales.* New York: Spring, 1977.

------. *Interpretation of Fairy Tales.* Zurich: Spring, 1975.

------. "On Active Imagination" in *Methods of Treatment in Analytical Psychology.* Stuttgart: Adolf Bonz, 1980.

------. *Shadow and Evil in Fairy Tales.* Irving: Spring, 1980.

------. *The Psychological Meaning of Redemption Motifs in Fairytales.* Toronto: Inner City Books, 1980.

------. *Puer Aeternus.* Santa Monica: Sigo Press, 1981.

------. *Aurora Consurgens: A Document Attributed to Thomas Aquinas on the Problem of Opposites in Alchemy.* Edited with a commentary by Marie-Louise von Franz, translated by R. F. C. Hull and A. S. B. Glover. Toronto: Inner City Books, 2000.

Wolff, Toni. *Structural Forms of the Feminine Psyche.* Küsnacht: C.G. Jung-Institute Zurich, 1985.

Index

R

regeneration 146, 147
ring 130, 134, 136-143, 145-147, 149, 151, 153, 154
rubedo 235, 237

S

salt 111, 118, 119, 183, 194
sea 31, 36, 57, 62, 69, 71-79, 81-88, 108, 113, 118, 154, 180-188, 191, 194, 195, 200, 210, 239, 240, 244, 266, 275, 280, 286, 289, 300
secret 64, 65, 71, 101, 120, 122, 142, 245, 265, 274, 282, 283, 298
Self 15, 27, 28, 34, 35, 53, 67, 69, 74. 76, 78, 81, 99, 108-119, 123, 131, 136, 143, 149, 152, 167, 169-173, 189, 190, 192, 198, 200, 212, 227, 230, 233, 236, 240, 244, 248, 261, 263, 271, 273, 278, 280, 284, 285, 291, 292, 300, 301, 304, 305, 307, 308
shadow 25, 33, 36-38, 40, 42, 63, 65, 72, 73, 74, 76, 84, 86, 99-101, 103, 106, 113-117, 119, 133, 134, 142, 183, 189, 194, 199, 206-208, 227, 235, 240, 243, 264-266, 281, 282, 300
shaman/shamanism 235, 237
ship 22, 38, 39, 238-240, 243-248
shoes 91-94, 106, 108, 112, 119, 202
signpost 14, 16, 176, 286
sister 19, 20, 23, 96, 103, 185, 208, 209, 213, 214, 228, 261, 268, 274, 275, 277, 306
sleep 27, 32, 36, 71, 104, 106, 115, 116, 117, 142, 146, 178, 184, 191, 193, 278, 290, 291
smith 106,107, 114, 117, 224, 234, 235, 237
soldier 66, 80, 171, 178-180, 187, 189, 191, 192, 194, 195, 200, 202, 203, 206-212, 214, 215
son 55, 69, 85, 99, 130-132, 138-141, 143, 150, 151, 183, 223, 226, 258, 282
spindle 108, 113

spinning wheel 27, 28, 108
Stages of Life 13, 42, 206
first half 13, 17, 24, 27, 37, 62, 73, 77, 87, 111, 184, 204, 206-208, 211, 212-214, 225, 270, 295
second half 13, 17, 21, 24, 28, 30, 37, 38, 42, 43, 65, 75, 87, 111, 204, 205, 206, 207, 208, 209, 211, 213, 214, 216, 217, 225, 229, 230, 240, 242, 282, 289, 300
stone 61, 106, 108, 112, 138, 139, 144, 197, 200-202, 206, 207, 209, 212, 226, 243-248, 291, 295, 306
philosopher's stone 61, 243
storm/lightning/thunder: 184, 261, 264, 278
suitor 261, 262, 266
sun 60-62, 78, 79, 81, 82, 84, 85, 87, 110, 179, 196, 206, 209, 212, 228, 243, 246, 264, 291
swamp 51-56, 59, 62, 65-67, 69, 70, 73, 80, 83, 84, 87, 263, 307
symbiosis 173, 174, 179, 209, 215
symbol 3-5, 14-17, 20-36, 41, 52-78, 83, 87, 96, 98, 102-123, 133-138, 141-152, 168-188, 202-216, 223-244, 258-266, 271-280, 283-299, 305, 307
sympathetic nervous system 192, 232, 287, 291

T

tear 117, 118, 119, 149, 171, 194
thief 227, 228, 238, 240, 241, 243, 247, 284, 304
thread 14, 54, 108, 109, 111
threshold phenomenon 103, 199, 202, 216
Toni Wolff 100, 120, 130
transcendent function 198
transformation 35, 38, 39, 40, 42, 54, 61, 62, 65, 74, 83, 96, 107, 115, 124, 150, 172, 176, 180, 184, 200, 201, 209, 213, 215, 231, 236, 243, 262, 263, 280, 281, 300, 303, 306
transition 13, 14, 17, 21, 22, 24, 34, 37, 38, 41, 42, 55, 59, 97, 98, 111, 116, 138, 139,

www.ingramcontent.com/pod-product-compliance
Lightning Source LLC
Chambersburg PA
CBHW020656270326
41928CB00005B/139